ACCIDENTALLY CLEVER

This compilation contains both fictional and true accounts. All characters, organizations, and events portrayed within the fictional segments are either products of the author's imagination or are used fictitiously. Those referenced in the non-fiction portions of this compilation are intended to express the opinions and experiences of the authors and not designed to offend or cause harm in any way.

Accidentally Clever

This book is dedicated to my lovely wife and my beautiful children.

I hope I get to meet you one day.

Foreword

I really wanted to start this off by seeing how many "Master Bates" jokes I could make... I didn't get very far.

I don't know what to say about Matt that you couldn't possibly glean from reading his stories; he's nuts. But he's nuts in a really endearing way. I'm not really sure if I say that because it's true or if it's because we just happen to be insane in very similar ways. I met Matt when we were 15 years old, working on a kids' TV show together for the Saban Empire. It was one of those Power Ranger spin off shows. I won't mention which one, but it was the best one... mainly because we were in it.

I'm not sure where or exactly how Matt and I met, but I'm pretty sure once we started spending time together in the tiny classroom where we were confined to for so many hours, we knew we were destined to be friends. We discussed our passion for the Beatles, quirky sketch-comedy, and the awe-inspiring Animaniacs. THAT'S where we really bonded. We spent HOURS dissecting the episodes we watched on our time away from set. We quoted them endlessly and sang every single song that we could possibly memorize. We discovered they had released albums and I believe I took his CDs home and burned tapes from them so I could listen to them on my commutes to and from set every week. On our downtime from the show, we decided it would be good to be pen pals. This is where the TRUE Matt began to show himself.

Matt fancied himself a Weird Al of our generation, if you will. I would receive letters with pages and pages of parody songs. Some of them even had themes. I believe one year I received a very thick envelope with almost an entire

Christmas Album penned by Mr. Bates with very recognizable songs, only the words had all been changed (He even brought a few to the classroom on rare occasion so I could look them over and offer my input). Even if I had just seen him on set, I'd return home and there would already be a letter waiting for me. Then I realized that I hadn't only become a pen pal with Matt, but I had become a writing buddy to several of the personas he had come up with in his brain. I believe there was the Happy Bunny (or something like that). There was a man named Jose who would write to me. Oh, and Forrest Gump wrote to me on several occasions. I found out later on that Matt was also using many of these characters for sketch writing that he was doing in school. He put together a group at his tiny high school in Yucaipa, CA called Commercial Parodies where he would come up with the silliest commercials or sketches he could possibly think of. He would send them to me via letter every once in awhile. Some were a hit, and some were not. But every single one of his letters had me rolling on the floor, laughing out loud, and tears streaming down my face. He always managed to make me laugh harder than anyone.

When our show was cancelled two years later, I was just about to graduate high school. I wasn't sad about not seeing Matt because I knew I had gained a friend for life. And life got tough and there were definitely times when I needed him for that gut busting laugh. It reminds me of when Spielberg said that he would call Robin Williams when he was making "Schindler's List" because the movie was so depressing to work on. Well, Matt was the Robin Williams to my Spielberg…. only I'm no Spielberg and Matt is way more intelligible than Robin Williams.

We don't talk as much as I'd like to these days, but his posts show up in my newsfeed daily on the Facebook and he still always makes me laugh. I even still have every letter he's every written me and every lyric to every song he's parodied that I was lucky enough to receive. When I need a good laugh, I go back and read them every now and then. I think I'll do that now.

And when you need a good laugh, pick up this book and know you're reading the ramblings of a mad genius and feel really lucky.

Libby Letlow

Ackowledgements

I have to start by thanking the team at Poorly Scribbled Pages for making this idea become a reality. I approached them with a pitch that basically consisted of, "Hi there! Me think can write book! You maybe say okay, yes?" and against their better judgment, they said "Okay."

My longtime friend and writing partner Patrick Quin Kermott was essential in many of these pieces coming to life. Since 1999, he has also had the thankless task of being my editor, which involves lots of patiently explaining to me that, just… no. No! I do not often understand "no," but somehow he gets through more often than not. Also, more than almost anybody else, he just flat out makes me laugh, something I assign great value to.

I could not have completed this project without the support and suggestions from the Five Wives, which sounds like a weird polygamist cult, but is really just my nickname for the five women who occupy a special place in my life… Nope, still sounds like a polygamist cult. Oh well. Needless to say, they each brought something special and specific to the making of the book and most importantly, when I told them I was thinking about doing this, they each thought it was a great idea. And trust me, if they didn't think it was a great idea, they totally would have told me. They are not exactly timid about telling me things I may not want to hear. Erin, Heather, Jennifer, Jessica, and Tiffany, if this were some weird episode of The Bachelor, I would totally give you all a rose.

Also, each one of them knows me well enough to know I put their names in that particular order because I'm completely OCD about alphabetizing things.

My 6th grade teacher Mrs. Taylor used to let me get up in front of the class and read stories I'd written when we could have been learning fractions. She seemed to realize I had some sort of natural inclination towards storytelling long before I'd even fully figured it out. I'm forever grateful to teachers like her, who fed the fire when it was just a spark, instead of snuffing it out.

Libby, thank you for taking on the monumental task of writing the Introduction. Even though Masked Rider has been off the air for seventeen years, I will always consider myself your sidekick, and I couldn't be happier about it. We may not see each other as much as I'd like, but I know we'll be quoting Animaniacs to each other for the rest of our lives.

The cast of Commercial Parodies, the loyal readership of the Bulletin, the Drama classes, people I've only known through social networking, my insane but undeniably awesome family… you're all responsible for this in one way or another, so don't even try to deny it.

To anyone who ever told me over the years that I should do something with my writing, and did not accept that shoving it in a drawer was "doing something," thank you for continuing to pester me about it. You were right. It just sometimes takes me fifteen years to figure these things out for myself.

Of course, I have to mention my dear sweet Mother, who is, often at the same time, the single craziest and yet most amazing person I've ever known. I'm an incredibly lucky son.

Finally, I'd like to thank all the people who noticed that I misspelled "acknowledgements" and are currently sending me helpful e-mails pointing out that fact. I regret to inform you that unfortunately, it's too late, because it's already in the book. All we can hope is that next time I will use a better spell-checking program.

```
U  S  E  L  I  B  O  M  O  T  U  A
A  C  C  I  D  E  N  T  A  L  L  Y
D  C  L  E  K  A  C  T  I  U  R  F
J  G  E  F  R  M  J  M  T  I  E  S
P  D  V  V  B  O  W  L  I  N  G  C
U  D  E  B  A  T  B  W  M  Y  A  H
N  A  R  P  D  H  Z  A  E  E  N  U
C  D  J  L  G  E  K  G  O  A  T  N
H  S  V  A  E  R  J  S  G  X  F  K
E  S  V  I  R  J  H  H  X  E  A  S
D  P  E  N  F  L  I  B  R  A  R  Y
L  C  E  L  L  P  H  O  N  E  M  H
D  M  T  M  A  T  T  P  A  F  V  G
P  I  B  I  Y  B  A  T  E  S  N  R
```

PoorlyScribbledPages

Table of Contents

Introduction

"Clever should have quote marks around it."

This is what my friend Pat said when I told him what I was going to call this book. He said it was because he'd had the sudden realization that all of my stories end with the moral that I'm not nearly as clever as I intend to be. Thus, Accidentally "Clever" was his thought. His point is valid but I still nixed the quote marks. I'm not ready to be THAT honest.

The truth is that I've been writing for over 20 years now and it came as a complete shock to me when I realized that I had enough material to put together an actual book with binding and a cover and everything. "Only Stephen King and Shakespeare can write books," I used to think. "Hopefully one day they can write one together! That would be awesome!"

Though in real life I can be exceptionally long-winded, I'm also very easily distracted so a long-form novel was never in the cards. If I was ever going to do a book, it was going to have to be a collection. Now I can turn the past tense of the first part of this sentence into present tense because that's exactly what the book is. This is a mixture of stories and anecdotes that I've written at various points over the last ten years or so. Some of the older pieces will be blatantly obvious just because of how dated the references are. I really wanted to go in and awkwardly insert timely things like "Iron Man 3" and "#The Twitter" into all the stories, but it just wasn't in the cards.

As you flip through the following pages, you will

discover three different varieties of storytelling, which hopefully will taste great together like when you combine chocolate, caramel, and a cookie crunch to make a Twix bar. Everything can be broken down into these three categories:

Short Stories (fiction)

There are seven short stories spanning exotic locations from Kenya to Bolivia. One of them takes place in a badger's living room. The story that leads things off, *Shadows of the Invisible*, is broken into eight parts and spread throughout the book, so don't become discouraged if you get to the end of *Part One* and feel no sense of closure whatsoever. A couple of these pieces have appeared elsewhere, but for the most part, you're getting exclusive, never-before-seen Grade A fiction here. Material which is meant to make you feel. To make you think. To take you on a journey to the depths of our innermost dreams and desires. But as I mentioned before, one of the stories takes place in a badger's living room, so I wouldn't get your hopes up too high about all THAT.

True-Life Tales (non-fiction)

I've never known what to call these. Several of them have been posted in various forms of social media over the years. MySpace called them "Blogs" while Facebook filed them under the heading "Notes." Personally, I always referred to them as "Columns." But none of that seemed to sound appropriate in this context, so after huddling up with my legal team, psychic advisors, and a guy on the off-ramp who promised to work for food, we came up with "True-Life Tales." Yes, it sounds like something you would find in Reader's Digest, but I've decided I'm fine with that.

Basically, these are things that happened to me, and I

wrote them down.

Advertisements (some weird grey area between fiction and non-fiction)

Each one of the True-Life Tales is preceded by a short advertisement because I am for sale. Every time you read one of the ads, I make something like three cents. Before taxes.

Once you make it to the end of the book, I have included a Director's Commentary section where I will go into the origins of some of the stories within for those interested. Sometimes the story behind the story is just as interesting as the story itself! (Although a lot of times, it's more along the lines of "I wondered what would happen if there was a goat in the road, and then I put a bunch of words together to explore that concept!")

In conclusion, because I read somewhere every concluding paragraph should start with some variation of "in conclusion," I'm very excited that you are reading my book, and I hope you think Jon Hamm should play me in the movie version. So I invite you to take a seat, grab a cool beverage and please do not set the beverage directly on the book, because you will leave a water stain on it. This goes double if you are reading the book on a Kindle. The journey begins on the very next page, and if all goes well then maybe, just maybe, you will enjoy what I've written. On purpose.

Shadows of the Invisible
(a tale told in "real-time")

Week One: Downhill Caboose

FRIDAY, NOVEMBER 15th, 2002

6:00 am - Baltimore, MD

In a rundown room on the second floor of the Budget Plaza Motel, a watch begins beeping on the arm of William Williams. Williams shuts the watch off without looking and continues to stare out the window at the parking lot. More specifically, Williams is staring at a car in the parking lot. It is a black Honda Accord, and it currently has only three tires. This confuses Williams, because when he parked the car just last night, it had FOUR tires. And also the driver's side window hadn't been busted out. Although he hasn't been out to look at the car, intuition tells him that the stereo is probably gone as well. Williams clears his throat and absentmindedly cracks his knuckles. He doesn't care about the car, not really. After all, it IS just a rental. But he wasn't done with it, and that's what is causing the anger to bubble up under the surface.

Williams takes a deep breath, closes his eyes, and physically pushes his anger back down inside of him. Now is not the time to let minor obstacles cause him to lose focus. The car is not a pressing issue, not for a few hours, and therefore he will deal with it when the time comes. He nods his head once, very sharply, and turns around to face the room.

Laying on the bed in the middle of the room, contorted into a truly impressive position, mouth flopped open and snoring loudly, sleeps Duke Gravy. Duke is not the man Williams would've chosen for the job, but it wasn't up to him. Duke's foot twitches slightly, visible under the sheet. Williams stares at Duke for a second, then walks over to the bed and slugs him in the stomach as hard as he can. Duke's eyes whip open and he leaps out of bed, falls to the ground, and begins coughing and gasping for air. After he composes himself a little, he looks up at Williams with flashing eyes.

"What was THAT for?" he hisses.

Williams looks down at Duke, says nothing, then points toward the dresser, where a cell phone sits on a charger.

Duke continues to glare at Williams. "You didn't answer my question. Why did you punch me in the stomach? With your FIST!"

"It's 6:01am, Duke. Make the call. You're late."

"I'm not late." Duke points at Williams, with two fingers. "YOU'RE late, late boy. And I'm early! Early like the Early Show on CBS. So SUCK IT!"

Williams shakes his head, grabs the cell phone and throws it at Duke, hitting him right between the eyes. The contact makes a satisfying THWACK sound, and it makes Williams smile. Duke, on the other hand, doesn't smile. Instead he puts his hands to his forehead and shrieks.

"OW! OW! You hit me with the phone! With the phone!" He checks his fingers for blood, finds none, then presses his hands back to his forehead. "The CELL phone!!"

Williams crosses his arms across his chest and continues to stare at Duke. He feels the anger rising back up within him, and he doubts he's going to be able to repress it much longer. Not while surrounded by this incompetence. He opens his mouth and speaks through his teeth. "It's now 6:02, Duke. Make the call."

Duke glares at Williams, flips him the bird with the wrong finger, and reaches down to pick up the phone. He dials a number with one hand while massaging his forehead with the other, and then puts the phone to his ear. After less than a full ring, the person on the other end picks up and Duke begins to speak. "Joe? It's Duke. It's time. Count down three minutes, and make your move. We'll be in touch." He hangs up the phone, and looks up at Williams. "They're at the house and ready for action."

Williams nods. "Good. We're at the Point of No Return, Duke. It's all been set in motion. Make the next call, and let's do this thing."

Duke smiles and begins dialing another number. Right before he hits send, however, he looks up and frowns at Williams. "Um... actually, can we not use my cell phone for this? I think I'm over my mobile-to-mobile limit, and it's like eighty-seven cents a minute, not to mention long-distance and roaming charges."

William's eye twitches ever-so-slightly, and the dam bursts.

6:04 am - Library of Congress, Washington D.C.

Jacques Vargas strolls into his office at the Library of Congress, throws his coat on the couch and flops down in his chair. He sits for a second with his eyes closed and his head back, and tries desperately to remember anything about last night. It's all such a blur and it gives him a headache to think about, but it seems important to figure out exactly what happened. He remembers watching Friends, then remembers hearing a knock at the door. It was his hot neighbor, he remembers, asking for a cup of sugar. But why would she have been asking for sugar in an outfit that was so slinky? And why was she holding a bottle of rum? And why did he wake up on the roof with his pants on his forehead? These are all questions that Jacques plans to deal with as soon as he gets a free moment. He opens his eyes, looks at the bright florescent light overhead, squints and covers his face with his hands. This is going to be a long day, he thinks, and as if to drive that point home, there is a knock on his office door.

"Jacques? Are you busy?" says a female voice. Jacques opens his fingers just far enough to see his co-worker Irma at the door with a file folder. He groans, but she pays no attention as she walks into the office and takes a seat. "I know it's early, but we've got some problems already. We were supposed to get a shipment of the new non-fiction books three days ago, and nobody can find them even though FedEx insists that they were delivered." Jacques shakes his head, but Irma continues. "Senator Chafee put in a request for some book on the history of forestry in Rhode Island. Lord only knows what he's up to now. Also, Chuck has found an anomaly in some of the international data. You know, the typesetting nonsense? He says that someone forgot to enter some information into the system, and it's causing all kinds of bugs overseas."

Jacques drops his hands and slams his head onto the desk. "Can this wait until later, Irma? I had a long night, or so I'm led to believe."

"Woke up in the bathroom at the Denny's again?"

"No, no. The roof. I think I might have a problem."

Irma gets up and tosses the file folder on the desk, to

the right of Jacques' head. "Well, whatever problems you're having at home, you need to leave them there and focus on your work. You're a high-ranking official in the L.O.C., Jacques, and with that position comes a certain responsibility." Irma waves her hands in frustration. "This isn't a normal library!! You either need to take some time off or get yourself together, because covering for you is getting old, and it's not really my job… boss."

With great effort, Jacques pulls his head off the table and rubs his eyes. He looks up and Irma and manages a weak grin. "You're a real firecracker, Irma."

"And I've got a short fuse. How long until we can get some work done?"

Jacques sits up straight, adjusts his wrinkled tie, and begins to leaf through the file folder. Papers, papers and more papers. He thinks back briefly to the time when he actually had passion for his work. It seems like such a long time ago, back before cups of sugar, waking up tied to things, and tattoos of his own name, misspelled. Irma looks at him expectantly. "So, where do you want to start?"

Deciding that the best way to start would be to get a cup of coffee, Jacques begins to stand up and speak when he is interrupted by the arrival of Chuck Williams, a talented up-and-comer in the L.O.C. Chuck comes in early, goes home late, and does things by the book (a common joke around the L.O.C. It's a laugh-a-minute in these parts!) Chuck also doesn't really care for Jacques, and makes no secret of his desire to one day occupy the very office he has just entered. He walks up to the desk and salutes. He doesn't like Jacques, but he believes in respect, even if he has to fake it. "Good morning, Mr. Vargas." he says.

Jacques sits back down. "Good morning, Chuck. Please stop saluting me. You know how I hate that. I'm not

Captain Crunch, for God's sake."

Chuck brings down his hand, but allows it to linger in the air several moments longer than he really should. With a small, quickly suppressed smirk, he gets down to business. "You have a phone call, Mr. Vargas."

"A phone call? You had to march all the way down the hall and into my office to verbally tell me I have a phone call, when it's a hundred times easier to transfer me the call… on the phone?"

"The man on the other end says it's urgent. You're not usually in your office this early, so I thought I'd check before I bothered putting him through to your voice mail."

Jacques shrugs and grabs the phone. "Good work, Chuck," he says before putting the receiver to his ear. "You really went above and beyond the call of duty this time. You're a good American." Sarcasm deployed, he presses a button and takes the call off hold. "L.O.C., this is Vargas."

"Mr. Vargas. Good morning." says a cold, calculating voice.

"Yeah, this is Vargas. How can I help you?"

"You can do exactly what we say and no one will get hurt. That's how you can HELP me."

Jacques looks up at Irma, who is looking back inquisitively. His glance shifts to the back of Chuck Williams, who is walking down the hall in his annoying good posture way. Jacques speaks in a calm voice, considering it's still too early in the morning for panic. "And what exactly do you mean by that, sir?"

"I mean, you're going to do whatever I tell you to, and if you do it right, you just might get to see your family again."

Eyebrows raised, Jacques replies. "I see… well, that's all fine and dandy, but I don't have a family. Sorry. But thanks for calling. Nice try."

"No family? But what about Lily?"

This is getting interesting, Jacques thinks, but the guy on the other end of the line has no idea what it's like to wake up on a roof. That kind of thing changes a man. He answers, still in a steady voice. "Lily? What ABOUT Lily?"

"She's your wife, isn't she?"

"My EX-wife."

"Yeah," says the voice. "But what about the kids!"

"STEP-kids."

The voice begins to sound slightly unsure of himself. "But... we spent all this... you know what, hold on a second..." Jacques hears the phone drop, and then the sound of two men arguing in the background. This goes on for nearly a minute, then the phone is picked back up and the cold, calculating voice comes on the line. "Is there anything particular you really care about? Something real specific?"

"I'm really into my golden retriever, Mr. Woofs."

A slight pause, added for dramatic effect. "We have Mr. Woofs."

"Mr. Woofs! No! You black-hearted fiends! Why have you done this?!"

"You'll find out soon enough... in fact, you'll find out on... November 22nd."

Jacques scratches his head. "But, wait. If you're not going to tell me for a week, why even bother calling me TODAY?"

The voice stutters and stammers again, unsure of how to answer. As they begin to reply with, "Uh..." Chuck darts back into the office, eyes-wide. Irma turns toward him with alarm. "What is it, Chuck? What's wrong?"

He hands Jacques an official looking file folder. "I just received this report from the FBI or the CIA or one of those other initial places. They've detected an assassination threat against the President of Antarctica... and they need our help!"

Irma's jaw drops, and Jacques drops the phone. This is too much for one day, he thinks. I'm going to need at least a WEEK to figure out what to do. This is a request we can easily accommodate.

To Be Continued...

The following True-Life Tale is being brought to you by…

Man's Best Reduced Price Friend

Everybody needs a pet! But at today's prices, getting a brand new pet is getting harder and harder. That's why you need to come to The Used Pet Showroom® and get a perfectly good pet without taking such a big hit to your wallet. We got dogs, we got cats, we got gerbils and hamsters and guinea pigs. Yes, we got just about any pet you could want and believe you me, these pets are comparable to any pet you'd find at one of those brand-name dealers.

Each pet at The Used Pet Showroom® goes through a 19-point inspection and must match our high quality standards before we ever let them near the showroom floor. And it doesn't matter if you've got good credit, bad credit or no credit at all, WE WILL finance you. Let me say that again. The Used Pet Showroom® WILL FINANCE YOU. You will not be turned down! Let's take a look at some of the fine animals we're selling right now! These animals MUST GO! No reasonable offer will be turned down!

Links - A four-year old kitty with six remaining lives. Six!

Rover - Nine-year old hound dog. Comes equipped with leash and doggy dish. His liver medication can be added on for only $59.99

Stanley G. Barx (FIXER-UPPER) - Middle aged dog with strange growths and a limp. Great first dog for the kiddies!

Sheldon - 1972 tortoise. Classic! Recently waxed shell!

Polly - Brightly colored parrot. 50,000 miles. Still flies like a charm. Does not move because he's... um... resting!

Whiskers - Genetically-engineered cat from Honda Corporation. Has AM-FM cassette deck. Can easily be upgraded to Sirius/XM Radio. Also comes with air bag and power whiskers. May have grudge against humans!

That doesn't even scratch the surface of what you can find at The Used Pet Showroom® so come on down and visit us today. If you live near a major metropolitan area, or an easily broken into animal shelter, chances are there's a Used Pet Showroom® near you.

The Used Pet Showroom®
New Pet Quality at Used Pet Prices!

You Can't Spell "Can't" Without "Ant"

It started as a compromise.

When my roommate Heather and I first moved in together, we had differing opinions about how many animals we should get. There was my opinion ("none") and there was her opinion ("all the animals in the world, including animals that are technically extinct"). We went around and around about the animal issue for much of the first year we were living together. She would say something crazy like, "I think I want a hedgehog because they are soft and cute," and I would roll my eyes, slink back into my room and spend the next hour or so trying to restrain myself from waiting until she fell asleep, then smothering her to death with a pillow. (Ha-ha! I'm just joking! I would never try and smother my roommate! More likely, I would poison her wine.)

One time, I came home from work and there was a turtle in the living room. This was particularly strange to me because when I had left for work earlier that day, there was no turtle in the living room. When I pressed Heather for an explanation, she said that the turtle was kind of an impulse buy, but that it was the "last animal" she wanted and that she had "no desire" to get any other creatures. So of course, a couple of months later, she brought home a rabbit. And then a fish. And then a frog. And two birds. And then she started babysitting a wiener dog. It was becoming apparent that when I put my foot down and declared that there would be no animals, nobody was listening to me.

Eventually, most of the animals went to other homes,

and we reached a truce on the animal issue. Although it was one of those kinds of truces like when Israel and Palestine are all like, "Oh yes! We should totally have peace! This is such a great idea!" and then six days later, someone drives a car bomb into an internet café. Still, I am not completely heartless and could see that dear sweet Heather still pined for some sort of animal companionship. So with Christmas coming up, I came up with a brilliant solution.

I would get her an ant farm.

Yes! An ant farm! A completely self-contained world featuring animals that did not make loud noises or diddle on the carpet or use my DVDs as chew toys. And the best part was that you could fit lots of ants in an ant farm, so it was like getting fifteen pets in one! I patted myself on the back and told myself that not only was I a genius, but I was really very smart as well.

Christmas Day dawned, and Heather opened her ant farm, then looked at me with a look as if to say, "What the hell?"

But I quickly went into PR mode and explained that she could finally have all the animals she wanted as long as they all lived in the ant farm, which was about 18 inches tall. Somehow I was able to convince her that this was going to be very exciting, and a few days later I sent away for the ants, which cost me $3.00 plus a $5.00 charge for shipping. You know something is going to be awesome if the shipping charge costs more than the actual item that is being shipped.

The ants arrived two weeks later in a small plastic tube and by then, even I was looking forward to experiencing The Incredible World of Ants. We were going to have the best ant farm in the world and were already discussing getting other ant farms and connecting them together so that the ants would have some sort of wonderful

Ant Universe to explore and conquer.

And then a week and a half later, all the ants were dead.

I still don't know what happened, but I should have seen it coming when my first act of assembling the ant farm was to dump the sand in the wrong half. If one is having trouble building the world itself, one cannot be expected to have a much easier time caring for the inhabitants of said world. But I was not the only one to blame. Heather bears just as much responsibility for the destruction of the ants as I do. The first thing SHE did to the ants was to decide that they were hungry and then drop a hunk of cornbread into the ant farm that was the equivalent of dropping a thirty ton cheeseburger on Los Angeles. That hunk of cornbread could've fed Ant Ethiopia for a hundred years.

I scolded her for overfeeding the ants then turned right around and tried to drown them. The Ant Farm Manual says the ants only need one to two drops of water every other day, so I intended to follow that suggestion to the letter. Instead, I accidentally ended up dropping... oh... six hundred drops of water into the ant farm. Watching the ants flee for their lives and having to crawl over the hunk of cornbread during the process was a lot like watching the video footage from the tidal wave that hit Thailand a few years ago.

So needless to say, the ants were under a lot of stress the whole time they were living with us. But ants are hardworking insects, so even as we kept trying to kill them by mistake, they persevered and started digging tunnels, and it was fascinating. It wasn't too unusual to walk into the living room to see how the ants were doing, then get lost in watching them to the point where fifteen minutes would be gone, just like that. Ant farms are hypnotic. If someone had come over to visit us during that week and a half, they would have found Heather and I hunched over opposite sides of the ant farm, silently staring at it with our jaws hanging open, and the person that came to visit would have been able to tell right away that the two of us totally knew how to party.

But eventually, one by one, the ants starting dying off, and nothing we did seemed to delay the inevitable. At one point, Heather dropped some birdseed into the farm, and the ants completely ignored it, perhaps because it was birdseed and not antseed. But lo and behold, the birdseed took root and BEGAN TO GROW, proving that we were doing terrible with the "ant" part, but we were naturals at the "farm" part.

A few days later, all the ants had gone to Ant Heaven, and to commemorate this emotional situation and to pay proper respect to these ants which we had grown so close to, Heather took the ant farm and threw it in the trash. Amen.

I've had a couple of weeks to think about what went wrong, and I think I've finally figured it out. See, it had nothing to do with overfeeding the ants or trying to make them live underwater or trying to get them to harvest their own crops to survive. No, it's much simpler than that. The company sent us a little plastic tube full of ants with cancer. And that, when you really look at things, is the only possible explanation.

This column is dedicated to the ants who gave their lives so that my roommate and I could be entertained for the better part of two weeks. You will not be forgotten!

The following True-Life Tale is being brought to you by…

Because It's Not Like You're Going To Throw Anything Away

Is your closet too cluttered? Are your filing cabinets too full? Are those stacks of old newspapers dating back to 1957 getting ready to collapse?

We know how frustrating it is to run out of room and we're here to help. We're Under Construction Storage®, the best place in town to store your stuff, or at least we will be once we're done building.

Under Construction Storage® strives to be America's storage leader with over 1,500 locations nationwide, but we're still working on finishing up the first one. We're getting pretty close. If you drive by the lot, you can see that the frame is up and the foundation has been poured. There have been some problems with the contractor, although that should be worked out sooner or later. As soon as we're open though, you're definitely going to want to make us your first choice for storing your valuable possessions.

At Under Construction Storage®, our self-storage units range in size from approximately 25 square feet to nearly 300 square feet according to the blueprints I'm looking at right now. We'll even have special climate controlled units to help protect your most sensitive belongings. But probably not right at first. The parts for the climate controlled units come from overseas and they've been tied up in customs for the better part of a month. We were even planning on providing computerized gates that would only allow access to authorized people, but the construction delays have caused our costs to spiral out of control. Still, we meant to do it. That's more than you can say for some other storage companies, including some that are currently open for business.

The fact is that you've got a lot of stuff and nowhere to put it. Why not put it at Under Construction Storage®? Because we're still under construction, you say? Well, yeah. That is a pretty good point. But it's really the only negative. Why not look at all the positives? Great prices! Excellent customer service! Clean, well lit facilities! All of those things could potentially await you at Under Construction Storage® at our soon to be completed site two miles down the unpaved road between the abandoned warehouse and the vacant lot.

Preorder today so you can be sure to have a unit reserved once we have our Grand Opening sometime between October 2015 and January 2017!

Under Construction Storage®

We Have Everything You Need To Store Everything You've Got... Eventually

A Lover, Not A Fighter

There are moments at my job where it is very apparent that we don't have enough work to keep us occupied.

One of those instances happened a while back during a shift that was not too busy, though what ended up happening had been brewing for a while. At the time I worked with two brothers named Hector and Jose who were, in their spare time, training to enter the world of professional boxing. They would talk about it off and on, and we would all joke that maybe one day they would bring all their boxing equipment to work and we could have a sparring session. Ha-ha-ha! Jokes are fun to make when you are at work! Ha-ha-ha!

I also worked with a guy named Jason, who was a few years younger than me and who, at the time, was one of the only other white people I worked with. I had maybe six inches on him, although he probably had about thirty pounds on me (this is not unusual; newborns occasionally outweigh me). So when we would all joke (Ha-ha!) about boxing each other, I would always challenge poor Jason. "Oh, yeah!" I would say, trying to sound like Macho Man Randy Savage but probably instead sounding like I had a serious throat infection. "You are going DOWN, little man! I am the king of the ring! There are going to be two sounds: Me hitting you and you hitting the floor!" And then I would flex, first making sure there were no women around, because the fact is that when I start flexing, women cannot handle the raw sexiness and often start ovulating on the spot.

Jason was always very soft-spoken, so he never really

responded too much to my mock cocky talking, and I say "mock" cocky talking, because I never really expected that we were going to box each other, because that is not the kind of thing that happens at a professional workplace.

So it was to my great surprise a couple weeks later when Hector and Jose brought in their boxing gloves.

They were going to spar with each other, but they (and everyone else really) wanted to see the great Battle of the Scrawny White Guys, so it was determined that Jason vs. Matt would be the undercard. On some level, I still didn't think we were actually going to go through with this so I continued my completely over-the-top trash talking. Bellowing about how victory would be mine and how I was going to win this thing for all the fans and that I would be pummeling Jason so badly that his family was going to need DNA testing to identify the body and on and on and on. I have no off-button when I think I'm being funny.

After a couple of hours of working, we all took our break at the same time and headed outside where we made a sizable square on the ground that was going to be our boxing ring. Hector brought over his gloves and put them on my hands while Jose was putting his gloves on Jason. It was decided that we would box for three rounds, each round being three minutes long, and at the end the audience which numbered somewhere around 8 (Madison Square Garden had nothing on us) would determine the winner, who would be crowned Champion of White People.

The audience did not end up playing a factor in the decision, as we never made it out of the first round.

Jason and I retreated to our separate corners of the boxing square, and Hector looked at his watch and said, "Okay... GO!!" The thing is, even as Jason and I were walking towards each other, boxing gloves in the ready position, I still did not honestly believe that we were going to box each other. It was insane. We were good work buddies, he and I, and we were at work, on the clock. People simply do not box under these circumstances. In my head, I was still amazed at how far we were taking this hilarious joke. "Ho-ho!" I was thinking, and I know I was grinning like an idiot as I danced around, showing off my fancy footwork. "This is crazy! I can't wait to go home and tell people about how I pretended to box somebody at work!"

And then he punched me in the face.

Up until that point in my life, I'd never been hit in the face. Going through school, I always prided myself in the way I was able to talk myself OUT of fights. "There is no reason for this fussin' and a-feudin,'" I would tell the bullies. "Instead, let's all go out for some frosty chocolate milkshakes!" Or something like that. I don't remember exactly, but I must've said SOMETHING clever, because I was able to avoid getting socked a bunch of times. So getting slugged between the eyes was a completely foreign sensation to me. I distinctly remember thinking to myself, as my head rocked backwards, "Hey... he just HIT ME! What the hell did he do that for?" It actually took him hitting me a second time to realize that we were seriously boxing each other.

And that was when I fought back...

(We will pause here briefly for dramatic effect)

Once I'd finally gotten it through my head that Jason and I were really boxing, I realized that I was going to need to hit him back at some point. This was not going to be easy because just as I'd never been hit before, I'd also never hit anyone else before. I didn't really know what was going to happen when I took a swing at him. It was possible that I had so much power in my arm that when I made contact with his head, I might collapse his skull. These were powerful weapons hanging from my shoulders, and they were unregistered.

My first punch barely grazed his shirt. He took the opportunity to pop me in the mouth.

My second punch hit him in the upper body but, to my surprise, it did not shatter his ribcage. Was it possible that I was not as strong as I had been loudly claiming I was, without any proof whatsoever to back up said claims? No, of course not. I was pulling my punches, afraid to hurt someone who I was friends with outside of the ring. At least this is what I will tell myself until my dying day.

It went on like this for maybe forty-five seconds or so. I would reach back with all my might and throw a deadly fist in Jason's direction, and after he absorbed the blow, he would make contact with a part of my body that would be sore the next day. I felt I was winning the match on points, but in an instant, everything changed.

I did not see the punch that knocked me down.

I mean, I know it happened. One moment, I was standing in the middle of a parking lot, surrounded by hysterically laughing co-workers, and the next I was lying face down ON the parking lot. Later on, it was explained to me that Jason hit me in the side of the head and I "went flying." However it happened, I was stunned to find myself that close to the asphalt. So was everyone else, because it took a couple of seconds for someone to jump up and start counting me out. I regained my senses somewhere between "three" and "four" and I thought to myself, "Oh, no! I may lose this fight, but there's no way I'm losing it on the ground!" It's this kind of macho mindset that has no business being in my head and the reason why a couple of minutes later, I would be bleeding.

I leapt to my feet right about "six" and turned back to Jason, ready to make him pay for what he had done. Observers noted that I was "very wobbly" and that my eyes were "kind of out of it". What these observers did not know, however, was that I was about to bring the thunder.

You remember that scene in Braveheart where Mel Gibson and his army are running full-speed towards the enemy, screaming about freedom? That was pretty much what I did next. I charged at Jason, arm cocked back, ready to unleash hell. However, I forgot an important element of boxing, which is that a powerful offense is pointless if you don't have any defense. Basically, I ran face first into his fist. And my nose exploded.

I almost went down again from the force of the impact, but instead, I stumbled backwards a few steps and managed to regain my balance. It was then that I looked down and saw the blood dripping onto my shirt. I reached up, brushed my nose with my wrist, held it up to my face, and sure enough... more blood. MY blood. Coming from my own personal body. This was not what I was expecting when I'd joked that Jason and I should box one day ha-ha-ha.

It was a strange moment, because when it clicked in my head that I was bleeding, I instantly went into this primal state. I didn't hear my co-workers anymore. I didn't see them. I had no idea that I was even at work, wearing my work clothes which were slowly turning red. I just knew that I was bleeding, that Jason had done it, and that I had to beat him to death. The only thought in my head was, and I quote, "Raaaaaaaaaaaarrr!!!"

As I went charging at Jason, about to make orphans

of his children, Hector noticed the blood and jumped out in front of me, blocking my path. "Okay, that's enough," he said, waving his hands in the air. "I think the fight's over." There was much laughing and clapping from the crowd, and I snapped back to reality, stumbled over to Jason and congratulated him on a good fight. "I guess we're going to have to call this a tie," I said as we tapped gloves.

"I'm really sorry about your nose," he replied.

My face hurt for a couple of days, but it ended up being fine. I also got quite a bit of newfound respect from everyone because even after I got knocked down, I got back up and went right back in to give blood. But I never quit, even long after the point where I should have. There were plenty of calls for a rematch, perhaps because it is hilarious to watch a skinny white dude who has no idea what he's doing get pummeled about the face. But I decided right then and there to retire from professional boxing. It is a sweet science, this I will not deny, but it's not for me. I'll let my career record of no wins and one loss sit in the record books, collecting dust.

But I will be happy to continue talking trash, because it is there where I remain undefeated.

Shadows of the Invisible
(a tale told in "real-time")

Week Two - The Four Shadows

"Last week, my ex-wife and step-children were kidnapped. Also, the President of Antarctica received an assassination threat. My name is Librarian of Congress Jacques Vargas, and these... are the longest eight weeks of my life..."

FRIDAY, NOVEMBER 22nd, 2002

11:00pm - Library of Congress, Washington D.C.

A timid knock comes to Jacques Vargas' office door, and he looks up from the book of Antarctica he's been staring at for an hour. Standing in the doorway, looking at meek as his knock would suggest, is Todd Herring, a recently hired assistant at the L.O.C. He holds some file folders and shifts his feet nervously. "Um... Mr. Vargas. Am I disturbing you?"

Jacques leans back in his chair and manages a small transparent grin. "No, Todd. Just doing some research. What can I do for you?"

"Well, Mr. Vargas, I've been doing some work for Mr. Williams, learning more about Antarctica that I ever cared to know really, and um... it's just that, I'm beginning to suspect that there's more going on here than I'm being told." Jacques opens his mouth to reply, but Todd cuts him off and begins speaking nervously, faster and faster. "I mean, I know I'm the new guy and all, and there's a certain amount of information that's probably none of my business, but this CAN'T just be about polar ice caps, sir! I stayed up all night doing calculations on how much it would cost to equip a penguin with flippers that fire bullets! And then I had to multiply that by the cost of equipping an ARMY of penguins with bullet flippers… and grenade launchers! And I don't mind telling you, sir, it's really EXPENSIVE! These costs can't be justified, and it doesn't make any sense…" Todd looks up at Jacques, pauses, and then his shoulders slump and he meekly finishes his thought. "… I've really overstepped my bounds with this rant, haven't I? I'm so sorry. I'll just clean out my desk and be on my way. Sorry to bother you." Todd stares at the wall for a moment and then turns to walk out.

"Todd, stop." Todd turns around slowly, eyes wide, sweat seeping through the file folders in his hand. "Look, I'll just level with you, because we're in a situation right now where everybody needs to be on the same page." Jacques stands up and walks over to Todd. "You work for the Library of Congress, Todd. And what does that mean to you?"

Todd frowns. "Books?" he asks tentatively.

"Exactly! Books! Because that's what a library is all about. Or so we've led this country to believe. See, Todd, the Library of Congress isn't what you think it is. That's just our front. In reality, we're a high-tech secret government agency that deals with serious threats against the country and the world."

"You mean like the C.I.A.?"

"Well, sort of. It's not the…"

"And the F.B.I.?"

"Right, well, you're kind of missing the point…"

"And the U.S. Postal Service?"

Jacques puts his hand up. "Okay, stop. We're getting off track. See, we're a very, very specialized branch of the government. We're not the same as the others. We're different."

"In what way?"

Jacques stares at Todd for a couple of seconds, blinks, and then looks off into space, as if trying to find an answer. Finally, he shakes his head and looks back at Todd. "That's almost certainly not important. But in answer to your original question, the reason you're doing so much work with War Penguins is because we're trying to find a way to protect the President of Antarctica, who has recently had his life threatened."

Todd gives a look of minor confusion. "Antarctica has a President?"

"Yes. And he is in danger."

Todd's look of confusion upgrades itself from minor to major. "The President is in danger... the one in Antarctica? And the Library of Congress is in charge of protecting his life?"

"Yes, Todd. What's so odd about all of that?"

Todd opens his mouth to tell Jacques EXACTLY what's so odd about all of that when Jacques speakerphone beeps. On the other end is Irma, the L.O.C.'s second in command. "Jacques, it's Irma. Are you there?"

"Yeah, Irma. I'm just telling the new kid here about how this isn't a typical library."

"Did you point out that you can't check out books from here? That's always a powerful point to make."

"Not yet, but I think he's catching on anyway. What's going on?"

"Well, Jacques, um... I've got Lily on the phone here. She says it's an emergency."

Jacques grimaces at hearing the name of his ex-wife. She never calls to just to say hello. It's always something that turns into a big ol' hassle. And this "emergency" nonsense... she probably needs money for something ridiculous, like food. He walks back over to the phone and picks up the receiver. "Irma, tell her I'm busy. Busy at my JOB. Maybe that'll give her a great idea on a different way to obtain income."

Irma speaks back in an uncharacteristically nervous fashion. "Actually, Jacques, I think you need to take this call. I think it's for real."

11:04pm - Budget Plaza Motel, Baltimore, MD

On the other end of the line, Lily Rodham-Vargas tightly grips a small cell phone. Her two kids sleep peacefully in the room's sole bed, blissfully unaware of what is occurring. They still think they're on a field trip, but Lily wonders how much longer she can keep up that charade. She sits in an uncomfortable chair, flanked on each side by a man. To her right, holding a gun and several index cards, is Joe. To her left, wearing a cloak and staring at her neck is Vlad. Vlad has been staring at her neck all week, and whereas it was creepy at first, now it's just annoying. She finds herself wishing it was daylight so he'd go back to sleep.

Joe pokes the gun into her side. "What's going on, lady? This is taking too long."

Lily glares at her abductor. "They put me on hold, okay? It's not like calling Pizza Hut."

"Pizza Hut..." sighs Joe. "That sounds great. I'm starving."

"As am I," says Vlad, running his tongue over his pointy teeth.

"Then it's a deal. After we make the drop, we'll order some dinner. I want pepperoni. Or do I want extra cheese? Pepperoni... extra cheese..." Joe goes into deep thought. "I dunno, Vlad. I could choose either one. They're really neck-and-neck." Vlad begins to drool, although nobody notices.

The phone clicks and suddenly Jacques' voice is on the line. "Lily, what are you DOING calling me at work? You KNOW I'm busy! I'm right in the middle of something!"

"Jacques..."

Upon hearing the name spoken, Joe and Vlad look up sharply. Joe jams the index cards in Lily's face. "You read the cards, you understand?" he hisses. "Nothing more, nothing less."

Lily looks at the cards, then the gun, then at Vlad, then notices for the first time that Vlad doesn't seem to cast a reflection in the big mirror in the room. Deciding to worry about that later, she nods and begins to read. "Jacques. This is Lily. I have been kidnapped."

"Hey, that sounds kind of familiar." Jacques says.

"You were contacted last week and informed of this kidnapping. Your efforts to locate me have failed."

"Efforts to locate you? Oh... yeah. THOSE efforts!" Jacques snaps his fingers. "Nuts and darn!"

Lily reads on, with Joe and Vlad hanging on every word, certainly moreso than Jacques. "If you ever wish to see me and the children alive again, you must be at the Kaffa House by 11:15 tonight. Failure to do so will result in my dearth." Lily squints at the cards. "Sorry. Death. I mean death."

"The Kaffa House? That restaurant on U Street? There's no way I could get there in time, even if I was interested in trying."

Joe snatches the phone from Lily's hand, accidentally giving her a paper cut with the index cards. "You'd better do what we say, Vargas. We're crazy! We'll kill her, the kids, each other! We're out of our gourds!"

"Listen, fellas. I don't know what to tell you. It's my ex. I never even liked her when we were married. You think I'm gonna go speeding around D.C. at 11:00 at night when I've got work to do, just because you've got Lily?"

Joe smiles. "I think you will, Vargas, because it's not just about your precious Lily. I think you'll find that by being at The Kaffa House in seven minutes, you just might be able to save the President of Antarctica."

Jacques speaks with disbelief. "How do you know about that? That's confidential Library of Congress information!"

"11:15. The Kaffa House. Take your cell phone. We'll be in touch."

Joe ends the call and tosses the phone on the dresser. "All right. I think he's on his way." Joe looks over and sees Lily holding her cut hand. A single drop of blood seeps out from between her fingers and drips off her hand.

Vlad dives to the ground, mouth flopping open. "Bllllllooooood!!!" he bellows, as he slams to the floor, knocking the cell phone off the dresser. He begins to vigorously lick the carpet as he emits a high-pitched squeal. Joe shakes his head, rolls his eyes, and picks up the phone. He dials up William's number and confirms that things are going according to plan.

11:08pm - North Capitol Street, Washington D.C.

Jacques speeds along the street, weaving in and out of traffic, wondering what his ex-wife could possibly have to do with the assassination attempt. Maybe she's the killer, he thinks. It's certainly within the realm of possibility. After all, she IS originally from North Dakota. But no, his L.O.C. intuition tells him it's something else. Something... else.

He swerves sharply, barely missing a Girl Scout and a Senator, when his cell phone rings to the familiar tone of "Brick House". He answers it. "L.O.C. Vargas."

"Jacques. On your way, I hope." It's a different voice, yet still very familiar.

"Who is this? What does this have to do with the President of Antarctica?"

"Please, Jacques. You know we're not going to tell you, so why waste your time by asking? You'd be more productive asking us about the Wizards game."

Jacques thinks about this. "Okay. Who won the Wizards game?"

"Silence, Vargas! I've had enough of your mind games! Now listen close, because I'm only going to say this once, or perhaps twice, if you don't understand it the first time. When you get to The Kaffa House, drive around to the east side of the building. There, you will see a piece of abstract art. It's four pillars, and they're lit with a backlight, causing four shadows to be cast on the sidewalk. Where these four shadows intersect is where you will find what we have left for you. Do you understand?"

"Four pillars with a backlight? That's an odd feature."

"It's called foreshadowing! It's very popular in the northern states. Now shut up and pay attention. It is very important that you retrieve this object at 11:15pm sharp. That's less than three minutes from now, Jacques. I hope you're close."

"I'm close enough." Jacques says through gritted teeth. He runs over a possum.

"Good. Then you'll be hearing from us at 11:15, on the dot. You pull this off, Jacques… and maybe the President of Antarctica won't have to die. Because just between you and me, those War Penguins… they're lame." The phone goes dead in Jacques ear. How on Earth did he know about the penguins, Jacques wonders. They're a top-secret project. Only a limited number of people within the L.O.C. have access to such information. And if this kind of information is being leaked…

Jacques doesn't have a chance to process this thought any further, because he suddenly realizes that his car has stopped moving. He looks around, looks up for some reason, then his gaze focuses on his fuel meter. Empty. He has run out of gas. He smacks himself in the forehead. "Nuts and DARN!!" he shouts, and this time he means it. He throws open his door, starts to get out of the car, and is narrowly missed by a speeding motorist. "Hey, watch it, jerk!" yells Jacques, waving his fist in the air. "I'm a pedestrian! I've got the right-of-way!" And Jacques the Pedestrian glances at the watch which is attached to this fist. The watch informs him quite matter-of-factly, that it's 11:14:58… 11:14:59… 11:15:00.

His cell phone rings.

To Be Continued…

The following True-Life Tale is being brought to you by...

Water Water Everywhere

No matter who you are or where you come from, one fact rings true. Water is the single most important substance on the planet aside from maybe oil. Health officials suggest that each person drink at least eight gallons of water a day and that if you don't then it is very possible that you will keel over and die right there on the spot. But what many consumers don't realize is that while water is readily available these days, not all water is the same. How do you decide which is the RIGHT water for you and your family or mistress? The answer is simple: Genius Water®.

Genius Water® is the latest creation from Hydra Labs®, and represents the very latest in state-of-the-art water technology. Whereas most water just quenches your thirst and keeps you alive, Genius Water goes a step further and actually makes you smarter. How does it accomplish such an amazing feat? Because Hydra Labs® engineers it that way. We take water from our patented SmartTap®, purify it then send it through our incredible quadruple osmosis machine. After that, we dump it in a vat and add electrolytes and carbohydrates and other secret brain ingredients, specifically formulated to increase your genius smarts. You know Genius Water® makes you smarter, because it says so on the label.

Not convinced? We asked our unbiased Hydra Lab® science team, the same team that manufactures and distributes Genius Water®, if Genius Water® would make you smarter and they said, and I quote, "Yes." Unquote. How can you argue with scientists? Look, you can drink your Aquafina® and your Dasani®, and you can walk around town wearing your underwear as a shirt going, "Duh, I am a water drinky man! All the time is water time!" Or you can choose Genius Water® and suddenly be able to name all nine planets. What? There are only eight planets now? Really? Huh… I hadn't heard about that.

Critics have said that Genius Water® is actually no different from regular water and that Hydra Labs® is just preying on people who are so stupid that they would actually think special fairy water could increase your intelligence. This is an outrageous accusation. We've got all kinds of facts and data that back up our claims, but we misplaced them when we went to lunch. Don't worry. We've got the secretary looking for them. The only thing you need to know is this: Genius Water® make you smart. Drink. DRINK! And if you want to get even SMARTER, reach for Advanced Formula Genius Water®, now containing hydrogen AND oxygen. We'll probably release some flavored Genius Water® too, because somebody accidentally dropped a strawberry in the vat.

So what are you waiting for, dummy? Get down to the store and buy Genius Water®. Sure, it's a little more expensive than regular water, but the more something costs, the better it is!

Genius Water®

You Would Have To Be Stupid Not To Drink Genius Water®

I'm Not So Much Lovin' It

There is a McDonald's I go to that is smarter than me. In saying that, I do not mean that the employees at the McDonald's are smarter than I am (although it's certainly possible, but I don't have the time nor the energy to sit all the McWorker's down and give them an IQ test). What I am referring to is the McDonald's itself, and more specifically, the drive-thru.

Several months ago, I pulled up to the drive-thru speaker at this particular McDonald's and before I'd even come to a complete stop, a lady's voice said to me, "Welcome to McDonald's. What can we make for you today?"

I ordered my usual, a ten-piece Chicken McNugget meal, because I always order my usual. That is why it is my usual. If I was ever to go to a McDonald's and they told me they were out of McNuggets, I would probably have a nervous breakdown right there in front of the register, because as far as I'm concerned the only thing on the menu at McDonald's is Chicken McNuggets and, once in a while, a strawberry sundae. When people ask me, "Hey, have you tried that new McRib Sandwich or funky chicken wrap?" I look at them as if they just asked me if I would like to spend the afternoon dropkicking kittens. It just isn't right.

So I ordered my meal, the Number Ten, large-sized with a Coke, and a NEW voice came out of the speaker. A deeper voice. A man voice. The man voice said, "Thank you. Please pull up to the second window." I wasn't sure what happened to the lady voice, but at the time I was too hungry to really give it a second thought.

After that day, the voice switch kept happening

every time I was in that drive-thru. The lady voice would greet me and the man voice would tell me how much my order was. I felt like I was dining at McJekyll and Hyde's. Eventually, I figured out what was going on, because my brain is like a detective and it is always on the case. The lady voice was a recording, and the man voice was the guy that was actually listening to me as I ordered McNuggets (large-sized, with a Coke!) The whole thing seemed kind of stupid to me. Why bother using the recording if there's a live person listening to you? And if they absolutely had to use the recorded greeting, couldn't they have a man greeting and a woman greeting, depending on which gender was manning (or woman-ing) the headset on that shift?

Well, like I said, this McDonald's is WAY ahead of me. I drove up to the speaker a couple weeks later and to my surprise, a male voice said, "Thank you for choosing McDonald's! What can we make for you today?"

Assuming that they'd finally heard all the complaints I'd been making in my mind and that they'd finally gotten rid of the idiotic recording, I ordered my Number Ten. A moment passed, and then a LADY replied, "Please pull forward." It was a double switch! I had been foiled by the McDonald's again!

It wasn't always like this. For the longest time, this McDonald's had a live person on the drive-thru speaker. His name was Joe, and Joe was the grumpiest man in the McWorld. If you did not order in exactly the right way, Joe would get angry at you and say, "Excuse me?" in a way that made you feel as if you had done something wrong. I dealt with Joe enough times to learn the proper way to order, and it was like this:

(Pull up to speaker. Wait for Joe to speak.

Sometimes, this would take several minutes. Do not attempt to order before Joe is ready, or he will say, "I'll be right with you", and then you will have to wait longer. Joe needs to be in his Zen place to accept an order.)
Joe - May I help you?
Dumb Customer - I would like a Number Ten.
Joe - Medium or large size?
Dumb Customer - Large.
Joe - What would you like to drink?
Dumb Customer - Coke.
Joe - Any sauce?
Dumb Customer - Barbeque.
Joe - Is there anything else?
Dumb Customer - No.
Joe - That'll be $5.67.

Do you see the way it worked there? You kept it short and sweet or else Joe became enraged. You only answered the questions he asked when he asked them, because if you tried to give him too much information at once, he would sigh loudly and snap at you, "Excuse me?"

Early on, I used to say, "I'd like a Number Ten, large-sized, with a Coke," but Joe broke me of that real quick. He did not want to hear your entire order all at once. It needed to be given to him in excruciating detail. God help you if you wanted to order food for four or five people when Joe was working. You'd be sitting there at the speaker until you run out of gas.

But I'll give Joe credit. He never once screwed up my order. How could he? Ordering from Joe left no room for error.

Honestly, I wish Joe was still there, because this recording drives me up the wall. I never know if there's actually a human person listening, and I feel stupid telling a recording that I want McNuggets. More than once, I've told the voice what I want, and then had the different-gendered human break in and say, "I'm sorry. What was that?"

And the McDonald's continues to get smarter each and every day. Just last week I pulled up, and the recording did something it had never done before. It began offering food suggestions to me!

"Thank you for choosing McDonald's," it said. "Would you like to try one of our new Cinnamon Melts?"

How the hell am I supposed to respond to that? Do I just start ordering? Should I answer the question and then wait for a different recording to give me the go-ahead to choose something else? In time, is this drive-thru going to turn into some sort of fast food Choose Your Own Adventure story? I think I already know how this is going to end...

> *(Ten years in the future, a car pulls up to the speaker. Before the driver can say a word, he hears a voice)*
> **McRecording** - Thank you for choosing McDonald's. Today you will be having a Filet O' Fish, medium-sized, with a cup of ice. Please pull forward and exit the drive-thru without stopping, as we have already eaten your meal.

The Dinner Party

The dinner party was going swimmingly. An aura of sophistication filled the air. This was a true grownups party, with political talk and glasses of fine wine. No tennis shoes full of bourbon at this dinner party. Not a chance. This was a gathering of upwardly mobile young adults, burned out on keggers and ecstasy-fueled raves. These partygoers were the future of America, looking ahead. They'd crawled out of the gutters long ago and the only toilets they'd be puking into from now on would be the toilets of success.

Chad and Marsha had worked tirelessly for nearly a month to make sure the dinner party would be perfect, and as they looked around the room, they saw nothing that would make them doubt that they'd accomplished their goal. How many guests were here? Forty-five. Maybe fifty. Each one meticulously invited for specific reasons. Putting together this guest list had been like constructing a house of cards in a hurricane, but dammit, these cards were standing tall, meant to be, and the result was visually stunning and deeply satisfying. Blow as hard as you like, Mister Wind, but realize that you're just wasting your breath.

Chad mingled to the left. Marsha to the right. Chad found himself in the middle of a truly intellectual discussion about the overseas agricultural markets and the fiscal effect on the American farmer. Fascinating. Would you like another glass of chardonnay? Don't mind if I do. Marsha quickly became engaged in a heated (but civil) argument contrasting the current governor with the governor of ten years ago. Which leader was better? Who's to say? What's important is that we're dressed business casually all at the same time and that we're using large words in actual conversation. Agreed? Indubitably!

Right on time, the religious discussion. Every good dinner party has one. Probing questions. Insightful, but appropriate. No reason to offend anybody. None of that "What if God was a gay black Republican mother of three" nonsense here. Dignified. And now, time to debate abortion! For it, against it, it doesn't matter. Just so long as everybody gets a chance to put in their one cent. (You never put in both cents at a classy dinner party. This fact is so well known that it needs not be said aloud) Have you seen any good theater lately? Of course. Read that popular novel, perhaps? Yes, yes, and what a pretentious piece of claptrap! I much prefer this obscure title by this little known author. Cheers all around! It's fun to know things!

After chuckling politely at an amusing anecdote about a clueless CEO, Marsha sidles alongside Chad for a status report. She speaks without looking at him. It's bad form to discuss things with each other at a dinner party. That is, if you're the host and hostess of the dinner party.

"This is working out great, right? Everything's perfect, isn't it?"

"Of course it is," Chad replies without turning his head and, in fact, barely moving his mouth. "It couldn't possibly be going any better."

"I'm so excited, Chad. After tonight, we gain an entirely new status. It's caviar and champagne from here on out. No more macaroni and Diet Shasta."

"Hold off on thoughts like that, Marsha. We don't want to get ahead of ourselves. Wait until the dinner party is over. THEN we can evaluate. THEN we can ascend to glory. For now, we still have work to do."

Marsha nodded her head almost imperceptibly, her recently botoxed forehead wrinkling not a bit. "You're right.

It's the seventh inning stretch, but the game's not over yet. We're close, though. I can taste it!"

"It tastes like acceptance, and it's as sweet as candy." Chad took a perfect sip out of his wine glass. No gulping at a dinner party. Never not no way!

A partygoer approached. Dr. Brady, finest dentist in the city. Dentist to the stars. A man of great education and influence. The perfect dentist for the perfect dinner party. When he spoke, he flashed his immaculate teeth with every word.

"Chad. Marsha. What an absolutely fabulous dinner party! I couldn't be more pleased and impressed!"

Marsha waved her hand dismissively, but not too dismissively. No, just the proper amount to show her modesty while at the same time accepting this very nice compliment. That's the way it's done at a dinner party. At the top of his game, Chad was there to pick up the assist. "And where is your lovely wife Karen?" he asked, positively oozing with charm.

Dr. Brady gestured toward the other side of the room. "Oh, she's over there somewhere, no doubt lapping up all the latest gossip. I sometimes call her Mrs. Dr. Brady, The Gossip Lapper!" Laughter all around. Wry remarks of such astounding wit were the norm around an event as posh as this.

Once the general merriment had subsided, there was a brief uncomfortable silence. Short, yes, but disastrous if allowed to continue. Chad and Marsha gave each other a panicked look. Did they really want Dr. Brady to tell all his patients that Chad and Marsha hosted awkward dinner parties? Of course not! This single silence had the potential to undo all the good that had been done. Desperately searching for a conversational transition, Chad noticed a colleague of his strolling by with drink in hand. Chad reached out and grabbed the coworker by the arm.

"Greg! I'd like you to meet Dr. Brady, dentist D.D.S. Finest dentist in the city, he is!"

"Pleasure to meet you, Dr. Brady. Greg Lawrence. I'm in sales."

Handshakes and small talk commenced and disaster was averted. Greg, always a true gentleman and an ideal dinner party guest, conversed with Dr. Brady for minutes upon minutes. Chad and Marsha stood close by, not saying much, just drinking up the tangy nectar of a dinner party gone great. Eventually though, Greg had to mingle his way over to the hors d'oeuvres table, and Dr. Brady turned back to his hosts.

"Nice man, that Greg," Dr. Brady said. "It was a pleasure to make his acquaintance." He looked around, then leaned in slightly and spoke in a low voice. "I must admit, I'm looking forward to telling my friends at the country club about what a fine dinner party I went to recently." Then he winked.

Inside, Chad and Marsha squealed with the joy of six year old girls on the Christmas when they finally got that pony. Outside, however, they remained cool, calm and collected. Both of them waved their hands at the exact same time in the exact same "Oh, go on!" fashion. Inspired by this wholly unexpected rave review from a person who was somebody, Chad scanned the room for another fascinating person he could introduce Dr. Brady to.

Standing not too far away, loudly arguing with a lamp, was Chad's good friend Adam the Axe Murderer. Adam was dressed, as usual, in a bright orange jumpsuit with his dusty and battered San Diego Padres cap. Chad had never seen Adam without it. Also, he was holding his rusty blood-splattered axe. Chad had never seen Adam without that either. Chad noted with some distain that Adam had neglected to shave for the dinner party. His bushy beard covered his heavily scarred face. There were leaves and twigs in it as well. As Chad watched, Adam shrieked "LIAR!!" at the lamp, then punched it square in the shade. The lamp crumpled to the ground and Adam began to stomp on it, defiantly singing the Canadian National Anthem. His singing voice was surprisingly good.

Chad turned to Dr. Brady. "If you thought Greg was grand, you're simply going to adore my friend Adam." Marsha nodded in agreement. She had known Adam for many years and was always charmed and entertained by his wacky antics. She had briefly questioned his inclusion on the dinner party guest list, thinking that perhaps his antics would be TOO wacky for such a get together, but in the end, she relented. After all, Chad had reasoned, who wouldn't like Adam? He was very outgoing and had a great personality.

With a winning smile, Dr. Brady spoke. "Any friend of Chad and Marsha's is a friend of mine. I'd be honored to meet this Adam fellow."

"Awesome!" Chad said, then corrected himself. "Er... I mean, glorious!" Chad mentally chastised himself. That gutter language had no place at a dinner party. He might as well have whipped out his genitals and bellowed, "RADICAL!!" He didn't think Dr. Brady had noticed, but he would not let it happen again. He cupped his hands over his mouth and shouted in Adam's direction.

"Adam!"

Adam continued to dance upon the remains of the lamp. He made no indication that he had heard Chad's voice.

"Adam!"

Dance, dance, dance. Adam could do a serviceable moonwalk. It was kind of a shame the lamp wasn't around to see it.

A little louder this time. "Adam!!"

Adam quit dancing and looked around, both confused and annoyed. Someone, he didn't know who, but someone, had interrupted his victory dance. When he found out who it was... he tightened his grip on the axe.

"Adam, you homicidal sonuvabitch, I'm over here!"

Adam turned and saw his friend Greg waving at him. He liked Greg. Greg was one of the few people who didn't seem to be put off by Adam's various eccentricities. Greg and his wife were nice folks, he'd always thought. He'd kill them last. With a crooked toothy grin, he walked over to them, absentmindedly knocking over an end table on the way.

"Dr. Ross Brady," Greg said as Adam approached. "I'd like you to meet Adam. Adam, this is Dr. Brady."

Dr. Brady looked suspiciously at the grubby man in the orange jumpsuit, but only for a moment. An oddly dressed guest at a dinner party was not completely unheard of. Why, Dr. Brady himself knew an assemblyman named Brett who attended soirées with his dress shirt slightly untucked. It happened so often that Brett had been given the clever nickname "Assemblyman Brett the Shirt Untucked Guy," and it was a nickname he wore with curious pride. Remembering Brett, Dr. Brady decided to give this Adam fellow the benefit of the doubt, even though the jumpsuit had interesting stains around the crotch area.

He held out his hand. "Pleasure to meet you, Adam. Love your jumpsuit. Orange, is it?"

Adam grabbed Dr. Brady's hand, shook it

vigorously, then pulled it up to his mouth and bit it on the wrist, growling.

"Hey! Hey! What are you doing?! OW!!" cried Dr. Brady, trying to pull his arm back from Adam's mouth, but having no luck.

Looking bemused, Greg shook his head and clapped Dr. Brady on the shoulder. "I wouldn't do that. The more you fight it, the harder he bites."

"But he's breaking the skin!"

Greg took a sip of his drink and nodded. "Probably."

Surprised by the decidedly unsurprised reaction of his hosts, Dr. Brady stopped fighting to retrieve his arm and looked at them, unsure of what to say or do. Chad and Marsha both smiled but made no attempt to intervene. Adam continued to gnaw on Dr. Brady's wrist, shaking his head back and forth. And then as suddenly as it had all began, it stopped. Adam spit out the mangled wrist and stared up at the ceiling, transfixed by the sight of something that wasn't there.

Dr. Brady grabbed his wrist and winced in pain as he examined the damage. "He BIT me!"

"Yeah, he does that sometimes. Would you like another crab cake?"

But Dr. Brady didn't seem to be able to let it go. "He bit me!"

Adam held out the tray of crab cakes, but when Dr. Brady made no attempt to grab one, he handed it back to Marsha. "That's just his fancy way of saying hello. He normally grabs you by the sides of your head and tries to bite your nose off, but as this is kind of a formal gathering, we asked him to tone it down a little."

"How utterly… original…" said Dr. Brady, mentally scheduling a tetanus shot for Monday morning. He decided to try and be a good party guest and keep the conversation going, even though he was bleeding quite badly. "So... Adam... aside from biting people you've just met, what do you do for a living?"

Adam continued to stare upward, unblinking. His eyes narrowed. Whatever he was looking at, it was making him angry.

Greg gently tapped Adam on the shoulder. "Hey, Adam. The doctor just asked you a question. He wants to know what you do for a living."

Without looking down, Adam responded, "I'm an axe murderer."

Dr. Brady nodded once. "Yes, well, that would explain the axe. But what I meant is, what is your job?"

"I am an axe murderer." Adam spoke in the tone of voice you would use to explain things to a particularly dimwitted three year old child.

Taking off his necktie and applying it to his wrist as a tourniquet, Dr. Brady shook his head. "I still don't think you're following me here. Where do you go every day from 9:00 to 5:00? Whatever you do with that silly axe is a hobby. A job is something you get paid for."

Adam finally tore his gaze away from the ceiling and looked Dr. Brady directly in the eyes. He spoke very calmly. "Who says I don't get paid?"

And then with one swift, practiced movement, Adam swung the axe with all his might and decapitated Dr. Ross Brady. The doctor's head fell to the floor and bounced twice on the recently steam cleaned carpet. His body stood rigid for a brief moment, then collapsed. His left hand released its tight grip on the necktie wrapped around his right wrist. Adam bent down, pulled Dr. Brady's wallet out of his pants and ruffled through it until he found the cash. It was nearly

$200, mostly in twenties. Adam put the money in a pocket on the front of his jumpsuit and hissed, "See? I get paid. I get paid money. Money... that they PAY ME!!" With that statement, Adam flew into a rage and began hacking at Dr. Brady's body with powerful strokes.

Greg allowed this to continue briefly, then reached over and patted Adam on the back. "Hey buddy, hold off on that for a second. I have some other folks I'd like you to meet."

Breathing heavily, Adam ceased his actions and turned to Greg. The smiling face of his friend caused his murderous rage to subside slightly. He took off his Padres cap, wiped his brow, then re-adjusted the hat on his head. He looked at Greg expectantly.

"I've got to introduce you to my accountant, Brenda. She's an accountant. And even better than that, she's single!" Greg cocked his eyebrow and grinned. He pointed across the room at Brenda, who was standing by herself, admiring a modern work of abstract art on the wall. She was gorgeous in a very classic way. Her strapless red dress fit snugly onto her shapely form.

Even from this distance, Adam could smell her perfume. He had an incredible sense of smell. He could smell the fear on a hot dog. He could also smell music. It was quite a skill, and now the only scent that was entering his nose was this woman's lovely perfume. It was enchanting. She would, he thought, make a wonderful bride, if only he didn't have to kill her right away. Feeling somewhat sad, in a detached kind of way, he lifted his axe to his shoulder, sighed, then ran shrieking across the room toward this beautiful goddess who he had come to love so deeply.

Brenda never even saw Adam coming. One minute,

she didn't have an axe between her shoulder blades and the next minute, she did. She collapsed to the ground like a ton of bricks. Adam pulled the axe out of her back and a tear ran down his cheek. It was such a shame that she had to die, but at least it had been relatively painless and he hadn't ruined the nice dress she was wearing. It was the least he could do for his lovely bride, he thought. God, he loved her.

A woman by the name of Sheila, a publisher of some sort, walked over to Chad and Marsha, who were spraying Lysol on Dr. Brady's mangled corpse. She was on her third glass of wine and seemed unaware of the screaming, crying man with the axe on the other side of the room. "I must admit to you both that I had my doubts you were going to be able to pull this dinner party off, but I'm about ready to raise my glass in congratulations! Such class! Such elegance! Such..." Sheila looked down at the body on the floor. Her eyes grew wide and she emitted a small gasp. "My stars! Is that man... deceased? On your brand new white carpet?!"

Chad shrugged. "Yeah. That happens sometimes. Can I get you a slice of cheesecake, Sheila? It was prepared by five star chef Enrique Fontaine."

"I really shouldn't. I'm trying to watch my figure. Thank you, though." She looked back down. "Is this some sort of conceptual art piece?"

"Nope. It's just your run-of-the-mill corpse. You sure you don't want some cheesecake? It's to die for!"

"The cheesecake is to die for?" Sheila pointed down at Dr. Brady, then said with a small chuckle. "Is that what happened to HIM?"

Adam's axe came right down the middle of Sheila's head, nearly splitting her in half. Blood splattered everywhere. "No, actually," said Marsha. "THAT'S what happened to him." She sprayed some Lysol in Sheila's general direction.

"Adam, do YOU want some cheesecake?" asked Greg, holding out a plate. "I promise you'll think it's amazing."

Using his bare hand, Adam grabbed a hunk of cheesecake and shoved it in his mouth. He chewed thoughtfully, then gave a thumbs up. "Good." He wiped his hand on his jumpsuit, leaving a smear of cheesecake. "I need to use the potty room."

"The bathroom is down the hall, first door on the left, but I think someone is using it right now."

"We'll see about that," muttered Adam as he stumbled off in that direction.

Chad and Marsha watched him go, then Marsha suddenly shouted, "Oh-no!"

"What is it, dear?"

"The cheese trays! I forgot to bring them out! What good is putting together fancy cheese trays if you don't remember to serve them to your guests? I've ruined everything! And we've worked so hard!"

Chad smiled and hugged his wife. "It's okay, Marsha. Everything has been going so well that I doubt anyone has even noticed the lack of cheese."

"Do you really think that, or are you just trying to make me feel better?"

"I don't just think it. I know it." Somewhere down the hall, the sounds of commotion were coming from the bathroom. A window shattered. "Now let's go grab the cheese trays out of the kitchen and we'll get them out here, and nobody will be the wiser."

Marsha kissed Chad on the tip of the nose. "I love you, Chad."

"I love you too, Marsha." He grabbed her hand and

they walked off toward the kitchen. "People are going to talk about our dinner party for years. I promise." This turned out to be true.

A few minutes later, Chad and Marsha returned from the kitchen, each holding a tray covered with exotic and expensive cheeses. No cheddar or Velveeta singles on these trays. There was Gorau Glas and Bitto. Caciocavallo Podolico and Pule. Also a couple of packs of string cheese that Chad noticed and hastily shoved in his pocket before anyone else could see them. But as they got to the center of the living room and looked around, they realized something was amiss.

All of the guests were gone.

Well, except for Dr. Brady, Brenda and Sheila, who continued to lay where they fell, but nobody else was anywhere to be seen.

Chad laid his cheese tray on the coffee table and wrung his hands together. "This... isn't right."

Marsha bit her lower lip. "Everyone was mingling out here a couple of minutes ago." She glanced fearfully at her husband. "You don't think they left because of the lack of cheese, do you?"

"No, of course not. That's absurd," said Chad, although he was mostly just saying it to make Marsha feel better. He'd heard horror stories of dinner parties that had fallen apart when the temperature had fallen from 78 to 77. Something as serious as missing cheese trays was much worse than that. He wrung his hands even harder.

"Then where did they all go? It's like they were never even here in the first place!" Marsha put her cheese tray down as well, right underneath the modern work of abstract art on the wall, which now had several large gashes in it, as if it had been hacked at with a sharp object of some sort.

"There has to be an explanation. Maybe they all went out on the balcony to look at the stars?"

Marsha grabbed Chad by the arm. "Chad, we don't HAVE a balcony! I told you we shouldn't throw a dinner party until we got a balcony! I TOLD you that!" Her voice became hysterical. "We don't even have a wine cellar! What were we THINKING?!"

Chad held up his hand. "Wait. I hear something."

Marsha fell silent and after a moment, she heard it too. Once she really started listening, she found it difficult to believe she hadn't heard it all along. It was the sound of forty-five to fifty party guests screaming for help, and it was coming from down the hall. "Oh, thank God," Marsha said. "They didn't leave!"

"I told you so!" Chad said as he walked down the hall, closely followed by Marsha, who had, after some waffling, opted not to bring a cheese tray with her.

They passed the bathroom on the left and then got down to the end of the hall where Adam was standing, completely soaked, orange jumpsuit dripping water on the floor. He was wiping off his axe with a hand towel. In front of him was a closed door which led to Chad and Marsha's bedroom. Behind the door, Chad could hear all the partygoers, many of whom were frantically crying. Chad pointed at the hand towel Adam was using.

"You're not really supposed to use those towels. They're more just for looks."

Adam raised an eyebrow. Chad grinned.

"Eh, don't worry about it. That's more Marsha's rule than mine. I notice you're a little bit drenched. What happened?"

"I took a shower." Adam tossed the hand towel to

the ground and grabbed his axe with both hands, trying to find the perfect grip.

Chad nodded. "Oh, okay. That makes sense." He leaned over, picked up the towel, and handed it to Marsha. "Hey, question. Do you know why everybody went into the bedroom?"

Adam shrugged. "They always try and hide somewhere." Then he smiled. It was actually a very winning smile, except for all the missing teeth. "But don't worry. I'm gonna get 'em out." Adam took the axe and plunged it as hard as he could into the bedroom door. The screams behind the door grew more panicked. Adam reared back and drove the axe into the door a second time. A medium sized chunk of wood came loose, exposing a medium sized sliver of light from the other side.

Marsha now had somewhat of a view into the bedroom, and she was relieved to see all her guests in there, cowering in fear, trying to hide under the bed and trampling each other to get as far away from the door as possible. Her cheese tray faux pas had not ruined the dinner party. Marsha smiled. She'd really dodged a bullet with this one.

Adam took a couple more swings at the bedroom door, which was rapidly filling up with bigger and bigger holes. He put his face to one of the holes and looked inside the room, laughing psychotically. This was going to be a good day. He was so glad he'd decided to come to the dinner party.

From behind him, Chad chuckled and clapped his hands together. "Oh, I get it! You're doing that scene from The Shining! That's hysterical! I knew everyone here was going to love your sense of humor. Marsha, wasn't I saying that just this morning, that people were going to crack up when Adam started being funny?"

"It's true. He really did." Marsha said. "But when you're done with your little skit, I want to serve dinner, okay? If I wait too much longer to feed everyone, they're going to start to get grumpy."

"Chad! Marsha!" came a cry from inside the bedroom. "Please help us! Call the police! There's a maniac with an axe trying to kill us!"

"Jonathan Davis? Is that you?" Marsha bent over and looked through one of the axe holes in the door at a terrified middle aged man in a smoking jacket who was banging on the opposite wall of the bedroom with his fist. "I didn't know you were here yet! I'm so glad you could make it. Where's your lovely wife Sheila?"

Jonathan tried to answer, but Marsha could not hear him clearly over all the other commotion. She got up and looked at Chad. "Jonathan Davis is in there."

"He's a good guy. I really like him," said Chad, as with one more mighty swing, Adam completely demolished the bedroom door. He walked into the room, eyes bright and shining. He didn't know where to start.

Chad and Marsha walked back through the living room on the way to the kitchen so that they could begin setting up for the dinner portion of the dinner party. A cacophony of various noises came from the bedroom. "Chad?" Marsha said, stopping near Dr. Brady.

Chad stopped as well and looked at her questioningly.

Marsha didn't continue talking right away, instead shifting back and forth on the balls of her feet. This was one of her nervous habits, something she did when she was about to bring up something she didn't think Chad was going to like. He smiled. "It's okay, honey. What's the problem?"

"Well," she took a deep breath, then continued. "I don't want to make a whole big deal about this, but earlier, with the hand towel... I know you played it off like a joke and all, but it really upset me that Adam used one of those towels. You know, those belonged to my grandmother and I don't like to wash them, just because they're so delicate. I know you don't like being the big mean taskmaster, but can you please talk to him later and explain why this is so important to me?"

"Of course I will. Don't even worry about it." As he spoke, several of the partygoers who had managed to escape from the bedroom ran past him and out the front door, yelling and sobbing. "I think Adam just got a little overexcited tonight and forgot his manners. He almost never gets to have an upscale social outing like this. But he'll understand. I promise."

Marsha looked relieved. "I thought you were going to tell me I was being ridiculous."

Chad opened his mouth to respond, to reassure his wife that her request was perfectly reasonable, when he was run into from behind by Jonathan Davis, and they both tumbled to the ground. Chad moaned and tried to catch his breath, while Jonathan flailed his limbs around trying to get back on his feet.

Marsha reached down to help her guest up. "Jonathan! Where are you running off to? Did you get an important call from your stockbroker?"

Jonathan ignored Marsha's outstretched hand and managed to stand up on his own. He glared at Marsha. "Where am I running off to? Are you serious?" Marsha did not reply, but just looked at Jonathan with confusion. "There is a man with an axe in your house and he is murdering your party guests! I'm trying to get away so that he does not murder ME! THAT'S where I'm running off to, you idiots!"

Chad finally got to his feet and stood between Jonathan and Marsha. "Hey, hey, hey! That kind of language is not necessary." He waved his finger in Jonathan's face. "There is no excuse for speaking to us like that in our house."

Jonathan gestured wildly towards the bedroom. "Man with an axe!"

"He has a name, Jonathan! It's Adam!" Chad was becoming angry. His guest was being very rude. "Would you like it if I called you 'man with a scarf'?"

"I'm not wearing a scarf! It fell off when I was running away from the man with the axe!" Jonathan glanced over his shoulder. Adam had finished his business in the bedroom and was now slowly walking back down the hall towards the living room. He was humming softly to himself. Jonathan pushed Chad out of the way and ran toward the front door.

"Rude!" Chad barked. He couldn't hold it in any more. "Very rude!"

Jonathan was just about out the door when he stopped, turned around, pointed at Chad and Marsha and screamed, "This is the worst dinner party I have ever attended." Then he continued outside and out of sight.

Jonathan's statement hung in the air. Chad and Marsha stood perfectly still, mouths agape. Behind them, Adam was wildly swinging his axe in circles, occasionally putting it through a wall or a couch. Around his waist, he was now wearing a lovely scarf. Far off in the distance, sirens could be heard.

Nearly a minute went by before Chad looked at Marsha. He spoke in a small voice a single word. "Rude."

Marsha shook her head. "What if he was right?"

"No. That's not possible. Everyone was having such a good time. The dinner party was going swimmingly."

"It was, Chad. It was. But I think we might have made a slight error in judgment."

"What error? What are you talking about?"

Marsha shifted on the balls of her feet. "Adam."

"Adam what?" Chad couldn't figure out where Marsha was going with this. But then he heard sounds coming from the hall. He glanced over and saw several of his party guests limping out of the bedroom, most with gaping axe wounds. As Chad watched them, he realized something profound. They did not seem to be enjoying the party. "Oh," he said. He finally understood.

He turned around and saw his friend pulling his axe out of their entertainment center. Chad had rarely seen Adam so happy. But if Adam was the only one enjoying the dinner party, could the dinner party really be considered a success? Adam randomly began swinging his axe again as he stumbled through the living room, swinging and swinging, getting closer and closer until he was finally within a couple of feet of Chad and Marsha. Not realizing how close he was until the last moment, Adam pulled back and the axe stopped a fraction of an inch from Chad's face. Chad sadly spoke. "Adam, we need to talk."

Adam looked utterly confused as he lowered the axe to his side.

"Listen," Chad said, as he held Marsha's hand for support. "We love having you here. You're one of the most interesting people we know. But it's becoming apparent that this kind of gathering isn't really the place for you. You're great. And these people are great too. But it turns out that you don't really mix well with each other. It's not your fault. It's not their fault. It just kind of… is. You know what I mean?"

Adam didn't say anything. He continued to stand there, breathing heavily.

"So," Chad continued. "I think I'm going to have to ask you to leave. This is one of the hardest things I've ever had to do, and I feel like such a scumbag..."

"But it's the right thing to do," Marsha said.

Adam stared at them for a moment, occasionally opening and closing his eyes. Then he snarled and raised the axe over his head. Chad put up a hand. "No, Adam. You really have to go."

Reluctantly, Adam lowered his axe again. He seemed to be struggling with something internally. Finally, he grabbed his head with both hands and screamed to the heavens. A tear rolled down Marsha's cheek. The sirens in the distance began to grow louder.

Adam hung his head and started walking towards the front door, dragging his axe behind him. He stopped after a few steps and looked back. "May I take the accountant with me? She is my bride."

Chad shook his head. "I don't think that would be a very good idea. I'm sorry."

Adam nodded once, as if he expected this answer. Then he resumed moving towards the door.

Chad couldn't let him leave like this. He ran towards Adam. "Wait!" Adam stopped again. Chad approached him, reached into his pocket, and pulled out a package of string cheese. He held it out and Adam stared at it. "It's for you. Something for the road, you know, since you didn't get to stay long enough to have dinner." His voice caught in his throat. "And because we're still friends, okay?"

Adam took the string cheese, stuck it behind his ear, then spoke one last time. "I liked your dinner party." With that he turned, walked out the door, and never looked back.

Chad and Marsha watched him go. Chad almost called out to him, but before he could, Marsha said, "He'll be fine. I know Adam can come off as being kind of fragile and sensitive, but he's a lot more resilient than he lets on."

"Yeah, you're probably right. It was just a difficult decision to have to make."

"We're about to have plenty of decisions to make that are going to be just as difficult, you know."

Chad cocked an eyebrow at Marsha. "What decisions?"

Marsha smiled. "How we're going to make the next dinner party even better than this one."

The couple laughed and embraced as the last of the surviving party guests crawled past them, out the front door and into the warm summer evening.

The following True-Life Tale is being brought to you by…

got dead?

It's happened to all of us. You've put together a perfect funeral. The flowers are fresh, the invitations are sent out and the hearse has been rented. But at the last minute you realize…

You don't have a corpse!

Then you're forced to either cancel the funeral or commit the socially awkward faux pas of trying to snuff out a family member. Well, no more! And it's all thanks to The Cadaver Barn®.

The Cadaver Barn® offers the best selection and the best prices for all your cadaver needs. Our stiffs are the deadest! Other low class cadaver companies have bodies that are only mostly dead, but our cadavers are 100% dead, 100% of the time. That's our promise to you! You've tried the rest, now try the best. Our comprehensive screening process weeds out the low quality and leaves you with absolutely the best dead for your hard earned dollar. It doesn't matter what you're looking for. We've got all races, colors, ages, shapes and sizes. And you don't have to worry about rigor mortis, because all our cadavers are fresh. Once it's been in The Cadaver Barn® for 24 hours, it gets tossed in the dumpster out back. That's our commitment to quality!

So stop worrying about where you're gonna find your next corpse for whatever you need them for. We don't ask questions or make moral judgments. We just sell the dead and we do it better than anyone that has ever lived.

The Cadaver Barn®
The Best Dead For Your Dollar

Throat Or Die

My throat hurts.

It's not the worst sore throat I've had this year, but it's just sore enough to be mildly annoying. I've been sucking on cough drops for the last few days (I'm sorry. Not cough drops. These are "Halls Mentho-Lyptus Oral Anesthetic with Advanced Vapor Action." I guess there's a difference.), but it's not doing a whole lot of good. Such is the sore throat, though. It'll hurt for a few days, then it will be gone, and I'll have to find something else to complain about. Maybe the weather. (Here is a preview: "Man! It's hot! What the hell, you know?!")

When I was little, all the medical advice I received came from my mother, who was incredibly predictable. Whenever I complained that I wasn't feeling well, whatever the symptoms, it was always because I needed to go to bed earlier. It didn't matter whether I had a headache or I was bleeding from a gaping head wound.

I'd come limping up to her, holding my severed foot in my hand, and I'd say, "Mom! My stump hurts!"

She would look at me and say, "It's probably because you stay up too late. Why don't you go to bed early tonight and we'll see how you feel in the morning." It was a strange thing to tell me, because at the time, I was going to bed at around 8:00pm. Any earlier, and I would be getting close to going to bed late in the afternoon. I also enjoyed the implication that whatever was wrong with me, in a way it was my own fault because I wasn't going to bed at the crack of noon.

Occasionally, Early Bedtime did not solve the problem and she was forced to medicate me. But again, there was a certain level of predictability in her medical care. For example, as a child, anytime I had a sore throat, her solution was to make me gargle with salt water. Now, from what I've read, this is actually a very good home remedy for a sore throat, but it was one of the most unpleasant experiences I ever had every single time. The first time she made me do it, the whole thing was kind of interesting. I was a scrawny little seven year-old with a sore throat but dang it, my mommy is going to make everything all better. I watched with wonder as she grabbed my little green plastic cup and then filled it with a little bit of water. Then she grabbed the salt and poured and poured and poured and poured and poured. After a quick flick of her wrist to swirl the mixture around, she handed it to me and said, "Okay, this isn't going to taste very good, but if you gargle with it for a minute straight then it's going to make your throat feel better."

So I, like the trusting child I briefly was, took a great big sip and after roughly two-fifths of a second, I spit it halfway across the kitchen. "BLECK!!" I shouted, and then burst into tears. My mother was not too happy and suggested that if I wasn't going to gargle the salt water, maybe I would be better off going to bed.

That ended up being the most successful of the many salt water gargling treatments that I had to endure over the years. From that point on, any time she pulled out the salt and the little plastic green cup, I'd stand there shivering and sniveling and basically praying for death or anything that would save me from having to put the evil potion in my mouth. Looking back, I think the main problem with her home remedy was that the ratio of salt to water was WAY off. Salt water, I can handle. But what she was making me gargle was a cup of moist salt. I assume she was trying to cure all the sore throats I was ever going to have in my life, just all at once.

But where my mother really shined was not in treatment. It was in diagnosis. No matter what I was complaining about, she was able to tell me, in an instant, exactly what was wrong. Somehow it was always the worst thing it could possibly be.

Symptom: "My throat is sore"
Diagnosis: "You've got strep throat"
Symptom: "My stomach hurts a little"
Diagnosis: "Must be an ulcer"
Symptom: "I have a headache"
Diagnosis: "You're probably dying"

Not that it mattered WHAT she thought was wrong with me. The cure was always the same thing. I had no idea that a spoonful of Robitussin and a 7:30 bedtime could cure cancer, but for me, it worked every time.

I know now that a lot of the time, she was just being sarcastic as a way to cope with a child who whined too much, but for a long time, I seriously thought I'd survived a number of truly terrifying medical illnesses and about ninety-five cases of strep throat, a malady that I am now pretty sure I've never had. (She did sarcastic pretty well. At the dinner table, I would occasionally see something on my plate I didn't recognize, and I would ask her what it was, to which she would inevitably answer, "Poison," which going by her tone of voice, was not such a big deal and did not ever get me out of eating it. I wonder if that's why I'm such a picky eater today, because as far as I know, anything that isn't a McNugget is poison.)

Not that it really mattered WHAT she said I was sick

with, because we almost never went to the doctor. Oh, I got all my shots and checkups, but when it came to just seeing the doctor because I didn't feel well, I had to be REALLY sick. Way beyond the healing power of salt and slumber. If I wanted a trip to the doctor, I'd better be throwing up, or have a nose that's been running for a week, or I'd better be bleeding from the ear. Unless I had fluid coming out of my face, we weren't going anywhere.

That became something I've carried with me to this day, because now I've got a severe and completely irrational distrust of doctors. I never go to the doctor. Never, never, never. It's because I'm certain that with a little trial and error, I can fix it myself. This theory has actually worked pretty well for me, except for the time a couple of years ago I got a brutal case of food poisoning and was sicker than I'd ever been in my life for the better part of a week. In retrospect, a visit to Mister Doctor would have been beneficial, as opposed to what I was doing instead, which was laying on the floor of my bathroom, writhing in agony. But eh... live and learn.

But the funny part is, as much I might have questioned Mother's methods, the whole thing has turned out pretty well. Here I am, twenty years later, with general good health, and I get sick maybe twice a year and it's never anything major. The occasional cold, a few aches and pains, a sore throat here and there, but overall I guess there's something to what she was doing all those years. She should really write a book. I, on the other hand, will just continue writing these columns, which go a long way toward making me feel better, until the time comes when I get hit by a bus.

One last medical note, for all you sufferers out there, and this one comes from recent personal experience. Like, within the last thirty seconds. If you have a sore throat and you think drinking a glass of orange juice will make you feel better because orange juice is supposed to be good for you, you are an idiot. It is going to burn like hell. You're welcome.

Shadows of the Invisible
(a tale told in "real-time")

Week Three: Twists, Turns and Other Twists

"Last week, I failed to save my ex-wife and step-kids from two kidnappers. The President of Antarctica continued to be targeted with an assassination threat. And people that I work with may be involved in both. My name is Librarian of Congress Jacques Vargas, and these... are the longest eight weeks of my life..."

FRIDAY, NOVEMBER 29th, 2002

3:00pm - Library of Congress, Washington D.C.

Behind the closed door of his corner office, Jacques Vargas sits with Chuck and Irma, going over reports on the assassination threat against the Antarctican president. "What I don't understand," Jacques says, "is why anybody would want to kill this guy in the first place. Who in their right mind could possibly be anti-Antarctica?"

Chuck Williams shakes his head, looking very annoyed at his boss. "You're looking at the wrong question, Jacques. That's why we're not getting anywhere! It's been two weeks now, and we're at the same place we were when we started because you have no clue what you're doing! You're like a sea captain trying to fly a fire truck to the sun!"

Irma sighs. "Maybe the reason we're not getting anywhere is because you two won't stop bickering. We're working towards the same goal, you know. The President of

Antarctica is a very important man, and it's very important that he lives."

"That's what I'm trying to do, Irma." Chuck says, throwing his hands in the air. "But this guy here has the leadership skills of a Speak and Spell. The difference being that I don't think Jacques can spell."

Jacques sighs much too loudly. "All right, Chuck. You're so smart, why don't you tell me what we should do. And then, when the President gets blown to teeny-tiny bits, I can laugh and laugh and laugh... at you, I mean. Not the President. That's going to be a tragedy."

"Look, you're so busy trying to find out WHO, that you've totally overlooked the question of WHY. You seem to have forgotten the rather obvious fact that very few people in the entire world even know that there IS a President of Antarctica. The Antarctic government is top secret and highly classified. Therefore, somebody IN THE KNOW would have to have a very specific reason to want him gotten rid of. Something like this risks exposing the President to the general public. And I think I've figured out a very rational explanation. See, about six weeks ago, there was a change in Antarctic foreign policy, and it caused..."

The door to the office bursts open and rookie Todd Herring falls to the ground from the other side. Everyone turns and looks, and Jacques quickly stands up. "Todd? What's going on?"

"Nothing, sir. I'm sorry, sir. I fell." Todd gets to his feet and brushes off his clothes. As he does this, a small tape recorder falls out of his shirt pocket. All eyes in the room follow it to the ground, and then three pairs look back at the highly-flustered Todd.

"Were you leaning on the door and recording our conversation, Todd?" Jacques shakes his head disapprovingly. "Cause that sure looks like what you were doing."

"No, sir. Not at all, sir. I just... I was just sort of, like, walking by the office, and I lost my balance and fell through the door... the one right there." Todd points weakly at the office door without making any eye contact with anyone else in the room.

"What's on the tape recorder, Todd?"

"Um... I don't know?"

Jacques walks around his desk and picks up the recorder. He rewinds it slightly, then hits play. Chuck's voice comes out of the tiny speaker. "...exposing the President to the general public. And I think I've figured out a very rational explanation. See, about six weeks ago..." Jacques stops the tape and looks at Todd. "Todd, do you have something you want to tell us?"

Chuck interjects. "Do I really sound like that? My voice is so... squeaky!"

"Chuck, please. We'll deal with your Chip and Dale voice later. Right now, Todd's about to tell us something. Right, Todd?"

Todd starts to shake his head, then licks his lips nervously and opens his mouth. "Um... yeah. You... um... you have a phone call. Sir."

"A phone call? I haven't heard any phones ring."

Todd nods and reaches into his other shirt pocket. He pulls out a small cell phone. "It's my own personal phone. I don't know how they got the number, but they're asking for you."

For a long moment, Jacques looks at the phone, then back at Irma. She gives a very slight nod. He shrugs. "All right. I'll bite." He grabs the phone, which is slick with sweat, holds it for a moment, then hands it to Irma. "You take this one, Irma. I think I'm just going to stand here and stare at Todd with my powerful gaze." He gazes powerfully at Todd, who cringes.

Irma frowns. "Are you sure you want me to get this, Jacques? They did ask for YOU."

"Can't talk. Gazing." Todd shakes and lets out an involuntary whine.

Irma slowly puts the phone to her ear. "L.O.C. This is Damole. Who am I speaking to?"

A slight pause on the end of the line, then a male voice speaks. "This is Joe. I'm one of the men who is holding Vargas' wife hostage. Why is he not taking this call?"

"He's sort of busy. He's breaking someone's spirit with nothing more than a glance. May I pass along a message?"

"Please do. Tell him that we no longer need his assistance. His constant incompetence is no longer part of our plan. Tell him he's really bad at following directions, and if he heard some of the things his wife said about him... wow. Apparently, he couldn't wash a dish to save his life. Or take out the trash."

"I'll let him know. Thank you." Irma begins to hang up the phone, then thinks again. "Hey, Joe. What about his wife? Are you letting her go?"

"Not quite yet, Irma. Unlike your boss, she still serves a purpose." In the background, Irma hears a toilet flush. "I've got to go, Miss Damole. Good luck stopping the assassination. And by good luck, I mean BAD luck." The phone goes dead in Irma's ear.

"Hey, Jacques, I've got a question for you." Jacques turns toward Irma, having caused Todd to flee in terror with his Super Stare. "You remember last Friday when you had to go the restaurant to pick up the mystery item so that the kidnappers would release Lily and the kids?"

"Vaguely."

"Okay, what exactly happened with all that, because the guy on the phone says he's still got her?"

Jacques shrugs unconvincingly. "Shoot, I don't know. It was so long ago. I've got too much on my mind to waste time with remembering things."

Chuck stands up and throws his hands in the air. "Yet another wholly unproductive meeting. Way to go, Jacques. You're really all over this Antarctica issue. We sure are lucky to have you around. Now if you'll excuse me, I'm going back to work. I have some ideas on how to save a life. See, what I'm going to do is to use all the resources of the Library of Congress."

"You sound like a junior high school field trip, Chuck."

Glaring at Jacques with a Super Stare of his own, Chuck turns on his heels and stomps out of the office. Jacques sits back down at his desk. "Just between you and me, that Chuck dude is, pardon my French, a le gars que je n'aime pas beaucoup."

"Yeah, that French IS pretty terrible, but we're getting off the subject. What happened last week? You came back pretty late, and you never said anything about it to me. Did you get whatever it was they told you to get?"

Jacques rolls his eyes. "Not TECHNICALLY. I sort of ran out of gas, and when they called me back, I just turned off my cell phone. Haven't had it on since, now that I think about it." Jacques cocks his head slightly. "I'll bet I have a lot of missed calls and voicemails."

Looking somewhat surprised, Irma snaps at him. "You just ignored these people? The ones that have your ex-wife? That's a little cold-blooded, Jacques. I know she's your ex, but there IS a little more at stake here than just her. Weren't they supposed to give you information on the assassination?"

"I don't know. Maybe. It was late. I was cold. You wanna go get a burger?"

"I just HAD a burger. Right before the meeting. It was undercooked and flavorless."

"Yeah, sorry about that. I ran out of spices... and fire." He snaps his fingers. "Hey, I do remember something from that night, now that I think about it! The guy on the phone said something that made me suspect that we might have a dirty agent here in the L.O.C. We probably should've been looking into that all this time. My bad."

"A dirty agent?" Irma begins to pace back and forth. "That actually explains a lot of the information leaks." Comprehension dawns on her face. "What if it's Todd? He's been acting terribly suspicious, plus he's the newest member of the L.O.C. We don't really know him at all!"

Jacques begins to rock in his non-rocking chair. Although putting forth great effort, he nods. "You might be right, Irma. Maybe Todd Herring is the mole within the agency. Plus, he's a redhead!" He slams his fist on the desk and sits up straight, looking for the first time like the leader he's supposed to be. "Call security and have them monitor Todd's incoming and outgoing transmissions. If we can get just a little proof..."

Chuck dashes back into the office, wide-eyed and holding the receiver of his desk phone. The detached cord dangles back and forth. "Irma, Jacques. We got another call from the assassin. He gave us a date and a place."

"That's insanely convenient."

"Shut up, Jacques."

Irma looks at Chuck expectantly. "So what's the place

and the date?"

"He said they're going to hit the President at the National Zoo... on December 6th..."

3:11pm - Budget Plaza Motel, Baltimore, MD

Jacques ex-wife, Lily-Rodham Vargas, sits on the bed with a small vial in her hand. She's glad her kids aren't here to see this, but they've been at their Grandmother's house since Monday. Having two small children in a small motel room was finally starting to drive Joe and Vlad insane, so they decided it would be better off to make the children leave. This was fine with Lily, who was getting tired of the constant questions. "When are we going home?" "Why does the man in the cloak smell like the undead?" "Why does the man in the cloak turn into a bat sometimes?" Endless questions that she didn't really have any good answers for.

But speaking of the man in the cloak, he is currently punching himself in the face over and over again, while the other man, Joe, counts the punches. "Eight..." WHACK!! "Nine..." WHACK!! "Ten! Ten in a row, Vlad! I can't believe you actually did that!"

Vlad wobbles slightly as bruises begin to form on his pale cheeks. "I have done what you asked! I have played your games! Now GIVE ME MY PRIZE!!!"

Joe laughs and motions to Lily to throw Vlad the vial. She tosses it to him, and in one quick motion, Vlad pulls off the cover and begins madly drinking the contents. It's rather pathetic, but Lily finds that making Vlad do stupid things for the vial sure beats watching daytime TV. She wonders fleetingly if she's ever going to be set free. Silently, she asks for a sign. As if on cue, Joe's cell phone rings.

Joe walks to the dresser, steps over Vlad, who is trying to stick his tongue in the vial, and answers. "Hello? Oh, Mr. Williams. Good afternoon. No, no. We're just sitting here, bored out of our wits." He listens intently, then glances at Lily. "Yeah, she's still here... you're kidding? You did? So it's still on... Yeah, I called him, but he didn't take the call. It's not important. I've talked to our inside agent, and he's not going to be a problem. Okay, so you're coming down now? We'll be ready." He hangs up the phone and kicks Vlad in the side. "Get up, Vlad. We're going into action."

Vlad looks up sadly. "But I'm so thirsty... so very thirsty..."

Ignoring Vlad, Joe sits on the bed next to Lily. "That was my boss. He's coming over right now, and if everything goes right, you might actually get to go home soon." There's a knock at the door, and Lily and Joe both look up. "All right. There he is. It took forever, but he's finally found the man who's gonna help us get things done."

Joe goes to the door and opens it. Standing there, side by side, is a sharp-dressed William Williams, and his partner Duke, who's dressed like a cowboy. They enter the room without saying a word, and directly behind them, looking in with a smug grin... is Jacques Vargas.

To Be Continued...

The following True-Life Tale is being brought to you by…

Bartender! Verb Me A Noun!

In school I never did good in writing because I was not so good in writing. The problem was my writing. It was not so good. After I got out of school my writing did not get more good because I was so bad at writing that I never did any writing or wrote. This was a bad problem because I write books for a living and my books were not good written. In fact they were bad in written terms. Lucky for me my book editor told me about Susan Lee's Writing Course® and I took the course and now my writing has improved in a more good way than before when it was bad. New paragraph.

Susan Lee's Writing Course® is for one week and for all of the days Susan Lee teaches how to take your bad writing and make it better through improvement. Did you know that you can add zing to your writing by using nouns and question marks? I do now thanks Susan Lee? Susan Lee also tells you the way to use descriptive words to make your writing come alive. Now my writing comes alive. It does.

I went to Susan Lee's Writing Course® and I am a person who you can trust because my writing speaks for itself and comes alive. You should take Susan Lee's Writing Course® too because you need to be a writer even if you are a vet or a person from Idaho. Idaho is a noun and I wrote it. Thanks Susan Lee? I mean Lee! Maybe if you are good at your write then Susan Lee will let you write an ad for her because she let me write and ad for her and it only took me six weeks. Susan Lee you are a Writing Course person! In a good way!

Susan Lee's Writing Course®

The WRITE Course For You To Take.
Oops... I mean RIGHT Course.
Sorry.

Coming Through In The Clutch

It was a red Nineteen Ninety-Something Geo Metro and I never wanted it, but it was mine. It came to be in my possession after a particularly contentious day of car shopping with my mother. We had spent most of that Saturday driving from used car lot to used car lot looking for a vehicle that would fit my needs. Our ideas of what my "needs" were could not have been more different. What I thought I needed was a brand new car, bright and shiny. What Mother thought I needed was a "car," possibly with tires, but only if we could fit such an extravagance into our budget. Our budget was somewhere around $5000, money I had made the previous summer during my brief foray into television superstardom. But the more cars we looked at, the more I was beginning to see that a truly phat ride could not be purchased for such a small amount of Benjamins. My mood became progressively more sour as the afternoon wore on. My mother's followed suit.

At the time, just a few months away from my 16th birthday, the relationship between my mother and I was at its rockiest. When I wasn't surly, I was bitter. When I wasn't bitter, I was cynical. Mother was not too happy with this version of her son, and there was a great deal of tension all the time. She was Israel and I was Palestine, minus a few car bombs. We were always looking for something to fight about, and that something was never too hard to find.

When we pulled up to what would be the final car lot of the day, we weren't speaking to each other as we'd just had a row at the previous car lot. She accused me of not picking out a car because I was just "being difficult," to which I countered that it's not MY fault if the stupid car lots don't have a stupid car that I stupid like. But she was right. I WAS being difficult, because a part of me equated getting a car with letting her win and I wasn't going to let that happen. Sadly, my internal logic remains a lot like that to this very day.

We got out of her car and trudged up to the fine selection of used automobiles available for purchase. It dawned on me at that point that if I didn't pick a car soon, I was doomed to spend the rest of my young life being driven from lot to lot with an increasingly enraged mother who would eventually drive me out to the desert, a trip from which only she would return. So I made a spur of the moment decision. It was a very stupid decision that would be difficult to top (though that doesn't stop me from trying once in a while). What I decided was that I was going to buy the first car I saw that was less than $5000, no matter what it was, just to make this nightmare end. That car ended up being the sporty, stylish red Nineteen Ninety-Something Geo Metro.

I walked up to the Metro, put my hand on it and said, "This one. I want this one."

Mother peeked in the driver's side window. "It's a manual transmission. I thought you wanted an automatic."

"I don't care. Let's just get it."

"You don't know how to drive a stick shift," Mother said. "How are you planning to get it home?"

"I don't know. I guess I'll just have to learn. Whatever. Let's buy it."

"Are you SURE this is the one you want?" she asked. I couldn't figure out why she was asking me so many questions. It wasn't as if it was a major purchasing decision, like when I was trying to decide which Nintendo 64 game to buy (answer: Mario Kart).

"Yes. It's my favorite. Let's go." And with that, she gave up and motioned over to the car salesman, who had been watching this exchange with sadistic glee. He knew he was going to make a sale on this day. I got the feeling it was not the first time he had sold a car to an idiot teenager and one or more exasperated parents.

A few hours later, Matt's Very First Car was sitting in the street in front of the house, freshly washed and just begging to be driven. It should have been a very exciting and liberating moment. But I did not want to drive it. I hated it, because it had finally sunk in that I had just spent my entire savings on a car that I didn't want just to appease my mother. The car sat there untouched and I avoided it as if it had something contagious.

The Metro sat there for a month or so, slowly growing roots. Eventually, my stepdad was able to convince me to let him take me out for some driving lessons, where he would attempt to explain the great complexities of the manual transmission. My stepdad and I got along pretty well and he had a laidback teaching style, so even though I was completely terrified, there wasn't a great deal of pressure to get it right the first time, every time. He told me that I was going to make mistakes at first and that was okay. And I did and it was. By the third lesson, I was beginning to pick up on things. The clutch and I were becoming friends.

Several days went by and my mood about the Metro was beginning to lighten. I was finally starting to envision myself driving around in it which was a huge step in the right direction. I wasn't too happy with how small it was (It was like cramming myself into a Power Wheel. I'd get in the car, push the seat as far back as it would go, and my knees would still be banging against the steering wheel.), but I was willing to deal with that. I was a few tantalizing weeks away from getting my license and being mobile, which meant freedom, glorious freedom. I could do what I wanted, when I wanted! I could drive to Maui, if that's what I felt like! A couple more good lessons with the clutch, and I was gonna get all NASCAR on this city.

But there would only be one more lesson, and it would be the last time I ever drove the sporty, stylish Geo Metro.

That afternoon, my mother offered to take me out driving, and my defenses immediately went up. I told her I'd rather go out with my stepdad, but she said he had things to do around the house. I told her that if that was the case then I was okay with not going driving at all, but her tone of voice made it clear that she was not ASKING me, she was TELLING me. I kind of think now, looking back, that she just wanted to spend some time with me, perhaps working on repairing our fractured relationship with some sort of mother-son bonding, but what ended up happening was just the opposite.

On the Annoyed Scale of 1 to 10, I was already at a 5 when we walked out to the Metro. I didn't feel like going driving with my mother, whose teaching style was more abrasive than my stepdad's was. She wasn't as good at accepting it when I would make mistakes, thinking that I was doing it on purpose to enrage her. As a silent protest against this unlawful outing, I didn't even bother putting on shoes, instead just wearing a pair of loose fitting sandals. When I protest, I do it HARDCORE.

I started the car and pulled into the street. For the first four to five seconds, everything was fine. Then I got to a stop sign and stalled the car. Mother didn't say anything, but her lips pressed together. It would not take long before they were pressed together so hard that they would virtually be gone. I restarted the Metro and made a right turn. Mother started giving me directions. Turn here, turn there, make a left on this street. I acknowledged her commands with grunts and loud sighs, hoping to get across the message of exactly how much I was not enjoying this. Her Annoyed Level went up to 7.

Sweat beading at the top of my forehead and shrieking at myself inside my head not to mess up, I continued driving around for several more minutes. Eventually, we reached an intersection. There was an SUV waiting at a stop sign to my right, so I stopped because the SUV had reached the intersection first, and according to the DMV handbook I had flipped through maybe twice, that gave the other car the right of way. But the SUV did not go. The lady in it just looked at me.

It was a stalemate. She didn't go. I didn't go. She waved me across. I waved her across. I couldn't understand why stupid SUV Lady wouldn't just cross the stupid intersection and was pondering this when a maternal voice loudly broke the silence.

"What are you DOING?" Mother said, sounding the opposite of happy.

I pleaded my case. "That lady won't go! She's got the right-of-way!"

"Why would she have the right-of-way?!" Her Annoyed Level was rising, but I was not sure why, because I was pretty sure I was right.

"She got here first!"

Mother pointed angrily out the window. "This isn't a four-way stop! It's only a two way! YOU DON'T HAVE A STOP SIGN!!"

I looked at where she was pointing, and to my surprise, there was no stop sign. I had completely missed this in my internal panic. I should have never stopped in the first place and SUV Lady was actually not as stupid as I had decided she was. SUV Lady had, of course, already left the stop sign and driven away during the argument. SUV Lady knew the rules of the road, but she also had places to go.

I stuttered and stammered in the driver's seat, trying to explain that I didn't SEE the lack of a stop sign, but Mother did not want to hear it. And neither did the giant raised truck that had pulled up behind me. A loud horn honked. Giant Raised Truck had places to go too, and if it had to, it would drive right over Geo Metro.

Now completely freaking out, I completely forgot I was behind the wheel of a motor vehicle and turned to my Mother and continued pleading my case. Giant Raised Truck honked again, then roared around me. As it did so, Mother cut off my argument by screaming, "GO! GO! JUST GO!!" So I pressed pedals to the metal.

And stalled.

Mother's Annoyed Level went to 15. Mine did too, because now I blamed her for putting me in this position.

"START THE CAR! START THE CAR!" she bellowed.

"I'M TRYING!!" I yelled back, and turned the key. The engine roared to life and I slammed the clutch down, causing the Metro to lurch into the middle of the intersection, where I promptly stalled it again. She yelled. I yelled. There was more stalling.

I don't know how we made it out of that intersection alive, but eventually we got past it and Mother screamed at me to pull over and get out of the car. I did as I was loudly asked. I wasn't really sure what was going to happen at this point, but I suspected it was going to involve me having to convince people at school the next day that no, no, I just fell down the stairs.

Instead she motioned me over to the passenger side where, from her seat, she hissed at me, "You take a walk and when you cool down, then we can continue." I whirled around, turned my back on her and began pacing back and forth in front of this house, where an insane dog was snarling and barking from his yard, telling me exactly what he would be doing to me if he wasn't currently chained up. I did not care. I was madder than the dog.

After probably thirty seconds of "cooling down" in which I just got madder and madder, I returned to the car, got in the driver's seat and looked at Mother, who did not look back. Staring ramrod straight through the windshield, she said, "Take me home," in a voice that dropped the temperature in the car about thirty degrees.

I have no memory of the drive home except that it was completely silent. When we finally pulled up to the house, she didn't even let me stop the car all the way before she threw the passenger's side door open, got out, and slammed it so hard that it probably registered on the Richter Scale. She began stomping toward the house as I finished applying the brakes, then I got out and slammed my door just as hard. I started stomping towards the house as well. We are a lot alike, my mother and I.

Somewhere during the stomping, I looked down and noticed that at some point during the leisurely outing, I had cut open my big toe on the clutch, which never would have happened if I'd put on actual shoes. This made me angrier and I stomped with more force, drops of blood spattering on the driveway. She reached the front door, threw it open, and slammed it behind her. The windows in the entire house rattled. I opened the door and was getting ready to slam it just as hard, dammit, when I saw my stepdad in the front room, staring at Mother, who was making a beeline for her bedroom. He looked over at me and said, "What happened?"

I couldn't even put it into words, so I just pointed in the general direction of my mother as if that explained everything and kept walking towards my room. My mother's bedroom door slammed shut. The house shook.

It took a couple of days before she and I spoke to each other again, but the more lasting effect was that I would never touch the Geo Metro again. It was a completely moronic reaction on my part, but I didn't want to have anything to do with it. At all. Ever. My mom must have felt the same way because a few weeks later, we traded it in for the 1988 Dodge Shadow, which was what is known as a step down.

But at least it was an automatic.

The following True-Life Tale is being brought to you by…

Se Habla Breakfast!

You know, for nearly a century we've been producing delicious bottles of Mrs. Butterworth's® pancake syrup. Our product is an American icon that comes in one of the most distinctive packages on the market. It's the syrup that's shaped like a lady! But we hired a Diversity Consultant and he told us that Mrs. Butterworth's®, although rich and tasty, doesn't do enough to attract certain segments of the population. He claimed that we needed to offer a version of our syrup that would be appealing to the Hispanic community and that if we didn't, somebody might file a class action lawsuit claiming that we are racist. The Diversity Consultant scared the bejeezus out of us, and that's why we're proud to present our new and improved culturally diverse syrup, Senorita Buttersworth®.

Senorita Buttersworth® takes the classic syrup you've come to know and love and adds a little Hispanic flair. For instance, Senorita Buttersworth® wears a big ol' sombrero. That's pretty Hispanic, isn't it? Also, we added ground up jalapenos to the syrup. It's HOT HOT HOT! It's the kind of product that makes you think, "Boy, this sure would be tasty on my pancakes," and also, "I am not at all interested in suing the Mrs. Butterworth's® company," sometimes at the same time! Senorita Buttersworth® also comes with a convenient spill-proof pour spout, and when you squeeze her, the music to the Mexican Hat Dance plays. That part was the Diversity Consultant's idea. He said just putting Mrs. Butterworth® in a sombrero and adding hot peppers wasn't enough. He said we must go even further and strive to be politically correct. To be honest, we kind of think

Senorita Buttersworth® is the opposite of politically correct, but perhaps that is why we are not a Diversity Consultant.

In blind taste tests, consumers of all races seem to hate Senorita Buttersworth®. If they are not offended by the sombrero, they are turned off by the spicy flavor. They insist that syrup should not be HOT HOT HOT and that it doesn't really go with pancakes. The Diversity Consultant begs to differ. "Then tell them to put it on their burritos!" he shouts, banging his fist on the desk. Then he said a perfect slogan for Senorita Buttersworth® would be "Illegally Crossing the Border Every Morning To Get To Your Breakfast Table." A few minutes later, we fired the Diversity Consultant and as soon as we sell all the bottles we produced, we will be pulling Senorita Buttersworth® right off the market. That's muy bueno!

Senorita Buttersworth®

The Syrup In The Sombrero That Has Its Green Card

The Shadow Knows

After the debacle of Matt's First Car (which was presented in vibrant high definition in "Coming Through In The Clutch," a story you may have already read if you aren't just skimming the book at random), I traded it in for Matt's Second Car, which turned out to be the sporty and stylish 1988 Dodge Shadow. The Dodge Shadow was truly a mean machine. You can keep your Escalades and your ninth-generation Hummers. I will always choose the 1988 Dodge Shadow. Why, you might ask, because you have got at least half a brain in your head. Well, several reasons:

1) The 1988 Dodge Shadow is state-of-the-art.

My Dodge Shadow had several impressive features, including a speedometer, a fuel gauge, and a little light that said "check engine," which stayed on for the last two years that I had the car. It also had a world class radio, featuring both AM and FM. You learn to appreciate the subtle majesty of AM/FM radio when your car does not have a tape deck or a CD player. Basically, any time I wanted, I could turn to one of the fine L.A. based radio stations on my AM/FM dial and instantly be connected to an uninterrupted block of thirty commercials in a row. Either that or a Ricky Martin song. It was a special time to be alive.

The Dodge Shadow also came with automatic seat belts, which sound good in theory, but are in fact the most useless accessory Motor City ever came up with. Whenever you would sit in the car and close the door, the shoulder belt would automatically move itself into the Optimum Safety Position, which for some reason was directly across my face.

On top of that, the lap belt still had to be manually attached, so while I'm trying to buckle the lower belt and trying to remove the shoulder belt from my ear, I'm not paying attention to anything I'm doing, which probably means I'm rolling right into an intersection.

The other benefit of the automatic seat belt is that it makes you fail your driver's test, thereby depriving you of your license for six awesome weeks. Unfortunately, it's true. The 1988 Dodge Shadow was the car I took my first driver's test in, and there was a large unpleasant man who was sitting in my passenger seat with his little clipboard. He'd maybe made two marks on it more than halfway through the test and in the midst of my almost crippling nervousness, I was beginning to see the possibility that I might actually pass this thing. But right at that moment, he shifted in his seat, putting tension on the automatic shoulder belt, which came unbuckled, and smacked him right in the side of the head as it retracted. He gave me a look that I cannot really describe except that it was the opposite of friendly. I stammered to him that the belt sometimes comes loose if you don't make sure it's clicked in all the way. His response was to start making LOTS of angry checkmarks on his little clipboard. Suffice to say, when I left the DMV that day, I was not a licensed driver. Thanks a lot, Dodge Shadow! I really owe you one!

2) The 1988 Dodge Shadow helps you learn important vehicular lessons that you would never have to learn in a newer car.

My sporty, stylish Dodge Shadow had an eternal oil leak. Wherever I went, a helpful trail of oil drops followed me, which I could've used to find my way home if I'd ever gotten lost. Because of this exciting feature, I had to keep buying quarts of Pennzoil every month or so, which wasn't a huge deal because although gasoline is expensive as hell, motor oil is cheaper than a gallon of milk.

But I can be a little bit scatterbrained, so this one time I'd forgotten to buy oil for... oh... several months, and decided to take a drive. About halfway to my destination, zooming right along in the fast lane at the Shadow's terrifying top speed of maybe 75mph, the engine made a very peculiar noise, and then the car violently downshifted. As a skilled driver of almost six months, I knew that the best thing to do was to continue pressing on the gas pedal, which I did, and it went right to the floor without making the car go any faster. Quite the contrary, in fact. The Shadow kept going slower and slower until it finally stopped. Do you know what it means to "seize your engine?" I didn't then, but I sure do now! Thanks, Dodge Shadow!

Once the engine seized up, the Shadow was not so much a "car" anymore as it was a "large white thing that sat in the driveway so the cat could have something to lie under." Not that that isn't important as well. It took me nearly eight months to scrounge up enough money to get a new engine put in it, and even then only with the help of a very generous loan from my grandparents. But while it was rotting in the driveway, it was able to teach me another important lesson that I think everyone needs to experience at least once: The magic of siphoning.

The Shadow had a nearly full tank of gas when it tried to commit suicide that lovely Christmas Eve afternoon. (Yes, it was seriously Christmas Eve when that happened. I'll bet you feel sorry for me NOW, huh?) So a few months later, when our lawn mower ran out of gas, my stepdad suggested that it would be quicker to siphon some gas out of the sporty, stylish Dodge Shadow instead of driving all the way down to the gas station. Sure, why not? It's not like the car was using it.

He grabbed a short length of rubber hose, took me over to the car and started to explain to me how siphoning worked. Yeah, yeah, I said, cutting him off. Hose in the tank, suck, suck, suck, gas comes out. You'd have to be pretty stupid to mess up sucking gas through a hose, and I'm not pretty stupid. No, what I am is exceptionally stupid. There is a monumental difference. I jammed the hose into the tank, put it to my lips, and took a huge breath. No gas came out, but a huge wave of gas fumes flooded into my mouth, hit my throat, and literally knocked me onto my back.

I hacked and wretched for a couple of minutes while my stepdad wiped the tears out of his eyes and tried to stop laughing long enough to make sure I was all right. I actually enjoy the smell of gasoline (I'm one of THOSE people), but it turns out that just because something smells good not does mean it TASTES good. And those were just the fumes. A few minutes later, once I'd finally shut up from knowing it all long enough to let him tell me the proper way to siphon, I was able to successfully extract the gas from the tank and got a quick mouthful of gasoline in its liquid form. My dear friends, I'll tell you what, I would still rather gargle gas than eat a spoonful of mustard, but it's REALLY close.

3) Even with its flaws, The 1988 Dodge Shadow is still better than the 1984 Honda Accord.

At the time I was rollin' in the Shadow, impressing ALL the fly honeys with my ride, my friend Alan was driving a 1984 Honda Accord. Well, MOST of a 1984 Honda Accord. The way that car ran, I always suspected some pieces had to be missing and that if we looked around enough, maybe we would find them. One of the pieces that was missing was the piece that kept the engine from overheating. The only solution Alan and I were able to come up with was to make sure that whenever we were in his car, we had to keep the heater on full blast. This would have been all well and good if we lived in Wisconsin and it was January. But we lived in Southern California and it was August. We spent many wonderful 108-degree summer afternoons driving around in the 1984 Honda Accord, heater blowing 108-degree air out every available vent while we stuck our heads out of the open windows, choosing "sunburn" over "heatstroke."

When the 1984 Honda Accord was not trying to bake us alive, it was giving us whiplash. The Accord was a manual transmission, a kind of car I have been in many times. In every other stick shift I've ever experienced, the driver presses down on the clutch, moves the gear shift around, and the car gently moves from 1st to 2nd to 3rd and beyond. When Alan would attempt to manually change gears, the Honda Accord would fight back. We'd be coasting along in first gear and he'd attempt to put the Accord in 2nd, and after moving the gear shift to its appropriate position, there would be a slight pause, then a loud "CLUNK," at which point the Accord would violently lurch forward, engine screaming. A moment later, our heads would slam back into the headrests and the Accord, having made its point, would speed up slightly. Then Alan would shift the car into 3rd and I would brace myself yet again. "Eeeeeeee-THUNK!!"

The last straw came near the end of that summer, when the Accord made it personal. I was in the Shadow, following Alan back to his house as he drove the 1984

Honda Deathtrap a few feet in front of me. Not 20 yards in front of his house, the Accord made a sound I'd never heard before and began to belch smoke out of its exhaust pipe. Maybe the smoke was also coming out of the trunk and the engine. It would not surprise me. It was an excessive amount of smoke. The amount of smoke you would associate with a California wildfire as opposed to a driving machine that was slightly bigger than a Matchbox car. The smoke grew thicker and blacker and it continued to escape from the Accord and then, right in front of my unbelieving eyes, it began to change color.

It turned yellow and I'm fairly certain that I also saw some green. I'm also certain that if he hadn't shut the car off and coasted the rest of the way into his driveway that eventually pink hearts and blue moons would have come flying out of the exhaust, followed closely by purple horseshoes. And as I gazed enraptured by this magical sight, the Northern Lights of car emissions, I drove right into the toxic cloud. It was unpleasant, to say the least. I can't say with any certainly what that smoke was made of, but "oxygen" was not even a minor ingredient. Once I'd driven through the smoke, I pulled into his driveway, parked behind him, then jumped out and shrieked at him that his car was trying to kill me. The Accord Cloud of Death, meanwhile, drifted lazily into the summer sky, heading off to cause global warming.

So even though I was not exactly the biggest fan of the sporty, stylish 1988 Dodge Shadow, I know that it could have been much worse. It served me well, good little soldier that it was, and every so often, I find myself wishing I could drive it just one more time... That is a complete lie, of course, but "wistful" is always a good way to end things. Just leaves you feeling all warm and cozy, doesn't it?

The following True-Life Tale is being brought to you by…

Bugged By Bugs?

For years and years and years, you've been trying to find a way to get rid of those darned roaches, and for years and years and years, the roaches have refused to die. You buy more powerful bug sprays, full of higher concentrations of scientifically engineered roach-killing toxins, but it doesn't do any good, and it's time to just give up. Introducing White Flag® Bug Spray, the bug spray for quitters.

Roaches are the master race, and we're never going to defeat them. That's the concept we kept in mind when we developed White Flag®. Spraying them with poison is only going to piss them off, so White Flag® is made from vitamins and minerals that fulfill all the nutritional needs of a growing roach. This way, when roaches take over the world, they won't feel the need for revenge against humans and perhaps will let us live in peace, on a secluded island somewhere in the South Pacific. At White Flag, we're keeping our fingers crossed.

White Flag® Bug Spray also seems to make the roaches stronger and more aggressive, which wasn't something we really planned on, but maybe it's for the best. The sooner we accept the inevitable, the better off we're all going to be. So come on, folks! Join us in our unconditional surrender to our new roach leaders by buying a bottle of White Flag® Bug Spray. Maybe if we're lucky, instead of wiping out humanity the roaches will allow us to live side by side with them as equals. Perhaps we could even get a spot in the Roach Government. Wouldn't be ironic to be in their cabinet? No, really, I'm asking you. I've never had a clear grasp on the definition of irony.

White Flag® Bug Spray

Kills Bugs Dead In An Opposite Kind Of Way

Keeping My Ion The Ball

Back in 2005, I bought my first ever completely brand new car, the sporty and stylish 2006 Saturn Ion. Yes, that is correct. I bought a car from 2006 in 2005. For three months, I was driving around in a Future-Mobile like I was George Jetson or something. Then January 1st rolled around and I was driving around in a Present-Mobile. Twelve months later, it turned into a Past-Mobile and nobody was impressed anymore.

But the day I bought it was an extremely cool day and I looked forward to showing the Saturn off to people by pointing at it and excitedly proclaiming, "Look! Because of this, I'm $15,000 in the hole!" It would've been nice to head straight to Venice Beach to show off my new ride to all the fly honeys, but the whole car purchasing process took so long that I was almost late to work. The honeys would have to wait.

I got to work and everybody came out to take a look at the Saturn, giving the usual reactions, looking around the inside, asking how much I paid, commenting on the new car smell, asking if they could dropkick the dent resistant side panels, etc. etc. After a few minutes, the crowd dispersed and we all went back to work. A couple of hours later, the topic of lunch came up and we all began to discuss where we were going to go. As usual, nobody seemed to be able to agree on one specific fast food place, but there was a unanimous consensus amongst everyone else that no matter where we went, I was going to have to drive. This didn't make a lot of sense to me, and I argued that my car was not going to stay brand new if I was constantly having to drive it. But I was outnumbered and my objections were ignored (even when I am not outnumbered, my objections are usually ignored).

The dining destination was eventually agreed upon and it wasn't much longer before the sporty and stylish Saturn Ion was driving down the street containing myself and two of my coworkers, David and Juan. We were all enjoying the roomy interior and smooth handling when my eye happened upon the instrument panel, which informed me that I was a little low on fuel. I told them I wanted to swing by the gas station real quick and fill up the tank, and they had no problem with that, probably because they were hypnotized by the roomy interior and the smooth handling.

With a new destination programmed into my mental GPS, I continued driving along. But as the gas station came into view, it occurred to me that I didn't have any idea what side of the car the gas tank was on. I'm sure the dealer pointed it out when I bought the car, but I hadn't been paying attention (the best time to not pay attention is when you're purchasing a new vehicle). As I continued down the road, I became completely consumed by where on the car my gas tank might be. "Driver side? Passenger side? Driver side? Passenger side?" was the chorus ping-ponging back and forth inside my brain, getting louder and louder as the pumps got closer and closer.

Knowing the location of the gas tank BEFORE I got to the station was very important to me because I didn't want to park next to a pump, then get out and see that the tank was on the complete opposite side of the Saturn, which in turn would cause me to have to take an extra ten seconds to drive around and reposition the car. To me, the thought of having to do this is mortifying, akin to giving a speech to Congress while in my underwear. I can just see busloads of tourists pointing and laughing, taking videos with their phones and uploading them to YouTube, which would later go viral. I'd have to go through life as the Gas Tank Guy, eventually ending up on Season 27 of Dancing with the Stars.

So this is what I'm mentally wrestling with as I reached the intersection where the gas station was located. It's a quick right turn and then an immediate left, a bit of driving that I've done countless times. THIS time, however, I'd gotten myself so worked up about the gas tank thing that I wasn't paying attention to the road at all. I'd gotten this far solely on instinct. My eyes were open, but I wasn't actually seeing anything because my brain was devoting 100% of its resources to "Driver Side vs. Passenger Side."

I got up to the light and began to make my right-hand turn, staring at the gas station the whole time, which was now directly across the street to my left. In my mind, I'd finally come to a conclusion, which is that the tank was almost certainly on the passenger's side. Relieved to have finally made a decision, I completed the turn and stopped in the middle lane in preparation to make my left turn, which would take me into the station. The instant I finished braking, I became aware that something was amiss.

First I heard David saying something that sounded like, "Whoa! Whoa! What are you DOING?!" Then from the back seat, Juan made a very sharp intake of breath, as one would do when bracing for impact. I looked to my right and I saw what was causing all the commotion.

There was a giant fire truck barreling down on us, blasting its horn as if to say, "Hey! Idiot in the Saturn! Get out of our way!" It was only at that moment that I realized three very important pieces of information:

1) The lane I had stopped in was not a turn lane. It was a lane on the other side

of the turn lane, meant for opposing traffic.

2) I wasn't even really IN the lane so much as I was turned kind of diagonally in such a way that the fire truck was going to t-bone the hell out of the passenger side.

3) We were all going to die.

I stared dumbstruck at the fire truck as it slammed on its brakes never once considering that if I just lightly tapped on the gas pedal, I could have moved us out of harm's way. Instead, it was like watching some terrible movie in hyper-realistic 3D, where the fire truck on screen was moving closer and closer and closer.

I was jolted out of my movie watching by David, who had been shouting something at me the whole time. It turned out what he was shouting was, "DRIVE! DRIVE!!!" which at that moment seemed to be coming out of his mouth in a completely foreign language. It made absolutely zero sense to me. I think if there had been time, he would have grabbed me by the neck, thrown me out the window and into the street, and moved the car his own damn self. But everything happened too fast. Eventually, the fire truck came to a complete stop, perhaps four inches from the side of my brand new car. It was so close that I could clearly see the firefighters in the cab, all gesturing wildly at me and screaming words I could not hear, but which I assume were something along the lines of, "We really like your car! Have a lovely evening!"

They blasted their horn one more time and it finally jolted me out of my stupor. I accelerated out of the way, into the gas station, and pulled up to the pump. The fire truck drove away, giving me one last horn blast for good measure, one that I suspect I deserved. Actually, at that moment I probably deserved to be dragged out of the car and beaten, L.A. Riots style.

We sat in silence at the gas pump for a few moments. David had lost a little bit of the color in his face and looked as if he wished to murder me, was trying to think of a good reason not to, and was failing. Juan was in the backseat just staring out the window. He seemed as if he was trying to remember if he'd told his family he loved them before he'd left the house that day. As for me, I was suddenly completely overcome with a hysterical case of the giggles. Nothing that had just happened was exactly "funny," but all of the adrenaline left me with a kind of nervous energy that manifested itself into titters and chortles. A more accurate way to put it would be that I was sitting there braying like a hyena. And I giggled for the rest of the trip, uncontrollably. I also tried to assure both David and Juan that the car was dent proof, so the fire truck probably would've just bounced right off of us like a bumper car.

"It would have cut us in two," David said through gritted teeth. "Your car is made of plastic!"

"Yes, but at least if they'd hit us, we wouldn't have had to call 9-1-1," I said, trying to find the silver lining.

It was, without question, the single most head-up-my-own-rear-end moment I've ever had behind the wheel and hopefully will remain that way for the rest of my life. As for me and the Saturn, we had many exciting adventures over the next few years, but none as terrifying and completely avoidable as that memorable night.

Oh, and in the end, I was right. The gas tank was on the passenger's side.

Shadows of the Invisible
(a tale told in "real-time")

Week Four: Gettin' Some Action

"Right now, an assassin is targeting the president of Antarctica. My ex-wife has been kidnapped. And people that I work with may be involved in both. My name is Librarian of Congress Jacques Vargas, and these... are the longest eight weeks of my life..."

FRIDAY, DECEMBER 6th, 2002

2:00pm - National Zoo, Washington D.C. (bird house and flight exhibit)

The glass door to the bird house building slams open, and in runs the team from the Library of Congress. They're all bundled up and covered with snow. Jacques Vargas takes off his hat and shivers. He points outside where a huge storm rages. "Brrrrr! Out there... it is cold!"

Chuck Williams sweeps some snow off his coat. "What was your first clue, Jacques? The blizzard?"

The third member of the team, Irma, takes a long look around the bird house, where many high-ranking officials from many zoos around the country are gathered. "I just can't believe that there are still people outside, trying to see the animals. I could barely see my hand, and it was right in front of my face. I never got storms like this when I lived in Hawaii."

A nervous looking dark-haired woman trots briskly

over to the new arrivals. "I'm Lucy Spelman. Director of the Smithsonian National Zoological Park. You're the security team, am I correct?"

"Ten points, Dr. Spelman. We're from the L.O.C., and we're here to look after President Kemo." Jacques shakes Dr. Spelman's hand. "I'm Vargas. To my left is Williams, and to my right is Damole. Has the President arrived yet?"

"Absolutely. Would you like to speak to him before he gives his speech?"

Jacques gives a sugar-sweet smile. "That would be DELIGHTFUL, thanks."

Lucy gives a sharp nod and runs off. Chuck leans into Jacques. "Before we talk to the president, I'd really like to go over some research I've done. I think I've identified a prime suspect."

"Now's not really a good time, Chuck. I'm free on Monday, though. Why don't you run and get me a snow-cone?"

Jacques begins to walk further into the birdhouse, but Chuck stands directly in his way. "I know this is just some game to you, Jacques. I know you can't be expected to take anything seriously, not after the way you reacted to your wife getting kidnapped three weeks ago, but I happen to care about my work. Now I don't have any idea how you occupy such a prestigious position within the L.O.C., because you obviously have no clue what you're doing, but you're a necessary evil to me, and at this moment, I need you listen to what I have to say, or else the President of Antarctica might not live through the day."

With the exception of a slightly raised eyebrow, Jacques' expression remains motionless. He and Chuck stare each other down for a moment as Irma rolls her eyes. Jacques blinks first, and then speaks. "I asked you for a snow-cone, and that was a direct order. However, in light of the fact it's snowing outside, a snow-cone might not be the proper taste sensation for me at the moment. I can see that now. For that reason, and that reason only, I'm going to listen to what you have to say. Make it better than a snow-cone, Chuck, or I'll be very unhappy."

Chuck clinches his fists without realizing it, then reaches into his coat and pulls out a file. "Ever since this assassination threat was called in, I've been researching possible suspects. Lots of research. And I've narrowed hundreds of people down to a man who I believe is positively involved, if not the brains behind the operation." Opening the file, he pulls out a clear color picture of a man we've seen before. "His name is Duke Gravy. No criminal record, but he's always close to trouble. He's one of the most prominent writers of anti-Antarctican literature. He's one of these nuts who thinks the whole continent should be melted down so we can have better surf, year-round. Our intelligence confirms that he knows about the existence of the Antarctican government. We don't know how he knows, but he knows. And the kicker is, he hasn't been seen in nearly a month. I think if we keep an eye open for this man, at the zoo, we can stop this assassination before it happens." Chuck closes the file and looks up, as if expecting a grade.

Jacques rubs his chin and shakes his head. "I'm inclined to disagree, Chuck, although your research is admirable. I'm impressed, and that in itself is impressive, because I don't like you, so it makes me harder to impress. But the fact is, Gravy's not our man. Duke Gravy doesn't have the capacity or the motive to pull off something like this. Duke Gravy is nothing more than a flunky who hates Antarctica because he thinks it's the cool thing to do. He's bowing down to peer pressure. This is the same man who waged a "terror campaign" against Idaho three years ago because "potatoes suck". But someone failed to point out that walking around in downtown Boise with no pants on isn't really a terror campaign." Jacques looks around the birdhouse, taking everything in, including the approach of President Kemo, and looks back at Chuck. "Gravy may be around. He's got enough spare time to follow Kemo all over the place. But Gravy's not our man. Not by a longshot."

Chuck looks back at Jacques with a surprise and a slight loathing admiration. His mouth hangs open slightly and he starts to move it. "How do you... how do you know all that?"

Jacques holds up his hand. "I may be a putz and a drunk and a lowlife, but I'm also a damned good Librarian of Congress. I'm not a mistake. Now why don't you and Irma go take a look around? We're trying to stop an assassination, you know." Chuck stands down and walks past Jacques, into the bird house. Irma follows behind, while taking a long look at President Kemo, who is now standing right behind Jacques.

"Mr. Vargas, I presume!" The President says, in a big, booming voice. Jacques whirls around and smiles.

"You're sharp as a tack. I'm Jacques Vargas, head of the L.O.C. It's nice to finally meet you, Mr. President. I'm sorry it's so cold outside today."

"I live in Antarctica, Mr. Vargas. Three days of snow doesn't exactly faze me. I'm this close to stripping down to my boxers and tap-dancing down the street."

"That would probably get some press coverage." Jacques begins to walk slowly towards the middle of the room. The President walks by his side. "Now, Mr. President..."

"Please. Call me Dennis."

"I really don't think I can do that, sir."

The President chuckles. "Gotta be formal, eh? Fair enough. Call me Mr. Kemo."

"Okay. I'll give that a try." Jacques clears his throat. "Mr. Kemo, as you may know…"

"Actually, on second thought… call me Mr. President. Mr. Kemo sounds stupid."

Jacques misses a beat, but quickly gets back on track. "Fair enough. Mr. President, your advisors have probably told you that you're the target of a threat. My team is here to protect you, which we will do at all costs. We understand that you have to give your speech, but you'll understand if we have to implement a few security precautions."

President Kemo smiles and his eyes twinkle just so. "Mr. Vargas, I am very grateful for all your concern, but you'll forgive me if I seem a bit flip about this whole issue. I get death threats all the time. And not just from humans. There's a right-wing group of polar bears up there who want my head on a glacier. I've learned to deal with it, and if you'll notice… not a scratch."

As Jacques converses with the President, Chuck and Irma meet back by the glass front doors. The snow has let up temporarily, and several people can be seen outside, walking around and pointing at the places the animals would be if it wasn't so cold. Irma shakes her head. "There's nothing out of the ordinary here, Chuck. If anything's going to happen, it's coming from out there, not in here."

Chuck nods and crosses his arms. "I really feel like this is the place, Irma. It's supposed to happen today, and from an assassin's viewpoint, this is the ideal place to do it. No press, no public, just a bunch of zookeepers and six-hundred parrots." He gives the birdhouse another glance, and turns away frustrated.

Irma looks outside, giving Chuck a moment to gather his thoughts. For a moment, she stares into the distance, looking at nothing, but her gaze quickly fixes on three men, milling around by a huge birdbath, twenty feet away. Immediately, her eyes grow wide.

Almost instantly, Chuck picks up on this. "Irma? What's wrong? What're you looking at?" After seeing that Irma will be no help since she just keeps staring, Chuck takes matters into his own hands and looks for himself. His eyes grow just as wide as Irma's. "It's Gravy. That's Duke Gravy!"

Irma speaks in a tone of disbelief. "Maybe it's not. Maybe it's his identical twin brother who looks exactly the same."

"No, that's definitely Duke. Where's Jacques? We need to formulate a plan to get him into custody." Chuck spins around and sees Jacques talking to the President. He cups his hands around his mouth and shouts, "Jacques! Gravy! Gravy, Jacques, Gravy!!"

President Kemo gives Jacques a questioning look. "Is something wrong with your agent? It sounds like he's hungry."

"No, no. He's just hopped up on angel dust. If you can excuse me for just a moment, I'll be right back."

"Actually, Mr. Vargas, I'm going to be giving my speech in a moment, so I'll be up on stage. Feel free to protect me whatever way you feel you must. You Americans are so cute, what with your security and your Homeland Defense." Giving yet another grin, the President winds his way towards the stage.

Jacques quickly trots over to Chuck and Irma. "Okay, this had better be more important than anything ever. I was just in the middle of something!"

"Duke Gravy is out there, Jacques. Right there." Chuck points. "Him. Here. Now? That's not just a coincidence. He's the shooter. Those guys are probably his accomplices. We can stop this thing right now."

"You know, Chuck, and it kills me to say this because, as I mentioned before, I don't like you, but you might be right. Containing Gravy might be the best possible move."

With a sense of purpose, Chuck claps his hands. "All right! Let's do this! Duke might be armed, though. I think I need a gun."

"I have a gun, Chuck. I don't plan on using it. But it probably would be a good idea for SOMEONE to have a gun."

"Okay. May I have the gun?"

"I can give you these bullets."

"Just the bullets, Jacques?"

Jacques takes Chuck's hand and looks into his eyes. "I will always give you bullets. Because…that's all I have to give…"

"You know, you're really irritating right after you watch Spider-Man."

"That's me, your friendly neighborhood Librarian of Congress. Here's a gun." Jacques hands Chuck the gun, which Chuck snatches away with a scowl. Jacques points towards the stage. "I'm gonna stay here with the President, just in case. But good luck, the both of you."

Chuck puts the gun in his belt and looks at Irma, who is reluctantly drawing her own weapon. "Let's not shoot them, okay? Let's just scare them a little."

Not really listening, Chuck motions towards the door, and he and Irma walk outside. Jacques watches them approach Duke and his buddies, who all seem to be eating something out of a doggy bag from the Kaffa House, a D.C. area restaurant. He barely has time to register this fact when instinct makes him turn around. He whirls around, suddenly feeling a sense of panic, and sees the President up on stage. As Jacques watches, a man who looks exactly like Jacques himself walks up to the President and outstretches his hand. From where they stand, twenty yards away, Jacques can hear what is being said.

"Mr. President," says the imposter. "Hello. I'm Jacques Vargas, head of the L.O.C. It's nice to meet you. I was wondering if I could get a picture."

The President registers a look of slight confusion, and Jacques begins to run. He runs towards the stage as fast as his feet can carry him. "Noooooooooo!!!" he screams, doing a fine impression of any number of action movies, but he knows he's not going to be able to get there in time. Pushing himself harder, closing the gap, he has time to notice a small black X spray-painted on the stage. The imposter is leading the President over to the X. "Stand right here, sir. This is going to be a great picture!"

Five yards away now, and Jacques knocks a couple of zookeepers out of the way. President Kemo is now standing directly on the X, just noticing the man running towards him. He looks at Jacques, then to Jacques, then back to Jacques, and Jacques (the real one) dives towards the stage. Right before he hits the President, he distinctly hears gunfire coming from outside, but that sound is completely deafened by the incredible explosion of the bomb going off, coming from directly underneath the X.

To Be Continued…

The following True-Life Tale is being brought to you by…

These Prices Will Never Learn

When it comes to shopping for children's apparel, parents know there's no better place than Kids Korner®. Whether you're buying clothes for tweens, teens or anything in between, Kids Korner® has got you covered with the best selection in town at the very lowest prices. But in this shaky economic climate, even our everyday low prices aren't adequate. We understand that nowadays parents are on a tight budget, so Kids Korner® is slashing prices on everything in the store!

But slashing prices isn't enough. We took a good hard look at our prices, and you know what? They made us sick to our stomach. So we smacked our prices right in the mouth! The prices begged us to stop but that just made us madder. "Shut up," we bellowed. "Shut the hell up!" And then we kind of blacked out. When we came to, sweaters that used to be $25 were suddenly $13.99. What we did to the prices probably isn't even legal, but those prices were asking for it.

Some clothing stores have sales that only go on for a limited time. Not at Kids Korner®. When we knock prices down, they STAY down. But don't get the wrong idea. We only do this to the prices because we love them so much. It's for their own good. There's no reason to call the authorities. And what business is it of yours anyway? These are OUR prices, dammit! Stay out of it!

Um… Sorry. We sometimes get kind of carried away here at Kids Korner®, especially after we've had a few beers. Sure, we backhand the prices for getting a little out of line, but we think they kind of like it. Sometimes the prices say to us, "I want you to hit me as hard as you can!" And we're more than happy to comply, which is why you can get a $55 pair of sneakers for only $3.75 at Kids Korner®. You simply can't beat our prices, but we can. And we are going to beat these prices within an inch of their life!

We love cutting prices, but don't get the wrong idea. When we have to whack our prices with a belt, it hurts us just as much as it hurts the prices. But it also allows us to sell belts for nine cents, not to mention it's buy one, get one free! Sometimes tough love is the only love that gets the message across, especially after we've had a few beers.

We're just going to level with you. You should probably load the family in the car and get to Kids Korner® as quickly as possible, because these prices might never be found alive again. We have HAD IT with these damn prices and the way they dress like whores in public! I will NOT put the beer down! It's not the beer's fault that you prices are so high! Now get over here right now!

Kids Korner®
You Know We're Fun Cause We Spell "Corner" With A "K"!

Inevitable

There was no doubt that it was going to happen, but I was still surprised when it did.

A couple of weeks ago, I moved into my latest residence, a brand new house purchased by my roommate and her husband. There was never any doubt that I was going to be tagging along with them when they moved into the house. I am a barnacle, and the only way to get a barnacle off of your hull is with a high pressure hose. Fortunately for me, "high-pressure hose" was not one of the wedding gifts on their registry.

The house is probably the nicest place I've ever lived, due in no small part to the fact that everything in it is brand new. It's got that "new house" smell, or at least it did until we went two weeks without trash service and it started to have more of that "new landfill" smell. Not that I am complaining. I'm lucky to have ANYWHERE to live. Were it not for the roommate dragging me along with her like a special needs crack baby, I'd probably be living at the Y, getting in knife fights with people because they keep un-alphabetizing my DVD collection.

As much as I'm enjoying my new living quarters, it comes with a downside that has taken some serious adjustments on my part. You see, the house has three stories, and my room happens to be up on the third floor. In my entire life, I've never lived anywhere with stairs, so suddenly having to trudge down two flights of them every time I want a fork has not been easy to deal with.

It was the worst when we moved in, because when I was packing I had no concept of what it meant to carry heavy things up a bunch of stairs, so I was just filling up boxes with as much as I could fit in them. I had several giant boxes of books that weighed roughly as much as a baby elephant. Boxes that I was having trouble just picking up off the ground and walking out to my car. And because I have the reasoning ability of a tree stump, it did not occur to me that this was going to be a problem until I stood on the first floor, at the base of the stairs, struggling to remain upright while grasping a box containing a metric ton of books and DVD's. "Hmmm..." I thought to myself. "I wonder how this is going to work." It turns out the way that it works is that you put one foot in front of the other and sweat and grunt and gasp for air and think terrible hateful thoughts about the jackass who packed these boxes and how as soon as you can stand up under your own power again, you are going to wring his skinny little pencil neck. (It was pointed out to me later on that a better solution would have been to just take some of the items out of the boxes before taking them upstairs. It was a brilliant idea and allowed me to not only feel exhausted, but also stupid. Thanks!)

Eventually, I got everything upstairs and proceeded to start unpacking and getting settled in. But a nagging thought started burrowing into my head and the more I thought about it, the more I knew it was something that was very likely to happen. More than very likely, in fact. A near certainty. I started putting two and two together and came up with the following equation:

I am extremely clumsy + I am not used to stairs = Danger

It all added up, and I knew that it wouldn't be too long before my equation would be proven true. And today it finally was. For you see, today I fell down the stairs.

It came as a huge surprise to me, because when it

happened, I was still half-asleep. I'd just rolled out of bed and was stumbling downstairs to use the bathroom. About three steps down, instead of placing my foot on the middle of the stair ("Recommended"), my leg swung several inches too far forward and I ended up putting the heel of my foot on the very edge of the stair ("Not Recommended: Parental Advisory Suggested"). As soon as I put my weight on it, my heel slipped forward and off the stair into thin air. My leg shot up as if I was auditioning to be in the Rockettes. My upper body kind of bucked in reverse and my arm shot out to grab the handrail, although by then it was too late. The leg I was standing on buckled and I crashed backwards, landing on my back at this diagonal angle that absolutely cannot be ergonomically correct. I sort of bounced once, and then my momentum caused me to slide down the last few stairs until I finally came to a stop in a heap of flailing limbs.

The very first thing I did, before it had even fully registered in my brain what had occurred, was to leap to my feet and look around to make sure nobody had seen my little spill. On my list of mental priorities, "pain" and "common sense" are way behind "saving face." If there HAD been somebody standing there - and I would've known right away if someone was, because they would've been laughing so hard they probably would've had a heart attack (one true fact in life is that it is hysterical to watch tall, skinny people fall down) - I would have loudly stated, "I am fine! There is no problem here! I meant to do that! It didn't even hurt!" I would have said these things even if there were broken ribs protruding from my chest. And then I would have limped down the hall and locked myself in the bathroom for about a week. But as luck would have it, nobody was home, so I didn't have to hide my true feelings any longer. My true feeling was "ouch."

So now that I've finally fallen down the stairs, I've spent the rest of the day wondering if that was the one time and I don't have to worry about it anymore or if today's little spill was a sign of things to come. Sure, it's always a possibility when you live in a house with stairs that you might slip once in a while, but once you go crashing down the steps like I did, isn't it logical to assume that you've learned your lesson and that you will be just a little more careful when navigating the treacherous terrain of the suburban household?

I think I'm going to start looking into the rates at the Y.

The Big Dumb Goat

The Sheriff

As Sheriff Collins drove his cruiser down lonely Highway 12, he gazed up at the blue sky and yawned. It had been a slow day in his small town. A lazy day. The kind of day when a sheriff wants to just pull over to the side of the road, put his boots up on the dashboard, and take a lovely summer snooze. It was an appealing idea, and Sheriff Collins decided to find a secluded spot behind the trees and do just that. Smiling at the thought, the Sheriff looked back down towards the road and it's a good thing that he did or else he would have hit the goat.

Sheriff Collins slammed on his brakes causing the tires to screech and smoke as the cruiser came to an abrupt halt. Like any good officer, the Sheriff was wearing his seatbelt, but the large cup of coffee sitting in the passenger seat was not so lucky. It flew forward and slammed into the windshield, exploding on impact. Steaming hot latte drenched the dashboard, the on-board computer, the book of tickets, you name it. It was a gruesome end for what had been a delicious hot beverage.

The car finally came to a complete stop and the Sheriff slammed back into his seat, not yet noticing the brown stains spreading on his uniform, only looking straight ahead at the goat who hadn't reacted at all even though he came within a few feet of being run down. The Sheriff sat there for a moment, breathing hard, adrenaline pumping, then he slapped the steering wheel with his open palm. He stuck his head out of the window and shouted at the animal in the middle of the road.

"What the hell are you doing, you big dumb goat? Get on outta the road, y'hear?"

The goat made no attempt to reply.

The Sheriff thought perhaps he hadn't screamed loud enough, so he began to honk his horn to punctuate the point he was trying to make.

HONK!

"You big dumb..."

HONK!

"...goat! Move your..."

HONK!

"...big..."

HONK!

"...dumb self outta the middle..."

HONK!

"... of the dag..."

HONK!

"...blasted..."

HONK!

"...road!!"

The goat blinked but did not move towards the shoulder of the highway.

Sheriff Collins was not used to being disobeyed by man or beast, and this goat was getting on his bad side with alarming speed. He decided to honk his horn a few more times, but he had a nagging suspicion this tactic was not going to be successful.

HONK! HONK! HONK! HONK! HONK!

"Don't make me come out there, goat!"

HONK!

"You don't want me to come out there!!"

HONK!

But maybe the goat did, because he didn't move a

muscle.

Now the Sheriff was REALLY mad. Not only was this goat ruining his precious nap-time, he'd been responsible for the destruction of his beloved latte. The Sheriff loved his lattes even though the deputies liked to make fun. *To hell with them,* Sheriff Collins often thought. *A man shouldn't be ashamed of the things he loves.* And with that love in mind, the Sheriff unbuckled his seat belt, threw the driver's side door open, and emerged from the cruiser. Latte dripped from his gun-belt. He made to stomp over to the big, dumb goat and give him a peace of his mind, but years and years of tactical training reminded him that a good officer always gives the situation a good, hard look before he acts. Just because this situation involved a goat did not make it any less of a situation.

The Sheriff gave the goat a long, hard look. It was a big goat, not huge, but larger than normal. It was a dirty white color and one of its horns was chipped. It stood there in the middle of the road facing the tree-lined shoulder, but it didn't seem to be looking at anything in particular. It was just… standing there. If its big dumb eyes weren't open, the Sheriff would have thought the goat had fallen asleep standing up. Sheriff Collins was a strong man, and it would not have been a difficult thing for him to walk up and physically move the goat off the road, but Sheriff Collins was also a Sheriff, and he'd be horn-swaggled if he was going to wrap his arms around a filthy goat. That's what deputies are for. He reached down to his belt, pulled out his walkie-talkie, wiped latte off of it with his sleeve, then pressed down on the button marked *transmit.*

"Bernie, this is the Sheriff. Do you copy?"

A young voice quickly responded. "Yessir, this is Bernie. What can I help you with, Sheriff?"

"Listen, Bernie, are you anywhere near the part of Highway 12 with all the trees?"

"Pretty close, sir. Probably about five minutes away, although I'm in the process of taking someone in to the county jail at the moment."

The Sheriff glared at the goat. It drove him crazy that the stupid animal didn't have the decency to at least make eye contact with him. "Well look, Bernie, I'm gonna need you to come on over here to give me a hand with something. Shouldn't take but a couple of minutes. Go ahead and bring the prisoner along. Not like he's gonna be in a hurry to get where he's going."

"Sure thing, boss. I'll be there in a half a jiffy. Over and out."

The Sheriff re-holstered his radio and nodded. Bernie was a good kid. He'd take care of this big dumb goat, and then the Sheriff could be on his merry way, off to catch a few winks. A lazy July afternoon was for refreshing naps, not for goat pushing, and he was sure even the Pope would agree. Sheriff Collins turned back to his car and began wiping latte off of everything inside with some napkins. The goat did not seem to notice.

Bernie

By the time Bernie pulled up to the scene a few minutes later, the goat had made its first significant movement. Now instead of facing the shoulder, the goat was facing the road ahead, and its rear end was pointing directly at Sheriff Collins, who was not amused. The Sheriff couldn't figure out what had made the goat decide to move ever-so-slightly, and he shook his fist at the big dumb creature.

"You don't make a lick of sense, goat!" the Sheriff yelled. "If you're going to move, why not move out of the road? Why not move out of the road?! I swear, even for a goat, you're really stupid!" The Sheriff thought maybe the insult would hurt the goat's self-esteem, but if it did, the goat hid it well.

Deputy Kearny, or Bernie, as the Sheriff insisted on calling him, parked his car behind the Sheriff's cruiser, told his prisoner to sit tight, then got out of his car and wandered over to the Sheriff, who was standing about fifteen feet away from a big goat with his arms crossed.

"Howdy, Sheriff," Bernie said. "What can I help you with?"

The Sheriff pointed at the animal. "There's a goat in the road."

"Yes, sir. It sure appears that there is."

"I'm going to need you to move the goat."

Bernie frowned. "What, you mean you want me to just shove him off to the side of the road?"

"I don't particularly care HOW you move the goat, Bernie, but that damn goat can't stay where he is. Road's for driving, not for goat standing, and I think even the Prime Minister would agree."

Bernie wasn't really sure why the Sheriff couldn't move the goat by himself, but Sheriff Collins was his boss, and if your boss tells you to move a goat, you'd best move that goat. Bernie shrugged, rolled up his sleeves, and began to walk towards the goat. "Whatever you say, chief. One moved goat, coming up."

The Deputy got a couple of steps away from the goat, then stopped. He'd never moved a goat before and wasn't really sure how it was going to react. Did goats bite? Or kick? Or spray noxious fumes out of a sac? Bernie didn't think so, but you could never be too careful. He decided to poke the goat with his baton first just to see what it would do. He pulled the baton out of his gun-belt, waved it back and forth a couple of times, then glanced back at the Sheriff, who gave him a big thumbs-up.

"You move that goat," Collins said. "You show that goat who's the boss!"

Bernie turned back to the goat, took a deep breath, then tapped it lightly on the haunches with the baton. Nothing. The goat didn't even flinch. Bernie hit the goat a little harder, and added some words of explanation, in case the goat didn't understand what he was trying to do.

"Go on now!" he said. "You get on outta the road here! Get!" But the goat continued to stand firm. Bernie placed his baton back in his belt, then put both hands on the side of the goat and tried to push, but the goat stood firm. Bernie dug in his heels and pressed harder, but it was like pushing a hairy block of cement. That goat was staying put.

"What's the holdup, Bernie?" came the call from the Sheriff. "Why aren't you moving that goat?"

Bernie stood up and put his hands on his hips. "Goat doesn't seem to want to move, boss."

"Well then, you gotta push it harder. You've gotta put your whole body into it. Lower your center of gravity. Try and get some leverage. You can't give up already, boy. It's just a big dumb goat, for Pete's sake."

"With all due respect sir, maybe you should come over here and give it a push. This goat isn't as light as it looks. Doesn't smell so great, either."

The Sheriff could feel anger bubbling up inside him again. "I ain't pushing no goat, Bernie. The people of this town elected me to crush crime, not to shove livestock."

"Then maybe you've got another suggestion, because

I'm pretty sure just pushing isn't going to do a bit of good. The goat seems pretty stubborn."

Collins sighed. *What good is a deputy,* he thought, *if he can't even move a big dumb goat out of the middle of a highway?* The Sheriff decided to try something a little bit different, since Bernie was proving to be about as useless as a brush fire in a kindling factory. He went back to his unit and rifled around in the backseat until he found his trusty megaphone, then he walked over to Bernie and the goat and got down on one knee.

"What're you gonna do, Sheriff?"

"I'm gonna move the goat, Bernie, since you don't seem to be able to."

Sheriff Collins put the megaphone to his lips, then moved it a few inches from the goat's head.

"THIS IS SHERIFF COLLINS OF THE POLICE!!" came the shout from the megaphone, causing Deputy Kearny to jump slightly, and several crows to go tearing out of the trees into the afternoon sky. "GET OUT OF THE ROAD, GOAT, OR YOU WILL BE IN VIOLATION OF THE LAW OF THIS GREAT STATE! REMAINING IN THE MIDDLE OF THIS HIGHWAY IS A FELONY, GOAT! COMPLY WITH MY ORDERS IMMEDIATELY OR YOU WILL BE PROSECUTED!!" The goat twitched a little but made no attempt to obey. The Sheriff stood up and threw the megaphone to the ground. "Damn it all! This goat is really pissing me off now!!"

Bernie rubbed his chin. "Maybe the goat couldn't hear you, boss. Maybe it's deaf."

"A deaf goat? Don't be ridiculous, Bernie. Goats have got some of the best hearing of any creature in the animal kingdom. It's a documented fact!" The Sheriff turned and stomped back towards his car, muttering under his breath in disgust. "A deaf goat... What kind of stupid idiot would say something like that?" Bernie trotted after Collins. The goat remained where he was.

The Sheepherder

When the cops got back to the Sheriff's car, Collins rubbed his forehead with his hands. This was proving to be more difficult than he ever would have guessed. He had learned a lot in the police academy, but he must've been sick the day they taught how to deal with serious goat scenarios. If only he wasn't so drowsy, he could probably think straighter. *I wouldn't be so damn drowsy,* he thought, *if I'd been able to drink my latte instead of wearing it.* The Sheriff was not happy.

"You know, Sheriff," said Bernie, looking back at the prisoner in the back of his car, "The guy I arrested earlier is a sheepherder. Maybe he has an idea or two. You think we should ask him?"

Sheriff Collins blinked. "Why did you arrest a sheepherder?"

"He was selling crack."

"To the sheep?"

"Well, maybe, but the crime I arrested him for was selling crack to kids. I'm not sure if it's actually illegal to sell crack to a sheep."

"It might be. I'd like you to look into that."

There was a brief, uncomfortable silence. "Um... right now?"

"No, you fool. Later on. AFTER we deal with the goat. Goat first, then sheep. That's the American way."

Bernie was unsure how to respond to this patriotic

statement so instead he just nodded and went back to his unit to retrieve the sheepherder, who might have the solution they needed.

A couple of minutes later, Yancy the crack-dealing sheepherder was standing handcuffed in front of the Sheriff, looking bewildered. "I'm sorry, Sheriff, but I'm not sure I caught what you said. Can you repeat that?"

Collins snarled. "I asked you if you knew anything about moving goats. Did I stutter?"

"No, not really. It's just an odd thing to say."

"I'm not interested in your opinions on the weirdness of my statements. All I'm interested in is what you know about making a goat move." Collins pointed at the animal in the road. "Specifically, THAT goat."

Yancy shook his head. "Can't you just push it out of the way?"

"Don't be ridiculous. Goats don't respond to pushing. Everyone knows that. But perhaps they respond to one of the tricks of your trade, which is why I need you to tell me what you know." Collins leaned in close and put his arm around Yancy's shoulder. "There might be something in it for you, my friend. You help me with this goat issue, and I might be able to reduce a certain drug dealer's prison sentence, if you catch my drift."

"That sounds wonderful, Sheriff, but goats aren't really my area of expertise. I'm a sheepherder, not a goatshifter."

The arm was removed from Yancy's shoulder, and the hand it was attached to was thrown up in exasperation. "They're virtually the same animal! They're both small. They're both furry. They both go *Baa!* They're like Siamese cousins or something!"

"Actually, I'm pretty sure goats don't say *Baa.* I think

they say, *Meh-eh-eh*. It's more of an *M* sound."

"What the hell ever! I'm not here to discuss the mysterious language of the incredible goat! I'm just here to get it out of the middle of my road! Can you or can you not make it move?"

"I can try, I guess. I'm not a great sheepherder, though. I mostly use it as a front for selling the crack. You know, the whole 'legitimate business' thing. 'How can you afford the Benz, Yancy?' 'Oh, I had a good month of shepherding.' You know what I'm saying?"

Bernie looked impressed. "Really? A Benz? How much money IS in shepherding these days?"

"More than you'd expect. Especially if you're dealing drugs on the side. Still, I might know a thing or two. Of course… there is a small problem..."

"What problem?" asked the Sheriff.

Yancy held out his hands.

Bernie shook his head. "Your handcuffs? I don't really think we can remove those, Yancy. You may be helping us out here, but you're still under arrest."

With a practiced motion, Collins pulled his keys off his belt and unlocked Yancy's cuffs. Yancy rubbed his wrists and smiled. Collins returned the smile and patted him on the back. "You go get that goat, tiger!"

"You bet I will, Sheriff!" said Yancy, and ran towards the goat.

Deputy Kearny tapped Collins on the shoulder. "Sir, why did you just remove the handcuffs of a jail-bound criminal?"

"Because, Bernie, you can't expect a talented sheepherder to move a goat without full use of his extremities. That's just silly."

"I don't know if it is. It seems to me like that might

have been a bad call."

Collins turned to Bernie. "Good or bad, it was my call to make. Desperate times call for desperate measures. And these have become desperate times."

"With all due respect, sir, it's just a goat."

"I can't understand what you're so uptight about. It's very simple. He moves the goat, we put the handcuffs back on him, he goes back in the car, and it's off to prison for the crack-herder. There's nothing to worry about. He's only ten feet away, after all."

Bernie glanced behind the Sheriff. He saw a goat. That was all. "Um... there might be a small problem with your simple plan."

"And what's that?"

Bernie pointed. "The crack-herder seems to have vanished."

Sheriff Collins turned around and sure enough, Yancy was gone. Collins spun around in a circle, madly looking for any trace of the guy whose handcuffs he had removed, but there was no sign of him. "DAG-BLAST-IT!!" screamed the Sheriff, and threw his hat on the ground. It bounced once and hit Bernie on the leg. Both the officers stared at the hat for a minute, then Collins looked up and ran his hand through his hair. "You think that guy ran away, don't you?"

"Either that or the goat ate him."

In unison, they both turned and looked at the goat in the road, and for the first time, the goat was looking back. They all stared at each other for a minute, then the goat made a small bleating sound and went back to looking at the trees.

Bernie shook his head. "That was more than a little bit creepy."

"You can't let the goat get in your head, Bernie. If you do, then the goat wins."

"You're starting to sound a little paranoid."

"I'm not paranoid!" the Sheriff said, sounding a little defensive. "But I'm not going to let myself be thwarted by a big dumb goat! I'm just not!"

"He's just standing there! Besides, now we've got an escaped convict on the loose. He can't have gotten very far, so if we call the helicopter right now, we should be able to track him down. It shouldn't take more than..."

Sheriff Collins held up his hand. "Cram it, Bernie. We aren't doing anything else until we move this goat. My pride is at stake now. My pride and my dignity."

"Right. Pride and dignity." Bernie sighed and looked back over at the goat. "I dunno, I guess we could move it with the car."

"The car. The car..." The Sheriff's eyes lit up. "The car! That's brilliant! I get in my car, back it up about a hundred yards, rev the engine, then stomp down on that accelerator, and move... that... goat..."

"That's not exactly what I was talking about. I was thinking more along the lines of just kind of bumping the goat. One mile an hour as opposed to one hundred and ten miles an hour, you know?"

Collins opened his mouth to respond when the sound of an approaching motor cut through the stillness of the afternoon. Both men turned to look and saw a big blue news-van driving down the highway towards them. It was the first car that either one of them had seen the entire time they had been dealing with the goat issue. Neither one of them said a word as the news-van drew closer and closer and finally came to a stop right in front of them. Channel 37 Eyewitness News reporter Trisha Tanner exited from the passenger side and motioned to her cameraman, who was driving, to stay where he was. As she walked towards the officers, Sheriff Collins muttered to Bernie under his breath. "Oh, great," he said. "Now we've got the media involved."

The Media

Channel 37 Eyewitness News reporter Trisha Tanner reached out and shook the Sheriff's hand. "Good afternoon, Sheriff Collins. I'm Channel 37 Eyewitness News reporter Trisha Tanner." She looked around. "Is something going on here?"

Collins gave her the stink-eye and crossed his arms menacingly. "There is nothing to see here. Move along, media. We don't need you around blowing everything all out of proportion."

Channel 37 Eyewitness News reporter Trisha Tanner grinned. "So there IS a story here!" She snapped her fingers and her cameraman appeared at her side with stunning speed. She also generated a Channel 37 microphone seemingly out of thin air. It was like a magic trick. Bernie half-expected her to pull a rabbit out of her shoe and ask it to pick a card. Instead she shoved the microphone in the Sheriff's face. "How would you classify the situation at this moment, Sheriff? Is it volatile?"

Collins stuck his finger out and began waving it around. "Back off, media! I despise you people, and your liberal slant on the news, and I'm not giving you any information whatsoever. Scram, you hear me? Scram!"

But as with the goat, Sheriff Collins was having very little success getting things to move at his command. Channel 37 Eyewitness News reporter Trisha Tanner stood where she was and continued to pepper the Sheriff with questions, which he continued to elude. After several minutes, she finally put her microphone down and shook her head.

"Go ahead and turn the camera off, Carl," she said to her cameraman. "This guy isn't giving us anything we can use. We'll just have to investigate this our own way. Nobody hides a story from Channel 37 Eyewitness News reporter Trisha Tanner, and I've got three local Emmy awards that prove it."

Carl the Cameraman put down his camera and happened to catch a glimpse of an animal standing a few feet ahead of them. "Hey, look at that! There's a cute little goat in the road!" he said, and raised his camera back up to get a shot of it.

The Sheriff reached up and put his hand over the lens. "Turn that dag-blasted camera off! You people are going to ruin everything!"

And depending on who you asked later on, that's exactly what they did.

The Showdown

The story of the goat in the road and the cruel fascist police force that was trying to move it against its will was the top story on the five o' clock news on Channel 37. While no one would deny that it was a slow news day, the story still touched a nerve with the people of the town, and by 5:15 they were beginning to show up in droves. Some wanted to give Sheriff Collins and Deputy Kearny a piece of their minds. Some wanted to meet Channel 37 Eyewitness News reporter Trisha Tanner, who was hot and single. Some wanted to try and get on camera so they could wave at it like idiots. But most simply wanted to see the goat. There was no specific class of people who were coming down to Highway 12. It wasn't a black thing or a white thing, a poor thing or a teenager thing. It was a human thing. And as history has proven time and time again, nothing brings people together like a goat in the road.

The goat, for its part, seemed oblivious to the attention. Aside from the occasional blinking, it stood perfectly still, looking at nothing. Sheriff Collins had put up police tape around the goat, so nobody could get very close, but that didn't stop the quickly-growing crowd from shouting supportive things at it from behind the barricades.

"Don't give up!" came from the left.

"We're here for you!" came from the right.

"You go, goat!" came from the back.

"I support our President and the War in Iraq!" came from the front (although the liberal media didn't let that get on the air).

"Hey, goat! I wrote a screenplay and I was wondering if you'd like to read it! I totally think you'd be perfect for the lead role!" came from above, as people had taken to scaling the trees and climbing on top of their cars.

As the scene grew increasingly more chaotic, Sheriff Collins and his Deputy stood just inside the police tape, trying to keep people calm and also trying to dodge the occasional items being hurled at them from the irate crowd. A hubcap missed Bernie's head by about six inches as he leaned in to speak to Collins.

"We've got to do something about this, sir. This is getting out of control."

"Thank you for the observation. I hadn't noticed."

"There's got to be some way to get these people to

disperse."

"Well, what do you suggest, Bernie? They want us to leave the goat alone, but as public servants it's our DUTY to move the goat, but we can't get the damn goat to MOVE so we're stuck in what I believe is a Catch-22, and I think even the Mayor of Bolivia would agree."

A sock full of batteries flew out of the crowd and hit Bernie in the back of the neck. He sprawled to the ground in pain. The Sheriff tapped him with his boot. "Get UP, would you? You can't show weakness around these people. Or this goat. This horrible... evil... goat."

Without realizing he was even considering this action, Sheriff Collins yanked his gun out of his holster and pointed it right at the goat's head. The crowd shrieked, then fell silent. Everyone leaned forward in anticipation of what was going to happen next. Channel 37 Eyewitness News reporter Trisha Tanner poked Carl in the side and motioned toward the developing scene. He nodded and slung the camera on his shoulder. The little red light went on.

"This is Channel 37 Eyewitness News reporter Trisha Tanner," said Channel 37 Eyewitness News reporter Trisha Tanner, "and this is Breaking News. The goat we told you about during the five o' clock hour is currently involved in an intense stand-off with the local Sheriff. I'm live on the scene with the exclusive story," she continued, failing to notice that there were reporters from two other stations standing directly in her shot.

Collins continued to point the gun at the goat, finger on the trigger, hand shaking. In twenty-three years of law enforcement, he had never pulled his gun on anything, but this goat, this big dumb goat, had pushed him over the edge. A desperate voice shouted from the crowd.

"Don't do it, man! That goat never did anything to

you!"

Collins whirled around, almost stepping on Bernie, who although dazed, was trying to get back on his feet. "Never did anything to me? Are you out of your mind? This goat has done EVERYTHING to me! All I wanted is a nap. And now..." he motioned at the crowd with the hand not holding the gun. "... now I've got all THIS. What did you expect to happen? What the hell did you people expect?"

Suddenly from behind him, a group of about ten people slipped under the police tape. They were long-haired and un-washed and clad in mostly hemp. Yes, the hippies had finally made their move.

The Hippies

Before Sheriff Collins could do anything to stop them, the hippies held hands with each other and made a human chain around the goat, who yawned. A particularly tall hippie who gave off the air of being their leader, along with a few other distinctive scents, looked at the Sheriff and shook his head.

"For shame, Mister Cop, man. You have let yourself get lost in the blinding flash of the electric lollypop, but the world is deeper than that, man. It goes all the way down, and I think you've forgotten what that means."

Now the Sheriff wanted to point his gun at the hippies, but he resisted. Instead he just stood there looking incredulously at the people who were now surrounding his goat. "Are you freaks out of your mind? This is no ordinary goat. I can handle an ordinary goat. When it comes to an ordinary goat, I'm the GoatMaster of The 21st Century. But this is more than a goat, and I can't believe you people can't see that. This goat doesn't care about you." Collins turned to the crowd and raised his voice. "This goat doesn't care about ANY of you! You know who this goat cares about?"

"Asians?" said one of the hippies, and meant it.

"No! This goat only cares about this goat. And that's what's wrong with the world today." Bernie sidled up to the Sheriff and snatched the gun out of his hand, but the Sheriff didn't seem to notice. He was in the zone. "This goat epitomizes everything that's wrong with everything. And that's why it must be destroyed." Sheriff Collins looked at the sky, and a tear fell from his cheek. "And I must be the one to destroy it." His eyes narrowed, a look of determination came over his face, and he turned again to face his nemesis. "Now goat, your time is up. Now you will die."

The Goat

The Sheriff began to walk towards the goat, murder in his eyes, when the lead hippie looked down and jumped back. "The goat, man! Look at the goat!"

All eyes went to the goat, and a gasp came from the crowd. The goat, who had been standing in the middle of the road for most of the day, had lifted its front hoof in the air. It looked up at the hippies who were completely surrounding it and opened its bearded little mouth.

"Meh-eh-eh!" said the goat. "MEH-EH-EH!"

The chain of hippies instantly released each other's hands and took a step back. Both the Sheriff and Bernie stood frozen, watching in awe as the goat suddenly sprang to life. It took a few steps then stopped and turned back to the officers.

"Meh-eh-eh!" said the goat. "MEH-EH-EH!"

The goat then swung its head back around, walked under the police tape, and continued on its way, the sound of its hooves clomping rhythmically on the asphalt. The crowd parted silently as the goat approached then passed. Even Channel 37 Eyewitness News reporter Trisha Tanner, who had never been speechless for a moment in her entire career, was at a loss for words.

As the goat reached the end of the crowd, it passed a man dressed like a sheepherder. The man nodded at the goat, smiled, then began to slowly clap his hands. After a moment a kid standing next to sheepherder started clapping too, and before too long the applause spread to the entire gathering. Soon people were hooting and hollering and loudly cheering the goat, who continued to walk away, down the highway, not responding to the noise, only putting one hoof in front of the other.

Somewhere within the celebrating crowd, a police officer with latte stains all over his uniform began walking towards his vehicle. He reached it, opened the driver's side door, and got inside. Before he could close the door, however, Deputy Bernie Kearny ran over and leaned down, directly in the way. He looked confused.

"Where are you going, boss? We've still got some work to do here."

The Sheriff patted Bernie lightly on the top of the head. "You're more than capable of finishing up here, Deputy. I think I'd just be in the way."

"Are you going to be okay? You look pretty shaken."

Sheriff Collins looked into the distance, down the road where if you squinted, you could still see the shape of a goat walking into the sunset. "Did you hear the goat? He forgave me. He forgave me." And without another word, the

Sheriff started his car, turned around, and drove away.

The story of the goat became legend in that little town, but like all legends, in time the details got fuzzy and the story began to drift away from the reality. Nobody ever saw Sheriff Collins again, but Sheriff Kearny was an exceptional law enforcement officer, so his predecessor was not often missed. Channel 37 Eyewitness News reporter Trisha Tanner eventually made it to the big city, where all reporters hope to end up, and a few years down the road she even got to do a story on the arrest of a crack-dealing sheepherder who'd also made it to the big city.

Highway 12 stayed where it was, as highways often do, but every so often, when traffic was light and the weather was warm, the sound of four hooves could be heard, off in the distance. Hooves which bought a small town together one special summer day, and showed them the big dumb goat within us all.

"Meh-eh-eh! MEH-EH-EH!"

The End

The following True-Life Tale is being brought to you by…

You Want Some Candy? No Sweat!

Have you ever had a craving for a candy bar but couldn't stand the thought of choking down yet another dry, brittle hunk of chocolate and nougat? Well, stop your uncontrollable sobbing, because there's finally a candy bar just for you. It's called Moist®, and it's the world's first candy bar that's always moist!

Moist® is made with rich milk chocolate, chewy caramel, roasted peanuts and lukewarm water. When you bite into a Moist® and it makes that squishing sound, you'll know that you're eating a Moist® even though it says it pretty clearly on the wrapper.

When you want some chocolate but don't have anything to wash it down with, reach for a Moist®. Eating a Moist® is like eating a candy bar and drinking a glass of day old tap water… all in one! Moist® is the candy that people who want a Moist® ask for by name.

Why waste your sweet tooth on a boring old candy bar when there's Moist®, the candy bar with condensation on every square inch? Yes, when you really think about it and you've had a few too many drinks, you'll agree that there's no better thirst quenching candy than Moist®. Grab a Moist® today and wring out the goodness.

Moist®
The Wet Candy

Valley Of The Dolls

Of all the things I'm scared of, and that list goes on and on and on, perhaps my most shameful and irrational fear is talking dolls. I'm a little unnerved by dolls in general, especially the ones that are just a little too human-like for their own good, but when they start trying to have a friendly chat with me, the conversation goes nowhere, because I am hiding under my bed. I lay this talking doll fear at the feet of my father, because I blame everybody else for everything that is wrong with me.

When I was younger, I used to spend every Thanksgiving at my dad's house. At that time, there was a Thanksgiving Twilight Zone marathon that would air on Channel 5 (which later became The WB and is now home to The CW, home of many fine programs, such as *look up CW shows before publishing this*). Yes, something like 18 hours straight of all the finest, most child scarring episodes of The Twilight Zone, presented in unnerving black and white. This was before my sister was born so I was the only kid in the house, which meant that while the adults were mingling and waiting for dinner to be ready, I pretty much kept myself busy by playing Legend of Zelda or watching whatever was on the TV. And for some reason, my dad always had The Twilight Zone marathon on.

It was during one of these special Thanksgiving holidays that I first saw the episode about a doll named Talking Tina, who was cute as a button and would say adorable things like, "My name is Talking Tina, and I love you!" But when everyone except the dad (played by Telly Savalas) left the room, Talking Tina would say less adorable things to him like "My name is Talking Tina, and I am going to kill you!" Sure enough, that doll managed to kill poor Telly Savalas, and also the innocence of a skinny little seven year-old, who would have Talking Tina nightmares right up until Christmas.

The bitch of it was that every Thanksgiving, as much as I'd try to avoid it, I'd ALWAYS end up seeing that stupid Talking Tina episode at my dad's house. If I didn't see ANY other Twilight Zone that holiday, Talking Tina always found a way to air just as I got within sight of the TV screen. It was like Channel 5 was just waiting for me to walk in the room before hitting "play." So even if I'd managed to banish Talking Tina from my subconscious during the previous 12 months, the Twilight Zone marathon was always more than willing to remind me. For most of my childhood, instead of "pilgrims" and "turkey," I equated Thanksgiving with "cranberry sauce" and "terror," neither of which I care for.

Talking Tina would have been bad enough, but in 1989, my dad introduced me to something even worse, something that screwed me up on a much deeper level. I was spending a few days at Dad's house and he came home with a video (see, kids, back in 1989, we watched movies on something called a VCR, which is like a Video iPod with huge clunky tapes that you had to rewind, a concept that is so archaic, I can't even figure out how to explain it to you). Dad told me, and I will never forget this, that he had rented a "hilarious" movie that was "really funny" and he wanted me to watch it with him. I had no reason not to trust him, because the previous two movies he had said this about were "The Naked Gun" and "Monty Python and the Holy Grail," the two movies which laid the groundwork for my sense of humor.

But on this day, the movie he had brought home was a charming little romantic comedy called "Child's Play." Oh wait, did I say "charming little romantic comedy?" What I meant to say was "evil scary horror killer doll fright fest." I get the two confused sometimes. As I was still skittish from years of Talking Tina, I was in no way prepared to deal with Chucky, who takes the fun concept of "homicidal doll" and adds a butcher knife.

Now that I'm a little older, I understand what Dad meant by calling "Child's Play" a funny movie. It's a completely ridiculous film, so much so that by the 5th movie in the series, it actually became a parody of itself, on purpose. But I was nine years old and already completely freaked out by talking dolls, so there was no chance I was going to be able to enjoy "Child's Play" as a silly little horror movie. I was getting twitchy even before Chucky started throwing people out of windows. And by the time his killing spree really flared up, I became completely hysterical. I pleaded with my Dad to turn the movie off, which he wouldn't do, pointing out yet again that it was so stupid that it was almost a comedy. Chucky killed more people, and I asked if I could at least go in my room where I would lock the door, wrap myself up in a blanket, and cower in the corner away from the windows. Again, he turned down my request. But even at nine years old, I was a shrewd negotiator, and was able to convince him to let me hide behind the couch, which was in the living room, thereby meaning that I could still be able hear the movie as I rocked back and forth and prayed that Chucky would not find out my address.

And that is exactly what I did. I wedged myself behind the couch with an issue of Nintendo Power and tried to distract myself from the sounds of the wise cracking doll murdering people on the TV. Did I have nightmares that night? You bet I did. Did I have nightmares several times a month for many years after that? Of course! Did I even have the occasional nightmare where Talking Tina and Chucky were married and they were BOTH trying to kill me? So help me, I did. Pretty much any chance I had of growing up well-adjusted died that day.

So almost 20 years have gone by, and although I'm not what I would call a huge fan of horror movies, I don't actively avoid them. I've seen all the "Nightmare on Elm Street" movies, I own two of the "Halloween" flicks on DVD, and hell, I even drove to my local movie theater and bought a ticket to see "Freddy vs. Jason" on the big screen. But when it comes to "Child's Play," I can't do it. My logical side knows this is stupid, but my logical side is sickly and weak. My irrational side takes steroids. The good ones. The ones from BALCO. And when I'm in a toy store and I find myself in the doll aisle, I walk a little faster, because you never know. One day, the dolls may come to life and have their talking doll murder revolution, but I will be safe, because you can bet I will be hiding behind the couch.

Shadows of the Invisible
(a tale told in "real-time")

Week Five: Flashback - The Tragic Tale of Plan A

"Last week, an assassin attempted to assassinate the president of Antarctica. My ex-wife has been kidnapped and may still be held hostage. And people that I work with may be involved in both. My name is Librarian of Congress Jacques Vargas, and these... are the longest eight weeks of my life..."

FRIDAY, DECEMBER 13th, 2002

4:00pm - George Washington University Hospital, Washington D.C.

Jacques Vargas jumps as the door to his hospital room swings open. He doesn't jump too high though, as the various tubes in his body don't allow for much swift movement. He has been dozing on and off all day, a product of the constant glorious medication that has been circulating through his body for a week now. If there is a more wondrous invention then morphine, Jacques wants to know nothing about it, at least until the morphine wears off.

Entering his room, looking concerned but serious, is Chuck Williams, followed closely by fellow agents Irma and Todd. Chuck takes a seat and rubs his chin. "You look pretty bad, Jacques. How're you feeling?"

"Well gee, Chuck. I was three inches away from a bomb when it detonated. I think the fact I'm still in one piece should get me the MVP award."

Todd, the rookie, speaks up in his small voice. "Plus, you saved the President of Antarctica's life. You did the job you were supposed to do."

Jacques glances up at Todd and glares at him. "You sound like a Hallmark card, Todd. One of the stupid ones with the pictures of lilies on the cover."

Moving over to the other side of the bed and grabbing Jacques' hand, Irma shakes her head. "I didn't think you were going to survive, Jacques. The bomb. The exploding. The loud exploding of the bomb. I honestly expected that you and the President were going to be in a million pieces."

"Your optimism is very moving, Irma. Thanks. You should all know better. It's gonna take more than a bomb to stop Jacques Vargas. Remember when I got hit by that train? Not a scratch!"

"It was a Fisher Price train. The kid that threw it was four years old."

Jacques waves his hand dismissively. "There are always nay-sayers. Now you know why I've all called you here. I want a full report on last Friday. I understand Chuck and Irma shot two suspects while I was getting blown up. That would be nice to hear about, and now that the ringing in my ears has finally gone away, I actually CAN hear about it. Also, I want a status report on President Kemo. How's he doing?"

Surprisingly, it's Todd that steps forward. "He was discharged from the hospital this morning, sir. I had a file folder full of all the information we were going to present, but I must've misplaced the darn thing."

"That folder was highly classified, Todd!" Chuck barks. "You can't just be LOSING stuff when you work for the Library of Congress!"

"Calm down, Chuck," Irma says. "It probably fell behind his desk or something. Or it's under some paperwork. You know how much paperwork we all have since the assassination attempt."

"Look, I'm sorry I lost the folder, but it doesn't even matter right now, because I've memorized everything in it. For instance, the fact that the bomb was intended to blow that whole building up, but it was so badly constructed, that the blast radius was only about four feet. Some real idiot built that thing. It couldn't have popped a balloon." Todd glances over at Jacques and begins to stammer. "I mean, um... I mean, it was still a BOMB, but you know... I just meant..."

"Don't worry about it, Todd. I get your drift. I'm not really that badly injured anyway. Just some lacerations, abrasions, and one nipple that just couldn't be saved. Also some internal stuff but, hey, real men don't whine about lung failure." Jacques takes a very labored breath, then turns to Chuck. "What happened with the shooting? That's what I want to know next. I remember you saw some suspects, and you two took off after them. Why did you feel it was necessary to gun down two possibly innocent people in the middle of a crowded zoo?"

Chuck stands up, walks to the foot of Jacques' bed, and begins to pace. "We didn't WANT to shoot anybody, Jacques. We didn't really have a choice..."

FRIDAY, DECEMBER 6th, 2002

2:13pm - National Zoo, Washington D.C. (just outside the

bird house and flight exhibit)

Guns drawn, but down slightly to avoid attracting attention, Chuck and Irma began to walk slowly over to the three men, the one in the cloak holding a doggy bag from The Kaffa House, and the other two reaching into it. The one in the cowboy hat, Duke Gravy, pulled out a hunk of steak, and as he began gnawing on it, he looked up and saw the approaching agents. At first, he did nothing, but after a moment, a brief glimmer of recognition dawned on his face, and the steak fell out of his hands. He spoke very softly but very forcefully under his breath. "Joe. Vlad. Run."

Joe looked at Duke quizzically, and Vlad was too busy licking the juice off the outside of his own undercooked steak to give any sign he'd heard what had been said, but Duke said it again, slightly louder. "Run, you fools. Run now. It's the L.O.C."

Joe glanced over, made eye contact with Chuck, and shook his head. "That's not Vargas."

Duke scowled. "Not the point, Joe. It's still the L.O.C., and they're coming this..."

"You three! Freeze! Hands in the air! Drop the doggy bag!"

At the sound of Chuck's commands, all three of them turned towards Irma and Chuck. Chuck's gun was pointed directly at Duke's forehead. Irma, looking very scared, had her gun pointed at the ground. There was a brief moment of silence, in which the only sound was the highly inappropriate laughing of a hyena. The standoff was broken as Duke gave a huge smile, winked, and took off.

As Duke ran to the west, Joe and Vlad both ran towards the east, darting around confused zoo visitors. At first, neither Chuck nor Irma seemed to know who to chase, but operating under the idea that more is better than less, they darted after Joe and Vlad.

The chase went on for only a few seconds when Vlad suddenly screeched to a halt. He turned back around and began to stare lustfully at a tall blond woman who was looking at the camels, unaware of what was going on around her. Her long, creamy neck was sticking out from her sweater, looking like a delicious Popsicle, and considering the weather, probably the same temperature as well. As if in a trance, Vlad started to walk over to this woman, so gracefully that some witnesses later claimed he wasn't even touching the ground. Chuck and Irma stopped running and watched this occur, not exactly sure how to react.

Joe looked over his shoulder as he ran, saw that Vlad was no longer behind him, and slowed to a halt. He cursed under his breath, and then cursed loud enough for everyone to hear, just for good measure. "Vlad! This is SO not the time for your ridiculous FETISH!!" Joe began to stomp back towards his partner, fuming with anger, and reaching into his jacket pocket for the cross he always kept on his person for these exact situations.

As Vlad got within a few feet of Girl With The Neck, Chuck's eyes darted back over to the left, and he saw Joe coming towards him, reaching in his pocket for what was undoubtedly a weapon. Although he had never before been in a situation like this or even fired a gun, Chuck instinctively knew what he had to do. He had to fire first, or he wouldn't get a chance to fire at all. Chuck shouted to Irma, "Gun! GUN-GUN-GUN!!" and before she could even begin to react, Chuck had fired his weapon. Each bullet hit its target and Joe dropped like a bag of bricks. Adrenaline pumping as people began to scream and dive out of the way, Chuck turned his gun on Vlad. He fired three more times, hitting Vlad with each shot.

Vlad, who was inches away from the woman, mouth wide open, did not seem to be injured in any way by the bullets, but instead became very angry. He turned back towards Chuck and hissed. Actually hissed. Then he bellowed, "Don't you people have any MANNERS?!" He dashed towards Chuck at a staggering speed and Chuck kept firing, but it was doing no good.

It was dumb luck that one of the bullets hit a nearby picket fence, and that the force of the impact caused the struck stake to launch itself into the air and directly into the heart of Vlad, just as Vlad was about to reach Chuck's sub-par neck region. Instead of biting Chuck and turning him into his undead minion, Vlad clutched his chest, screeched loud enough to shatter glass, and instantly turned into a white powder. Nobody who witnessed this had any time to truly process what had just occurred though, because at that exact moment, a bomb went off, and the day got even MORE interesting, becoming WAY worth the price of admission.

FRIDAY, DECEMBER 13th, 2002

4:10pm - George Washington University Hospital, Washington D.C.

Chuck sits back down, after relating the tale to Jacques, while Irma looks at Chuck, highly agitated. "You just HAD to shoot him, didn't you? They probably had information we could've used if you weren't so trigger-happy! Now we're nowhere! We've made absolutely zero progress, and we're no closer to stopping this assassination than we were before we stopped the assassination!"

"That's not exactly true," says Todd, drawing back on his knowledge of the file folder he had so carelessly misplaced. "We found the detonator behind the bird house at the zoo. It had a single set of fingerprints on it that we were able to run through the L.O.C. database. It was a clean set of prints, and we got a match almost immediately."

"A match?" Chuck says suspiciously. "I wasn't informed of a match."

"It seemed to be in everyone's best interest if I let Mr. Vargas decide who had access to that information, so I kept it confidential."

Jacques grins, which pulls slightly at the stitches on his upper lip. "That's an excellent decision, Todd. We still don't know who we can trust within the Library, and we have to control information. But now that we're all here, with people we can trust, why don't you give us the results of the fingerprint scan."

"It came back to a man named William Williams, who I discovered is one of the Library of Congress' ten most wanted."

"He's on the most wanted list?" Irma asks. "For what?"

"Overdue books. A lot of them." Todd turns back to Jacques. "Sir, I think we have to assume that the assassination threat is still very severe. This man risked a lot to try and kill President Kemo, and he's not through. He had a very specific goal, and I don't think he's going to stop until he achieves it."

Jacques puts his head back, lost in thought. "William Williams... that name sounds very familiar." He looks at

Chuck. "Your last name is Williams, isn't it, Chuck?"

"My last name isn't exactly uncommon, Jacques. Robin, Vanessa, Hank and Hank Junior. Lots of people have my name."

"Including our prime suspect. Weird."

Chuck slams his fist on the foot of Jacques bed. "If you want to say something, Jacques, just come right out and say it! We can talk about names, if that's your pudding pop! What about YOUR name? Jacques?! You're not even French!!"

Jacques points angrily at Chuck. "I was good at sports!"

The argument begins to intensify, or probably would, if a nurse wasn't walking in the room at that very moment. "You're going to have to keep it down. The both of you. Your volume is excessive." Chuck throws up his hands and begins to protest, but the nurse snaps her fingers. "Excessive! In fact, you're all going to have to leave, because the President of Antarctica wishes to come in and have a word with Mr. Vargas."

As if on cue, Antarctican President Dennis S. Kemo majestically enters the room. He smiles at the sight of the broken man in the hospital bed and walks over to him. "Mr. Vargas! I'm leaving town tonight, not to be back in D.C. until next Friday, but there are things I need to know before I go. Things that I didn't think were so important until last week." What he wants to hear is the entire story of the assassination attempt, every last word and minor detail. But we're already up to speed on that particular tale, and there's something more important going on just across town.

4:13pm - The Kaffa House, Washington D.C.

Sitting at a booth in the back of a mostly-empty Kaffa House restaurant is William Williams and his partner-in-crime Duke. They've been sitting there for several minutes, waiting for the waitress, but they haven't spoken since they sat down. Duke is distracted with a never-ending stream of thoughts, and Williams just stares out the window, grinning ever so slightly. So slightly, in fact, that Duke doesn't notice. "Something got you boys down?" It is the voice of the waitress, holding two glasses of water, which she puts down on the table.

Williams glances at the waitress, allows the corners of his mouth to curl up just a little bit more, and nods his head. "Yeah, something IS getting us down..." He looks up at her name tag. "... Francine. Me and my friend here, we had a plan, and it didn't work out at all. And I'll tell you, I'm not sure what we're gonna do next."

Francine pulls out her ticket book and her pen. "Well, sugar, my grandma always used to say that if at first you don't succeed, you should really try Plan B. Can I get you boys an appetizer to start?"

"Plan B." Williams' eyes light up. "Yes! Plan B. You know, Francine, you're exactly right. We can't let a minor setback keep us down. Not when we've got a Plan B just sitting there, waiting to be put into effect!"

Francine smiles kindly. "That's the spirit, hon. Appetizer?"

Williams waves her away. "No, no. You're gonna have to give us a minute." Francine turns and walks away without saying a word. Williams looks over to Duke, finally grinning a grin that can be seen. "Duke, have you still got that Redskins jersey?"

"Sure do. But we're not actually going to try Plan B,

are we? That was always just a big joke?"

"Not anymore. Now it's the last chance we have to pull this off and get our money. You're gonna wear the jersey... and that mustache of yours is gonna have to go." William begins to laugh and he claps his hands a couple of times, causing other patrons and Francine to look over at the booth. And then, with a single swift motion, he reaches into his coat and pulls out a brown file folder, upon which is written the words "Library of Congress - Highly Confidential."

To Be Continued...

The following True-Life Tale is being brought to you by…

Delivery In 30 Minutes Or Less… Or You Still Pay!

Here at Pizza Prince®, figuring out a way to stand out in the crowded pizza market was our #1 dilemma. What distinguishes us from a Domino's® or a Papa John's®? So we asked our customers what we could do better and the response was unanimous: "Lower your prices and make tastier pizzas." And that really got us to thinking.

Let's face it, our pizzas aren't that great, and our prices are outrageously high. But instead of fixing our two biggest problems, we decided to take those problems and make them the solution. Our pizzas are terrible, our prices are ridiculous and we are OWNING it!

People are constantly screaming at us. I mean they are right up in our faces so that we end up covered in spittle. They shriek about how our pizzas gave them food poisoning and were so expensive that they couldn't afford to buy Pepto-Bismol® afterwards. You know what? THAT'S the kind of pizza you're going to remember, and remembering the name of a business is king in the advertising world. Seeing Pizza Prince® splashed across the front page of all those newspapers is great for business, even if the articles are usually about class action lawsuits. All publicity is good publicity, that's what we tell our lawyers!

Look, you can complain all you want about the pizza and the prices, but all we care about is that you're talking about it. The picketers in front of our restaurant have signs that say, "Pizza Prince® – Minimum Quality, Maximum Price," but we don't mind! Heck, we're so proud of it that we made it our slogan. A lot of people are so impressed with our honesty that they're able to overlook the shabbiness of our product. Truth is such a rare commodity these days. That should really count for something. You want truth? Here's another one: we make more profit by skimping on the ingredients. Don't you find our candor refreshing? Doesn't it sort of make you want to buy pizza from us? I'll bet it does!

We can sit here all day and try to convince you to come to Pizza Prince®, but in the end, there are only three things you need to know: its pizza, it's expensive and it sucks. Also, we do not offer specials or accept coupons. Aren't we just ADORABLE?!

Pizza Prince®
Minimum Quality, Maximum Price

Bowled Over

Dear Matt,
    I understand you went bowling the other day. Is it possible this experience reminded you of an amusing anecdote that you would like to share with the rest of the class?
                                Sincerely,
                                Loyal Reader

Thank you for writing in, Loyal Reader! It's the darnedest thing. I actually DO have a bowling story I have been looking for an excuse to tell! Thank you for writing in and giving me an excuse to pass it along without using some forced transition or contrived gimmick!

For a while, my friend Pat and I used to go bowling on a semi-regular basis. It was part of the "We're bored. What should we do?" rotation that did not yet include "going to Hooters," "picking up skanks at the bus station" or "doing blow off of the neck of a llama." Let's just say that the rotation has really kicked it up a few notches as we've gotten older.

Bowling was always a good choice because it's cheap and it sort of resembles physical activity if you squint hard enough. Plus, our bowling alley of choice contains an excellent air hockey table, which meant that if by some chance we hadn't injured ourselves bowling (we had), then we could attempt to injure EACH OTHER playing air hockey (we would). Frankly, I can't think of a single time we left the alley without at least one of us limping or bleeding.

So it was a pretty typical scenario that found us at

the bowling alley one afternoon, wearing our stylish bowling shoes and hurling our lopsided pockmarked alley balls down the lane. Pat and I had only one goal when bowling, and it had nothing to do with getting strikes. All we ever hoped for that one of us would hit the pins in such a way that one of the pins would end up in the gutter, juuuuuust ahead of where the pin-setter could reach. This meant that when the next ball was rolled, if you aimed just right and threw it hard enough, you could bounce the ball off the pin laying in the gutter, sending it rocketing in some random unpredictable direction, sometimes into the other lane, and always with a satisfying "CLUNK" noise that was way cooler than the sound of a third strike in a row. A game where the final score was in the neighborhood of 45 to 12 but contained at least one Gutter Pin was considered a success along the lines of winning the World Series.

Anyway, on this particular day, we were a game and a half into our bowling experience, and there was no excitement to report. I got up and made my throw down the lane, knocking over a handful of pins. The ball didn't return right away, but the pins reset themselves, so I grabbed a second ball and sent it into the remaining pins to complete my frame. Pat went over and picked up his ball, and as he was waiting for ten shiny new pins to appear on the lane before him, he turned to me and said, "Neither one of the balls you threw has come back yet."

I shrugged. "So? They're probably still working their way through the system. Go ahead and bowl."

Pat's single greatest mistake in this entire incident is that he listened to the garbage that was coming out of my mouth. This tends to be anyone's biggest mistake. But apparently he was convinced by my winning argument, so he turned back towards the lane and bowled. A few moments later, he bowled his second ball.

The first inkling that there was going to be a problem occurred to me when I walked over to the ball return machine to bowl my next frame. Contrary to the name of the machine, it had not yet returned any balls, even though we had fed four of them to the void behind the pins. When we had initially started playing, we'd grabbed two alley balls each, so now we had run out of things to bowl. At this point, the logical thing to do would have been to stop bowling, go to the front desk and report that we had a small issue. That is common sense, is it not? So it should surprise nobody that the thought never even crossed my mind. Instead, I looked around and saw row upon row of alley balls, just sitting there. It occurred to me that if I went and grabbed a couple more of these balls, I could continue bowling and would not have to concern myself with the Mystery of the Missing Bowling Balls. So, of course, that is exactly what I did.

Pat and I continued bowling for a few more frames, hurling ball after ball down the lane into the bottomless pit from which innocent bowling balls never returned. After every frame, we would wander over to the alley balls, grab two more, then return to our lane, ready to continue on our quest for the high score. Had I been by myself, I suspect that I would have bowled the rest of that game, then another one, then packed up and went home. But I had Pat with me, and he has something I do not: A Voice of Reason. It took a while for it to start shouting at him, but eventually shout is what it did.

I had just completed yet another frame, and at this point, I would estimate that we had thrown between twenty and twenty-five balls down the lane without seeing a single one come back to us. The shelves where we were grabbing the alley balls from were nearly empty, and we'd long since run out of balls that were our ideal weights. I typically bowl an 11 pound ball, but I'd been forced to start bowling 15's, 8's, 6's... whatever I could get my hands on. I sat back down and when Pat stood up, instead of bowling, he looked at me and said, "We should really tell somebody what's going on. This isn't right."

I was not following and expressed this opinion to him.

He shook his head. "Something is wrong here. One or two balls not coming back is one thing, but we've been bowling for twenty minutes. I think I'm going to go up to the front desk and tell them what's going on."

I nodded. "Yeah, maybe you're right," I said, but inside, I was more than a little bit disappointed. Plus, I knew there was a distinct possibility that we were going to be forcibly ejected from the bowling alley. I did not much care for that thought.

Pat made a beeline for the front desk and a couple of minutes later, he returned with a grumpy, bearded Kris Kringle-shaped old man who did not look like he wanted to be our friend.

"What the hell did you guys do?" he asked as he knelt down next to the ball-return.

"We were just bowling," I said, using my patented Puppy Dog Eyes. "The balls stopped coming back."

Angry Santa muttered something that wasn't very jolly to himself and began poking and prodding at the machine. Pat and I sat there and tried not to make eye contact with each other. If we did, we would've started laughing uncontrollably, and laughter would not have been the appropriate reaction at that moment. We continued to sit there in uncomfortable silence as Angry Santa pushed buttons and made adjustments, and finally, after a minute or so, a ball popped out of the machine. It was like the old man had done a magic trick. I was mildly impressed and thought to myself, "Well, that's good. Seems like everything is going to be allllll right."

And then the second ball came out of the ball return.

What was surprising about the second ball was the speed at which it emerged from the depths of the machine. It didn't so much slowly roll into the return tray as it rocketed from the hole as if shot out of a cannon. The whole machine rattled. Angry Santa glared at us. And Pat and I looked at each other, both thinking the same thing. There were twenty-some balls under there. And they were coming. Now.

The third ball flew out of the machine, clacking loudly the whole way. It was followed almost immediately by the fourth, which came out with such force that it slammed into the third one. As the next two balls launched themselves out of the ball return, I noticed that the ball return tray was nearly full, so I jumped to my feet, scurried over to the machine and began grabbing the balls and returning them to their shelves. Pat followed suit. But we were not nearly quick enough. The balls began coming even faster, blasting forward in a blur. "SHOOP! SHOOP! SHOOPSHOOPSHOOPSHOOP!" went the balls, until finally the machine could no longer handle it. A green ball was halfway out of the machine when the red ball coming from behind slammed into it from below, causing it to get wedged in the hole. From inside the machine, we heard a sound like "WHUMP!" as balls continued crashing upwards. Several more "WHUMPS" came from underneath, but the green ball was stuck and it was not going anywhere. The machine lurched a couple of times, then there was a horrible screeching sound and it completely shut down.

Pat and I exchanged a glance. Our glance said, "Uh-oh..."

Angry Santa exchanged a glance with us too. His glance made it quite clear that Pat and I were now on the Naughty List.

In the end, Angry Santa had to almost completely dismantle the ball return. He pulled off its outer shell, a couple of belts and had to yank the hell out of the green ball to get it loose. When he finally got it out, he looked at Pat and I, both sitting there staring at our feet, and said, "Oh, I'll bet you think this is reaaaaaaaally fucking funny, don't you?"

It was not the kind of statement I ever expected to come from either Santa Claus OR a bowling alley repairman, but I guess I couldn't blame him. I couldn't think of a response to his question, so I was glad when Pat said, "No." It was a good answer. Short and to the point. And the best part was that it got Angry Santa to stop giving us the evil eye. He grunted in our general direction, then continued pulling balls out of the machine.

The most amazing part of the entire experience was that after Angry Santa rescued all the balls and reassembled the machine, he did not grab us by the throats and toss us outside. He just walked away. Pat and I had a brief discussion about whether we should continue bowling or not, or if perhaps it would be better to escape while we had the chance. We chose to continue bowling, but after a frame or two, we decided to pack it in. A lot of people were staring at us and the whole vibe was unpleasant. We returned our stylish shoes to the front desk and slunk outside. We didn't even stop to play air hockey. We'd broken the bowling, and it seemed like a good idea to not push our luck.

It was several months before we went back to that

alley, sure that our pictures were going to be posted behind the desk under a heading that read, "If You See These Ruffians, Contact Police ASAP!" But our fears were unfounded. We've returned many times since then, but we've taken our learning experience to heart. Now, whenever a ball doesn't come back, we go right to the front desk, explain the situation, and wait until everything has been fixed before we continue our bowling activities. But we still aim to DESTROY those gutter pins…

A Story About Badgers

Billy Badger, Billy Badger, had a badger life.
And Billy Badger, Billy Badger had a badger wife.
Billy Badger and his wife, they loved to romp and play,
And spend their time together romping all the live long day.
Yes, Billy Badger, Billy Badger, never had a care.
He and Brenda Badger would go romping anywhere.
They'd run around and dig a hole and jump and laugh and crawl.
Billy Badger was the gladdest badger of them all!
(traditional children's rhyme - circa 1873)

Billy Badger pulled into the driveway of his small suburban house. As he turned off the engine to his beat-up Honda Accord, he looked at his home and noticed the chipped paint, the busted shutters and the roof which had needed new shingles for nearly five years. For a moment, Billy Badger simply sat in his car with his head on the steering wheel. This was not how he had envisioned his life turning out. He never thought he'd still be living in this run-down shack or still working at The Law Offices of Lerner, Moore, Strasser and Silva for a wage that was barely enough to pay the bills. He only took that job as a temporary way to make money while he pursued his dream of being a pediatrician. But where had all the time gone? How had so many years gone by with so little progress towards achieving a goal that seemed as elusive as ever? He took a long deep breath and tried to collect his thoughts. He knew he had to put on a happy face before he went in the house, so as not to worry poor Brenda. With a great effort, he bared his pointy teeth in a weak attempt at a smile, then grabbed his suitcase and exited the vehicle. He trudged up to his front door, and reached for the knob. The door was locked.

"Damn," muttered Billy Badger, under his breath. It wasn't the fact that the door was locked. He always told Brenda to keep it closed and locked when she was home alone. They lived in a bad part of town and it was a safety issue. However, Billy Badger hated having to use his house key. As an animal without opposable thumbs, getting a key in a lock was a chore that never seemed to get any easier. On top of that, Billy became aware that he had locked his keys in the car. "Damn-damn..." Billy muttered again. Billy Badger wished he could just keep his keys in his pants pockets to prevent this from happening all the time, but the local clothing stores never seemed to have attire that would properly fit a two-and-a-half-foot tall member of the weasel family. This seemed like discrimination to Billy Badger, but his constant pleas always fell on deaf ears.

Billy Badger knocked on the front door. "Brenda!" he yelled. "Brenda, it's Billy! Open up! I left my keys in the car again!" After a moment, Billy heard the sounds of movement coming from within, and then the door was unlocked and opened.

Brenda Badger was wearing her usual yellow apron with the comical writing on the front: 'Don't BADGER Me, Dinner Is Almost Ready!' She had found it at a yard sale, and spent $1.50 to purchase it. That was $1.50 more than Billy really thought it was worth, but he also noticed that he'd lost his sense of humor as the years had slipped by. Brenda stood there with a scowl on her furry face and shook her head. "Again, Billy? How many days in a row can you leave your keys in the car?"

Billy frowned and barged inside. "Just call the locksmith, all right. I've had a long day. I don't need a lecture from you right now."

"Call the locksmith. Call the locksmith. That seems to be your motto, Billy. You certainly say it more than, for instance, 'I love you, Brenda.'"

Billy Badger threw his suitcase on the couch and angrily loosened his tie, which was the only article of clothing he was wearing. "Don't start with me, Brenda! Just call the damn locksmith!"

Brenda stood very still and glared at Billy for a moment then turned and stomped off into the kitchen. Halfway there, she whirled back around and shot a fiery glance at her husband. "I like how we can't ever afford to go out to dinner, but we're putting the locksmith's children through college. That makes my day, Billy! I just want you to know that!"

Billy rubbed his face and sighed theatrically. "Shut up, Brenda. Just shut the hell up, all right?!" he said, but Brenda had already left the room. Billy bared his teeth, knowing that he and the wife were going to be fighting for the rest of the evening. A long day was going to turn into an even longer night, one which would no doubt end with him sleeping on the couch. Already accepting the inevitable, Billy Badger flopped his stocky body onto the couch and waited for Brenda to return so that the arguing could begin.

A couple of minutes passed, and when Brenda didn't come out of the kitchen right away, Billy Badger decided to watch some television. He grabbed the remote control and pressed the button marked 'POWER' with a lone claw. The TV clicked on, and Billy noticed that it was on The Discovery Channel again. He sighed. Brenda always watched The Discovery Channel, all day long, and it drove Billy nuts. He wasn't paying for 150 premium cable channels so that his wife could spend all her time watching nature documentaries. He had worked hard to get them out of that kind of life, and she should stop living in the past. Sure, the present wasn't much better, but at least here they had a future, not like when they lived in the wide open plains and deciduous woodlands of southern Saskatchewan.

Billy Badger flipped the channel to ESPN, in hopes that he could catch some of the late scores on SportsCenter. Of course, SportsCenter was on commercial, but this didn't surprise Billy. This was just his luck. As he sat there, staring at the TV but not really watching it, he heard the telephone ring. It rang and rang and rang, and for some reason, Brenda wasn't picking it up. Billy couldn't figure out why she wouldn't answer. It's not like she had to travel some great distance. There was a phone in the kitchen, after all. The sound of the ringing was like a jackhammer in his skull, and he finally sat up, turned toward the kitchen and shouted, "That phones not gonna answer itself, Brenda!"

Her snippy voice shot back almost instantly. "Don't worry about the phone, Bill. I'm only trying to get dinner out of the damn oven. I'll do six things at once, just like usual!" He heard her slam the oven door shut, and after a moment, the ringing ceased.

Billy could hear Brenda talking on the phone, but her words were muffled by the kitchen door, and to be honest, he didn't care who she was talking to anyway. SportsCenter had returned, and the highlights of the Maple Leafs game were far more interesting than anything his wife was going to be talking about.

A brief span of time passed by, and Billy Badger was enjoying himself for the first time all day. His teams had all won their games, and the banter of the sports anchors was especially amusing. Just as he allowed a small smile to creep onto his face, Billy heard Brenda emerge from the kitchen. His smile turned to a frown as he looked up to see her standing over him.

"What?" Billy Badger snapped at her, not attempting to mask his annoyance in any way.

"The phone was for you. It was The Law Offices of Lerner, Moore, Strasser and Silva. They wanted to know if you could come in an hour early tomorrow."

"Well, who was it, Brenda? Who did you actually talk to? Was it Lerner, Moore, Strasser or Silva?"

Brenda threw her tiny arms into the air, exasperated. "I don't KNOW, Billy. They all sound the same to me."

"Great! Just GREAT!" Billy said as he sat up and slid off the couch. "Now I don't have any idea who called, so I don't know who to prepare for! I prepare for Lerner differently than I prepare for Moore! You know that, Brenda! You KNOW that!"

"Well, maybe next time, you can answer the phone, and then I won't have to fail your little pop quizzes!"

Billy Badger pointed at his wife with his claws, the chocolate-brown stripes under his eyes blazing with anger. "Don't take that tone of voice with ME, Brenda! I have the job! I bring in the paycheck! Last time I checked, you don't do anything to keep this family going!"

"The hell with you, Billy! And the hell with your job! You think it's EASY living my life? I didn't want to spend all my time being a housewife! I wanted to go to school! I wanted to have a career! But do you have any idea how hard it is to try and get into a community college when you're a badger!?!"

"Oh, don't use that old excuse! The only reason you can't get into college is because you're not trying hard enough. You give up too easily, Brenda, and it makes me sick to my stomach!"

Brenda grabbed the remote control off the couch and threw it at Billy Badger with all her might. It missed him by a mile and struck the wall, shattering into several pieces. "How DARE you call me a quitter? I call that college every single day, and you know what they keep asking me for? My high school diploma! How in the hell can I have completed twelve years of schooling when I'm only three years old?!"

Billy rolled his eyes. "Excuses, excuses. That's all you give are excuses." He gestured toward the broken remote control. "And now you've destroyed the remote! Dammit, Brenda, I hope you're happy. I hope you're REAL happy!"

Her eyes beginning to fill with tears, Brenda spoke in a soft, cracking voice. "I haven't been happy for a long time, Billy. A very long time."

Billy Badger stood where he was for a moment, breathing deeply, and staring at the trembling female badger standing before him. It had been a long time since he'd looked at her, really looked hard at her. To his surprise, he noticed how beautiful she actually was. It was as if he was seeing her again for the first time. He saw her beady little eyes, her soft grayish color. He marveled at the way her subtle striping pattern accentuated her powerful legs, which were great for digging. He even found himself a little turned on by the way she had put on some body fat for the winter, while still staying a sleek thirteen and a half pounds. Yes, at that moment, Billy Badger remembered why he had fallen in love with Brenda in the first place. Grinning slightly, Billy began to walk towards his wife, wanting to comfort her, wanting to tell her that it was all going to be okay. But before he could reach the spot where she stood, a light rapping came at their front door. They both turned their heads to look at the door, then Brenda wiped her eyes and without a word, scampered back into the kitchen. Billy watched her go, feeling terrible that things had gotten this bad, then with a great effort, he plodded over to the door and swung it open.

Standing on the doorstep was Billy Badger's next door neighbor, Adam Horowitz. Adam towered over Billy, and Billy had to lean way back to look Adam in the eye. It was this way with most people for Billy Badger, especially someone as tall as Adam Horowitz, who stood five foot four. Adam looked down and grinned.

"Afternoon, neighbor!" Adam said pleasantly. "How's the world treating you?"

"Same old, same old. You know the story."

Adam laughed. "Don't I ever. The problem with the daily grind is that it happens every day!"

Billy Badger chuckled, even though the thing Adam said wasn't actually funny. "So, what can I do for you, Adam? To what do I owe the honor of your visit?"

Adam shuffled his feet and got a sheepish, almost embarrassed look on his face. He began to wring his hands together. "Well, see... the thing is... well, you know my daughter Katie, right?"

"Of course." Billy Badger liked Katie .She would often feed him peanuts and scratch him behind the ears.

"Yeah, well, um... this is kind of an odd request. Please don't take this the wrong way."

Billy Badger patted Adam on the ankle. "It's all right,

Adam. You and Katie are friends of mine. I'm sure nothing you could ask me is going to drive me into a burrowing rage."

Adam smiled, but still looked uncomfortable. "Okay, well... you know I have nothing but respect for you. You're a great neighbor. And see, Katie's third-grade class is having show-and-tell on Friday, and I thought that maybe, if you were okay with the idea, Katie could bring you in to show the class." Adam half-shrugged and looked down hopefully at Billy.

Billy Badger blinked a couple of times then rubbed his chin thoughtfully. "I'll tell you what, Adam. Let me talk to my associates at The Law Offices of Lerner, Moore, Strasser and Silva, and I'll see if I can get the afternoon off. I think visiting the kids could be a lot of fun."

Looking greatly relieved, Adam nodded. "Thank you so much, Billy. You've got no idea how much I appreciate this. You're such a unique creature, and I think the class is going to go wild over you." Adam laughed. "And to think I thought you might take this the wrong way."

"Oh, don't give it a second thought," said Billy Badger, grinning. "I'm a talking badger. I can see how a bunch of nine and ten years olds might find me interesting. I'm not offended at all."

"This is really great of you. I owe you a big one. You'll have to come over this weekend, and we can watch the game on my big-screen TV. I'll fire up the barbeque and the brewskis are on me!"

"I'll be there, neighbor!"

Adam bent over and shook Billy Badger's tiny front leg. "Sounds like a plan. I'll call you tomorrow to give you directions to Katie's school. Again, I really appreciate this. Really."

"Oh, get outta here. This is what neighbors are for. Now, if you'll excuse me, I've got to get back inside. I'm having one of those 'Big Discussions' with the wife."

"I heard that, bro." Adam whistled lightly. "Sometimes you just gotta deal with the old ball and chain. Good luck, Billy. I'll talk to you tomorrow." Adam stood up, turned and walked down the driveway back towards his house. Billy watched him go with a smile, then closed the front door.

When he turned around, Brenda Badger was standing there, arms crossed and ears twitching slightly. She spoke very softly, but with a solid conviction. "Dinner is on the table, Billy. Kangaroo rat and Cream of Marmot soup. It's your favorite and I hope you enjoy it. And now I'm going to go pack, because I'm leaving you." And without blinking, Brenda Badger swung on her heels and walked out of the room and down the hall.

What Billy Badger did next was pure instinct. Without thinking, he bounded down the hall, grabbed Brenda by the shoulder, whirled her around, bent her back, and planted a huge passionate kiss on her pointy snout.

Billy had never been the romantic kind of badger. Sure, he loved his wife, but he was never good at showing it. This sort of act was simply unheard of, and when he removed his lips from Brenda, she gazed at him, almost in fear. But as she looked into his eyes, and saw the sincerity behind them, she couldn't help but smile.

"Oh, Billy," she said. "I'm so sorry."

Billy Badger put a single claw to her lips and shook his head slightly. "Shhhhh..." he whispered. "Not another word. It's me who should be sorry. I see now that there are so many things I've done wrong, but I want to make them right. Tomorrow, I'm going to go into The Law Offices of

Lerner, Moore, Strasser and Silva, and I'm going to tell them that I'm taking a vacation. I'm taking my wife on a trip to the deciduous woodlands of southern Saskatchewan, where we grew up, and I'm going to spend the entire time reminding her why she's the only badger I want to spend the rest of my life with."

A tear of joy fell from Brenda Badger's eye, and immediately soaked into her fur. "Billy, you don't have to do that. I know how important your work is."

Billy Badger grinned seductively. "Not as important as my wife is. I can always find a new Law Office of Lerner, Moore, Strasser and Silva... but I can't ever find another Brenda Badger." He lovingly nuzzled under her chin, her favorite place to be nuzzled, and then looked at her with a look she hadn't seen in ages... pure animal lust. He leaned in ever closer and spoke softly into her ear. "Now let's get this silly apron off of you, and see if we can't make a litter of baby badgers."

"But Billy, isn't it getting kind of late?"

With a fluid motion, Billy Badger picked up Brenda Badger and slung her over his shoulder. "I think you've forgotten that badgers are nocturnal, Brenda. We're SUPPOSED to be up all night long..." And without another word, the Badgers retreated to their den, where several hours of feverish mating was about to commence. As the sun went down on their modest suburban home, Billy and Brenda had learned a valuable lesson. Whatever problems may have gotten them down, in the end, Billy Badger loved Brenda Badger and Brenda Badger loved Billy Badger. That was all that mattered.

The following True-Life Tale is being brought to you by…

Oh Wow Brown Cow!

The cow. One of nature's most versatile creatures. Cows can be used for meat and milk and leather furniture. But in the last thousand years or so, very little cow progress has been made. The cow of today is almost identical to the cow of yesteryear and in this age of technology, such a lack of improvement is unacceptable. It's the 21st Century, dad-gum-it! Your cow should not be stuck in the caveman times! And that is why for the last fifteen years, the federal government in association with this nation's top scientists and farmers has been developing the next generation of cow. At long last, this next-gen cow is about to be made available to the public.

Ladies and gentleman, please rise and say hello to the Wireless Cow®. It's the cow of the future and once you've experienced it, you'll wonder how you ever lived without it. First and foremost, the Wireless Cow® doesn't have to be plugged in. Let me say that again, because you probably think what I just said is a typo. The Wireless Cow® DOESN'T HAVE TO BE PLUGGED IN! Now you can do all your milking on the go in a way that compliments your busy lifestyle. And don't think that "wireless" means "slow." The Wireless Cow® works just as fast as a regular cow, sometimes even faster. That's because the Wireless Cow® is powered by satellites that were exclusively designed to handle this new Wi-Cow technology. This means fewer dropped "Moos," guaranteed! But that's not all! The Wireless Cow® comes equipped with hooves, an MP3 player and text messaging capabilities. COW SCIENCE FICTION IS NOW COW REALITY!

Security is an unavoidable issue these days as hackers and unsavory persons are working around the clock to get a hold of your personal information and also tip over your cow. But with the Wireless Cow®, you can rest easy knowing that we've installed the most advanced security features right into the cow's DNA. Every Wireless Cow® is outfitted with an assault rifle, a 75,000 volt cattle prod and a direct link to our 24 hour Cow Monitoring Center. If those smart-aleck kids from across the street get anywhere near your Wireless Cow®, THEY WILL REGRET IT. But if they treat the Wireless Cow® with respect, it might just let them play classic video games on its touch-screen hide. Also, every single Wireless Cow® is born with OnStar. Standard. You don't even need to ask. It's already there.

Why be the last dope in Lameville when you can be President of Awesomeburg? Get a Wireless Cow® today and start experiencing a world you've never even imagined. Once you've cowed wireless, you'll never want to cow any other way.

(Important Legal Note: Please do not attempt to mate your Wireless Cow with your Wireless Bull®. It does not make cute little Wireless Calves®. It just damages the internal software.)

The Wireless Cow®
The Cow That Proves Once Again That Science Rules!

Mother's Day

It was Thanksgiving, a day for family and gluttony, and that year the festivities were being held at my Mother's house. A few days prior to the holiday, we'd had an unusually strong snowstorm, which I considered to be a "terrifying blizzard," but someone from the East Coast would barely call a "dusting." Of course, in typical Southern California fashion, the next day the temperature broke into the low 70's and all the snow melted except for a large mound in Mother's backyard which sat in the shadow of her jacuzzi.

So Thanksgiving rolls around, and aunts and uncles and cousins and grandparents and various friends and acquaintances arrive, and the get-together is well on its way to being a stirring success. We were all hanging around the backyard waiting for dinner to be ready when my cousin Anthony walked up to the jacuzzi, grabbed a handful of hard, dirty snow from the mound in the shadows, and proceeded to lob it at his mom. As the snowball sailed lazily over her head, she whirled around, pointed at him, and hissed, "Anthony! Knock… it… off!"

We cousins all thought this was hysterical and we snickered and chuckled, and in the midst of all the laughter, a germ of an idea planted itself into my head. 'Anthony threw a snowball at his mother, and it was hilarious,' I said to myself, the idea germ quickly turning into a virus. 'So if I was to throw a snowball at MY mother, then I would be the one who is hilarious!' It made such perfect sense, I wondered why I'd never thought of it before.

So with a big, dumb grin on my face and barely able to contain my giddiness at the uproarious stunt I was about to pull off, I trotted over to the mound, grabbed some snow (which at this point was more like filthy shaved ice) and hurled it across the backyard at my mom, like a juiced-up Roger Clemens trying to strike out the side. The snowball missed my mom by about ten feet, which I am not proud to admit, because I was trying to hit her square in the back.

Like my aunt before her, Mother turned around and gave me the evil eye, but instead of just telling me to knock it off, she decided to go for something a little more ominous. "You'd better not do that again," she said, and I could tell by the tone of her voice that it was not exactly a 'threat' so much as it was a 'promise that bad tidings would befall me.'

I knew better than to challenge that particular tone of voice because when I was growing up, every time I continued pushing her buttons beyond that point, I always ended up in some sort of pain. There were several occasions, especially in my teen years, when I would get it into my head that I was stronger than my Mother and that she was old and slow. And I would share these thoughts with her, and she would agree with me by saying something like, "If you come near me, you're going to get hurt." Inevitably, this sort of statement would make me laugh out loud, because obviously her Alzheimer's was making her senile. So I'd start dancing around her like a boxer, poking her in the side or pushing her shoulder while cackling like a mental patient. The whole time I'd be doing this, she'd just stand there, looking at me. At the time, I would think the look was fear, but as the years went by, I came to learn that the look was pity, because she knew what was about to happen to her son.

It always happened so fast that I could never quite figure it out. One minute I'd be bouncing around, smacking her arm and telling her that after I beat her with my raw power, I was going to put her in a home, and the next minute, I would be on the ground and begging for mercy, usually with my arm yanked behind my back and my face being ground into the carpet. I'd struggle fruitlessly against her cop holds for a while, and then in an almost bored voice, she'd say, "Are you done?" Thoroughly defeated and humbled by a woman who was not quite as frail as I'd expected, I would agree that I was, in fact, quite done, and Mother would let me go. I'd slump into a heap, all red faced, sweaty, and gasping for breath, and she would go into the kitchen to start making dinner.

She would explain it to me sometimes. "I may be a girl, but I'm always going to win because when I fight, I cheat. I'll pull hair, I'll poke eyes, and I'll knee you in the crotch. So anytime you want any of those things to happen to you, you just let me know." Looking back, it was really sporting of her to tell me all her secrets. Not that it did any good, because I always ended up writhing on the ground regardless.

The thing was, the beat down would only stay in my head for about a year and then I would get amnesia, and inevitably it would occur to me that my Mother needed to be taken down a notch, and I was the one who was equipped with the strength and the skill to do it. Looking back, the best way to describe that time in my life was 'delusional.'

Now flash forward about ten years, and I've just been informed by my Mother at a Thanksgiving party that the snowball I just threw at her is the last snowball I am going to be throwing. The internal response to that should have had been something like, 'Well, Matt, you've had your fun. You threw the snowball. Ha-ha-ha! Best not to push your luck in front of so many people!' But instead, a much more interesting thought came into my head, and that thought was, 'Now, wait just a darn minute. That woman is in her 40's now. You can take her! Besides, she'd never do anything to you in front of so many people! Go ahead! Throw another snowball! Be hilarious!'

As soon as the snowball left my hand, I knew I had made a huge mistake. Not just that I was throwing it at her, but that this one was exactly on the mark. My first throw sailed wide. This one went right down the middle. The snowball smacked her right between the shoulder blades. She turned back around and looked at me, and for a moment, everyone froze.

In all the years that woman has been my Mother, I don't think I've ever seen her move as fast as she did that Thanksgiving afternoon. She was across the backyard before I even had time to mentally compute that she was coming at me. She grabbed me around the middle and started maneuvering me into a control hold, but I wriggled away from it and managed to mostly escape her grasp. As she went to grab me again, she widened her stance and without really thinking about it, I swept her legs out from under her.

In a quarter-century of living, it was the first time I had gotten the better of her in any way, shape or form while we were wrestling around. She fell onto the grass, but got a grip on me on the way down, and I went crashing on top of her. It was the single best opportunity I'd ever had to win one of these battles of ours... and I completely squandered the chance. I was so stunned that I'd gotten the drop on her that I let my guard down for a split second, but a split second is all she needed. And yet again, everything happened so fast that I couldn't quite figure it out.

What I do know is that somehow she got behind me and grabbed a fistful of my hair, then put me in some sort of an arm bar. She got her feet back under her and started barking out orders in short, clipped sentences.

"Get up!" "Walk over to the jacuzzi!" "Not so fast!"

Here I am in my mid-20's, 6 feet and 130 pounds of solid USDA-approved beef, and I'm getting thrown around the backyard by my mother in front of just about everyone I'm related to. It was not my proudest personal moment. I would not even put it in my Top Ten. But what struck me is that nobody came to my rescue, knocking my mom aside and shouting, "Hey, lady! You leave that 25-year old man alone!" I was on my own on this one.

I complied with her demands as she led me over to the mound of snow and ordered me to get to my knees, all the while never releasing her death grip on my hair and continuing to crank my arm behind my back. I knelt there in front of the mound and she said, "So, you like throwing snowballs at your mother?"

"No, not really," I said, hoping this was the correct answer.

"Are you going to throw any more snowballs at your mother?"

"It wasn't just me! Anthony was throwing them too!" I thought perhaps I could reason with her, but she was not about to be distracted from the point she wished to make.

"I'm asking if YOU are going to throw any more snowballs at YOUR mother!"

"No, of course not."

"Good. And now you're going to eat some snow."

I didn't even have time to process what she'd just said when she took my face and ground it into the icy, dirty, mound of snow. It was cold, and it was pointy, and it was not delicious in that way that a newly fallen snow can be. After a few moments of this, she pulled my head up and asked, "Do you want to eat some more snow?"

I spit out a mouthful of slush. "Not particularly, no."

"Then you'd better not throw any more snowballs at your mother."

And with that, she let me go, walked back across the backyard and continued having the conversation with my aunt she was having when the snowball hit her, as if nothing out of the ordinary had just happened. I, on the other hand, slowly staggered to my feet and took the walk of shame back over to my cousins. Needless to say, they found the entire incident to be EXTREMELY hilarious. So in a way, I'd achieved exactly what I had set out to do.

This incident taught me two important lessons. One, I need to not underestimate Mother's resourcefulness until she actually IS in a home (and probably not even then), and two, no matter how heart-wrenching your story is, it is very difficult to get the child abuse people to come out when the child is in his mid-20's.

It's been several years since that very special holiday memory, and I've gotten older, stronger, and craftier as I've reached my prime. And even though I know now that I could totally take her, I choose not to. This is because over the years, I have also learned wisdom.

Although... Christmas is right around the corner, and she'd totally never see it coming...

Shadows of the Invisible
(a tale told in "real-time")

Week Six: The Unlikely Hero

"Two weeks ago, an assassin attempted to assassinate the president of Antarctica. My ex-wife has been kidnapped and may still be held hostage. And people that I work with may be involved in both. My name is Librarian of Congress Jacques Vargas, and these... are the longest eight weeks of my life..."

FRIDAY, DECEMBER 20th, 2002

1:15pm - Library of Congress, Washington D.C.

Sitting at his desk, absentmindedly unbending paper clips, Jacques Vargas ponders a very important decision. Even though he's only been out of the hospital and back at work for two days, Jacques is still a big-shot, and as such, is responsible for many critical decisions. However, figuring this one out is causing him an unusual amount of trouble, due to the fact that so much rests on what he ultimately decides to do. The pointy edge of a paper clip stabs his thumb, drawing a small bead of blood. He doesn't really notice.

"Seasoned fries or onion rings..." he mutters to himself. "Onion rings or seasoned fries. So many pros and cons..." He begins to gnaw on the paper clip. His office door swings open, startling him and causing him to accidentally jam the paper clip through his tongue. He grunts in pain and yanks it out of his mouth, throws it on the ground, and stomps on it. "Stupid paper clips!" he shouts. Having told the paper clip what's what, he looks up to see who has barged into his private office.

Jacques is thoroughly surprised to see that his visitor is Lily Rodham-Vargas, his ex-wife and recent kidnapping victim. She looks at Jacques and the blood on his thumb and dripping from his mouth, and rolls her eyes. "Paper clips again, Jacques? You know better than that. Especially because you always end up getting onion rings."

Attempting to mask his surprise by appearing cool, calm and collected, Jacques grins and goes to sit on the corner of his desk. He misses by about three feet and tumbles backwards, falling to the ground with a mighty crash. The vibration causes a paper clip to fall off his desk and onto his arm. Actually, INTO his arm. He pulls it out and tosses it aside, not bothering to wipe off his newest blood droplet. In the coolest, most collected way possible, he sits up, crosses his legs Indian-style, adjusts his tie and points at Lily. "I thought YOU were still kidnapped."

"I sort of figured that by the way you were making absolutely no effort to find me. No, Jacques, I've been free for a couple of weeks now. Once they got me to confirm that the other guy looked exactly like you, they didn't need me anymore."

"The other guy? You mean you saw the clone? The mock-Jacques? The one that tried to blow up the President?"

Lily shakes her head and sits down. In a chair. "He wasn't a clone, Jacques. As far I as could understand it, it was just plastic surgery. He looked an awful lot like you, but you don't have a Columbian accent."

Jacques gets up, goes over to his desk, and successfully sits where he meant to sit before. He glances at the clock on the desk. 1:18pm. "Why did they need someone that looked like me, though? What's so special about me?"

Lily shrugs. "I was married to you for seven years and I was never able to figure that one out. But all I could tell was that it had to be you. I mean, you have no idea how mad they got when you didn't get the package in the four shadows at the Kaffa House. They were calling you Jacques the Inept Fool Who Ruins Our Exhaustively Plotted Plans. It was like your Indian name."

"I really tried to get that package, but you know how it is. If I'm not properly motivated, it's hard to light that fire under me."

Lily throws her arms in the air. "I had been kidnapped, you inept fool!"

Jacques reaches out his hand and puts it lightly on her shoulder. "You don't really mean that. It's just the stress." Lily looks at the hand on her shoulder, then back at Jacques. She pushes it off, leaving a thin streak of blood on her shirt. Jacques takes this all in stride as he gets up and begins to pace back and forth. "But what was in the package? THAT is the great mystery here! The contents... of the package..." He begins to hum the theme to Chariots of Fire.

Having heard that theme plenty of times during the course of their marriage, Lily cuts him off quickly. "It was a key. The key to the utility closet in the Bird Sanctuary, to be exact. The closet where the other Jacques was hiding while the President was getting ready to give his speech. The closet where YOU were SUPPOSED to be hiding, except that you are, as previously discussed, inept and a fool."

"You sure know a lot about this assassination business. It's very... suspicious..."

"I spent three weeks in a motel room with a petty thief and a vampire! There's not much else to do aside from discussing the details of the over-blown secret plan."

Still looking at her with suspicion, not noticing the paper clip he has stepped on which has gone through his shoe, Jacques stops pacing. "Then what I'd like to know, Lily, is why you're telling this to ME? Why, I ask you, why? WHY!?"

"Because, Jacques, you ARE the head of the L.O.C., and you ARE the man in charge of stopping the assassination, and you ARE so truly clueless that you'd never call me and ask me these questions on your own, so I figured I'd save you the trouble of looking like a dope when President Kemo gets gunned down." Lily looks around thoughtfully. "Although, now that I think about it, I really should've run this information by your staff. I imagine they're probably, you know, competent."

A knock comes to the Jacques' door, and it opens. Jacques' second-in-command Irma walks in and looks at Lily with mild surprise. "Miss Rodham-Vargas. I didn't realize you were here."

"That's all right. Jacques STILL doesn't realize I'm here. Besides, I was just leaving." Lily gets up, walks around the desk to Jacques, leans in close to his ear and cups her hands around her mouth. "I'M NOT KIDNAPPED ANYMORE! YOU CAN STOP YOUR TIRELESS SEARCH!!" Satisfied, she nods her head as Jacques clutches his, and she walks out of the office. Irma watches her go and then looks back at Jacques.

"It's nice to see the two of you getting along again."

Still grimacing, Jacques glares at his departing ex-wife. "I would respond to that, but I'm suddenly deaf." He shakes his head sharply, then turns his head back to Irma. "She did give me some really interesting information, though. We're going to have to look into some of it."

"We'll have to do that later, because President Kemo

is here. He's in Transmission Room Three right now waiting for you."

Jacques stands up, grabs a bunch of paper clips, and shoves them in his pocket. "It's about time. It's unlike a world leader to be late." He grabs his briefcase and he and Irma begin walking towards the Transmission Room. "How is his security?"

"Better than it was at the zoo. We had the Advanced Secret Service team travel with him from the airport, and they're waiting in the lobby to protect him on his way back once he's done here. He's completely safe, Jacques. Nobody is going to assassinate President Kemo while he's on American soil."

"Well-spoken, Irma. Very patriotic. Actually, I do have to compliment you. Having him broadcast his speech to the zookeepers via satellite is a fine idea, but having him broadcast it from the L.O.C. was inspired brilliance. Nobody can get to him here, and he's under our watch at all times. Well done, Irma. I'm gonna buy you half a bagel." He pats her on the shoulder twice, leaving two small red drops.

Irma smiles, but looks embarrassed. "I'm just doing my job, Jacques. You know that." They walk a few more steps, then she grabs him by the arm and stops. "Listen, Jacques, before you go in there, there's one last thing I want to tell you."

"I know, I know. You only like onion bagels. I don't understand it myself, but to each his own."

"No. It's this mole issue. I've been doing some research and some surveillance, and I'm pretty sure I've discovered exactly who it is that's been leaking information." Jacques says nothing, but listens very, very intently. "It's Herring. Todd Herring. I didn't want to believe it, because he seems so nice, but I've caught him accessing files he has no business looking at, and even more incriminating, I've got a recording of him talking to William Williams on the phone. It's pretty solid evidence, Jacques. We've got to get him into custody."

Jacques frowns and rubs the side of his face. "Herring. I guess it makes sense. My granddaddy always told me never to trust redheads. Or people from Vermont. Is Todd from Vermont?"

"Um... no. He's from Brooklyn, but Brooklyn is pretty close to Vermont. Look, I was thinking that while you're in with President Kemo, I could go find Todd and take him back to your office so that we can deal with him there. I'll gather up all my evidence, and we can confront him. It's the only way we're going to be able to find out who's really behind all this."

"You're exactly right, Irma. This is why you're second-in-command and not seventh or twelfth-in-command." Jacques checks his watch. 1:21pm. He's running behind. "You go do what you have to do. I've got to get in there with the President. I'll meet you back in the office at 1:45 sharp, and we'll get to the bottom of this."

Irma smiles professionally, turns on her heels and walks off toward Todd's office. Jacques watches her go, then quickly dashes over to Transmission Room Three. He runs in the door and sees the President of Antarctica standing in front of an elaborate series of monitors and cameras. President Kemo is going over his notes, and he turns around as Jacques darts in.

"Librarian Vargas!" he bellows in his usual jovial voice. "I was beginning to think you weren't going to be here to protect me from the big bad assassins! Oh, wait! Are you the REAL Jacques Vargas? I've been tricked before! KA-BOOM!!" He laughs and walks over to Jacques and shakes his hand. "It is good to see you again. I'm glad we both survived that pesky little bomb thing."

"That makes two of us. By which I mean you and me." Jacques opens up his briefcase and begins rifling through it. "Now, the main reason I'm here is just to keep an extra eye on you in the room. I'm not expecting anything to happen, but it can't hurt. Once you give your speech, we'll take you back to your car, and you'll be safely on your way back to Antarctica, away from the place where people seem to want to blast you into itty little bits. Once I find my..."

A new voice speaks. "Excuse me? President Kemo?" Jacques turns and looks and sees a clean-shaven man in a Washington Redskins jersey standing at the door. He's holding a small notepad and looking at the President with a slightly demented awe. "It IS you! I knew it! I just knew it!"

Jacques puts down his briefcase and walks over to the man. "Who are YOU, sir? This is an UNBELIEVELY restricted area!"

"My name is Duke... er... I mean Duncan. Yes, Duncan. And I'm President Kemo's BIGGEST #1 fan! I've been a fan ever since he was City Councilman Kemo. He's just the best!"

"How did you possibly get past security?"

Duncan glares at Jacques, then looks back at the President with incredibly wide eyes. "I know I'm not supposed to do this, but you're just SO awesome, Mr. President, and it would mean SO much to me if I could get an autograph." He holds out the notepad. "Please?"

President Kemo smiles. "You know, as the leader of a highly secret government, I don't get many fans. I can't agree with your choice of football teams, but I like your enthusiasm. I'd be honored to give you an autograph."

Duncan grins, and he reaches into his pocket. "Let me

just grab a pen."

Jacques realizes that something is horribly wrong, but can't quite put his finger on what it is. Just as his mind begins to toss out possible ideas, he sees that what Duncan is pulling out of his pocket is not a pen, but a gun. Jacques stomach drops as Duncan points the gun directly at President Kemo. "Here's YOUR tip, Mr. President," he growls.

Frozen in place, Jacques can only watch in horror and disbelief as Duncan begins to squeeze the trigger, but a gunshot rings out before he can fire, and Duncan collapses to the ground. Duncan looks down at his chest, where a gunshot wound has suddenly appeared. His eyes grow wider than ever. "I'm bleeding! I'm bleeding my own blood!"

Amazed and confused by what has taken place, Jacques turns to where the gunshot came from. Standing there, in the doorway, gun still raised, stands Todd Herring, looking highly satisfied, but shaking like a leaf. Not sure why, Jacques looks at his watch. The time is 1:30pm.

To Be Continued...

The following True-Life Tale is being brought to you by...

Mr. Sandman... Bring Me A Dream

In today's high stress world, getting a good night's sleep is critical. It's good for the body and it's good for the mind. But science proves to us that traditional mattresses aren't good enough. The problem is that a mattress that is comfortable for Person A may be the worst possible mattress for Person B. And let's not even get into what Person C thinks is comfortable. If only there was a mattress that allowed you to adjust the comfort level to your own personal comfort standards! Funny you should mention that, because the certified Mattress Scientists here at SnoozeCo® have come up with a revolutionary new product that will change the way you slumber. We call it the SleepNail® 5000!

The SleepNail® 5000 isn't your regular old mattress. It is the Mattress of the Future. Deep within its plush satin-feel 100% rayon sleeping surface are nails. Huge stainless steel 14-inch nails, pointy-side up, from head to toe. With the simple touch of a button, you can choose how much nail you want sticking out of the top of the mattress. Three inches? Six inches? A foot? It's up to you! Whatever meets your personal sleep needs! That's the great part about the SleepNail® 5000. It puts the power of choice right in your hands. Don't believe the hype? Then just listen to these true testimonials from actual satisfied SleepNail® 5000 customers:

> *"I used to have one of those mattresses without nails in it, but then I accidentally bought a SleepNail bed. Now I'll never go back to a regular mattress. Mostly because*

I'm currently skewered by five inches of nails and I can't move."
Elliot - New Jersey

"As a mother of three, I used to have a problem with the kids jumping on the bed. Not anymore. Thanks SleepNail 5000!"
Gail - Vermont (former mother of five)

"Why can't I choose a setting where the nails completely go away? That doesn't seem to be an option. It seems like the only reason I ever fall asleep on a SleepNail bed is because of the massive blood loss. Also, do the nails have to be rusty?"
Ted - South Dakota (widower)

You can't possibly need more convincing! But if you're still skeptical of the wonder of the SleepNail® 5000, we'll add in this special bonus: If you order within the next 20 minutes, we will include an exclusive SleepNail® pillow, free of charge! A SleepNail® pillow is the perfect companion to a SleepNail® mattress because it is full of nails. Also broken glass and old spark plugs. And on top of all that, when you purchase a SleepNail® bed, we let you have a 30 day in-home trial. If you don't agree that the SleepNail® 5000 provides the best night's sleep you ever had, we will take it back, and we won't charge you a dime!

(Note: If the mattress is stained with blood, we cannot accept your return. Sorry. It's a legal thing.)

So what are you waiting for? Pick up the phone and

order your SleepNail® 5000 bed today, and finally discover just how refreshing sleep can be when you've got 5000 nails digging into your flesh! The answer? Pretty darned refreshing! (gives thumbs-up)

SleepNail® 5000
We've Got This Sleep Thing Nailed!

Me, Myself And I

Ah, the internet.

There are many things we can point to as proof that the internet is the greatest invention since Taco Bell's new Doritos Locos Tacos. If you'd like to know what the weather is and do not feel like looking out the window, there's weather.com. If you absolutely need a huge clump of Britney Spears's hair, it's available on eBay at a reasonable price. If you're looking for the latest news on what Anna Nicole Smith was watching on TV before she died (because it matters and it matters a LOT), there's TMZ. The internet is all about making information available to whoever wants it whenever they want it, and the best part of all is that none of this information is ever wrong.

At least this is what I thought until just recently.

One of my personal favorite websites is Wikipedia which is, according to Wikipedia, "a multilingual, web-based, free content encyclopedia project." The idea behind Wikipedia is that anyone can edit any of the articles at any time, thereby allowing the collective knowledge of everyone in the world to come together, like those rings the kids from Captain Planet wore, to create the most accurate factual articles humanly possible.

It doesn't always work out that way. Sometimes people who are idiots edit the articles and sometimes Stephen Colbert tells everyone in the Colbert Nation to change facts on Wikipedia based on his whims. This is all fine and dandy, of course, until it affects you on a personal level. For you see, I am on Wikipedia, and my article is flawed.

Why does Wikipedia have an article about a doofus

like me, you ask? Good question. About twenty years ago, I achieved great fame and fortune as a television celebrity. I was on the legendary Saturday morning children's television program Masked Rider, a show that was so popular that it took more than a year for us to get cancelled. Masked Rider is the kind of show that, when people find out I was on it, they always have exactly the same reaction. They squint their eyes, scrunch up their lips, think way back and finally nod their heads almost imperceptibly, then say, "Oh, yeah. I think it's possible that maybe I sort of remember that show." It is much the same reaction Jerry Seinfeld gets when he runs into people at the Wal-Mart and tells them he was on Seinfeld.

Anyway, on the Wikipedia article for Masked Rider, there is a cast list, and listed next to the character Herbie is my name, because that was the character I played (please, no autograph requests). For the longest time, my name did not link to anything, but a couple of months ago, my friend Alan got in touch with me and had some distressing news.

"Do you ever go on Wikipedia?" he asked.

"Sure," I said.

"Have you ever looked at the Matthew Bates article that's linked to your name on the Masked Rider page?"

"There's no article for me," I pointed out. "I haven't done anything else worth writing about."

"Yeah," he said. "You might want to go take a look."

A few clicks later, I was at the Masked Rider page. I scrolled down, clicked the link with my name on it, and sure enough, up on my screen popped a page about Matthew Bates. But it did not seem to be a version of myself that I recognized.

"Matthew Bates is an English professional football player who currently plays as a defender for

Middlesbrough," said Wikipedia.

I looked around at my room, located in Southern California, and considered the possibility that there might be some sort of error. But you know what? It wasn't that big of a deal. So they got their Matthew Bates's confused. It's not like I have the most unique name in the world. It's a mistake that anyone could make. "No harm, no foul," I thought to myself. At least now I have an amusing story to tell people. But then my eye fell upon the next paragraph and I about fell out of my chair.

"Matthew made headline news in September 2006 when naked photographs of him were posted on the internet, showing full-frontal nudity. He had taken the pictures himself in a mirror whilst on holiday, and they were thought to have been released on the web by an ex-girlfriend."

And there were links to the pictures.

A few minutes later, I had come to two conclusions. 1) The internet occasionally makes mistakes and 2) I do not mind if people think Professional Football Player Matthew Bates and I are the same person, because this dude is very well-endowed. Matthew Bates should be in Equus. Those horses would be in awe of his terrifying package. Also, he seems to be quite good at soccer.

So, even though I could easily edit the page and fix the error, I'm going to leave it. We Matthew Bates's have to stick together, I always say. Besides, a slight identity mix-up on Wikipedia doesn't change the fact I still have a page on IMDB that is certainly accurate and up to date. In fact, I'll check it right now. Yep. There it is. Apparently, in addition to my work on Masked Rider, I was also in "Bridget Jones' Diary" and "V For Vendetta."

If you see it on the internet, it must be true.

The Time Time Flew

I.

I have no reason not to go inside the supermarket, so I go inside the supermarket. I find myself here because less than thirty minutes ago, I opened my refrigerator only to find that there was not much food left. Some milk, a jar of peanut butter, a half-eaten Twix bar in the butter dish, but nothing that was going to silence the hunger in my stomach. When I first came to this country from Kenya, I would not have felt this way. I would have been grateful to eat whatever I could get my hands on. A Twix bar would last me for a week and after I finished off the peanut butter, I would have eaten the jar. But ever since I started living in America, I find myself becoming picky, a concept that would be completely foreign to any of my fifty-seven brothers and sisters who remain in Kenya.

I walk down the produce aisle, pondering whether I desire fruit or vegetable. Even after two years of American life, the choice between the two can be overwhelming for me. Fruit. Vegetable. Fruit. Vegetable. During my youth, the choice was much simpler: Nothing. Due to this, I never developed any decision making skills as a child, which has certainly affected my adulthood. Sometimes, the voice in the drive-thru speaker box will ask me if I "want fries with that." I never know how to respond. Oftentimes I burst into tears before I ever make it to the second window. There is just so much pressure.

Suddenly, I see a bunch of tomatoes. They are red and ripe and each one has a little sticker on it. It occurs to me that I do not know whether a tomato is a fruit or a vegetable, and this uncertainty has a calming effect on me. It reminds me of another time when I was uncertain, and the way that one special girl helped me find an answer that I could not discover on my own.

Her name was Akate, and truly she was the plainest girl in my village. It is likely I saw her ten thousand times while I was growing up, but until that special day, I had never actually SEEN her. The eye has a tendency to overlook plain things because they are boring. The eye would rather look at something attractive wearing something skimpy, and Akate was not the former and would never wear the latter.

It was a typical 125 degree spring morning in Kenya and I was on my way out of my home with a basket my mother had woven. I was to take it down to the bazaar and attempt to sell it so we would have some money that night to buy food. I was not a very good salesman, so we often went hungry. I don't know why I am the only one who ever had to go and sell mother's baskets, especially because I had fifty-seven able bodied brothers and sisters, but I knew better than to question my parents.

As I strolled down the dirt road, I tripped on a rock and lost my grip on the basket, which went flying out of my hands. It bounced twice, rolled, and came to a stop only when it hit a pair of bare feet. The owner of the feet bent down and picked up the basket. It was Akate. I had no idea who she was.

--- A basket, she said. Either you are going down to the bazaar to sell it, or you really like carrying around baskets so you can drop them in the street!

--- No. It's the first thing.

--- I was just joking, she said, then laughed as if her so-called joke was amusing.

Tomatoes, I cannot explain to you how irritating her laugh was, but every "ha" that came out of her big mouth was like a railroad spike going into my brain. Still, I was taught to be polite to females (at least until I married them), so I gave a halfhearted grin and coughed out half of a chuckle.

--- Yes, very nice, I said. May I have my basket back now?

Akate walked over to me, put my basket back on the ground and looked into my eyes. She then grabbed my hand in hers and spoke to me in a breathy voice.

--- It is so nice to meet a hilarious awesome guy like you in a place like this. My name is Akate. I go to school down the street.

--- Of course you do, I said. It is the only school in the village.

She laughed again, and I had to resist the urge to pull my hand out of hers and put it over my ears.

--- You are so funny. Maybe I will see you in class one day. What's your name?

--- Bujune, I replied, even though I did not really want to tell her. I wondered how long I was going to have to stand here being polite.

--- That is SUCH a great name, she said, squeezing my hand even harder and grinning like an idiot. Well, I have to go get some water from the river now, but I hope we can talk again soon. I would stay longer, but I don't want you to think I'm a BASKET case. Ha-ha-ha!

Her agonizing laugh made it impossible to even pretend to be entertained by her pathetic attempt at humor.

--- That was a joke. I said "basket" case and you and I met because of a BASKET. And then she let go of my hand and actually pointed at the basket on the ground.

--- Yes. The basket. I understand. And I turned around, picked up the basket and ran away as fast as my legs could carry me. When I reached the end of my street, I looked back over my shoulder and she was still standing there waving at me with her right hand while her left hand rested on her heart.

II.

As I walk into the beverage aisle, I am approached by an employee of the supermarket. She is a pretty brunette girl with a lovely smile and a smoking hot body. I would like very much to tap that ass, but I have learned over the years that it is inappropriate to come right out and say that in this country. This was difficult when I first arrived here, because I found myself wanting to tap many asses. There are many attractive females in your country, and I'm sure I feel this way partly because I spent so much time with Akate, who is average even amongst average people. If Akate was a number between one and ten, she would be the space between the "I" and the "V" in the number five.

The supermarket girl smiles and asks if she can help me find anything. What I really want to find are the directions to the inside of her pants, but instead I shake my head.

"I am doing all right, thank you. I am simply trying to decide which of these many Pepsi products I would like to buy. There are so many different choices!"

"Yes, there really are." I find it incredibly hot that she agrees with me. "My favorite is the Strawberries and Cream Diet Pepsi. It's really good, plus its diet, so it helps me watch my figure!"

Watching her figure seems like an excellent idea. I would like to watch it shower. I lick my lips without realizing it. Supermarket Girl sees me do this.

"You must like that flavor too!"

"What? Oh... yes. It is most... delicious. Maybe I will get it and drink it." Supermarket Girl has got amazing lips. I begin to wonder what they are capable of. I clear my throat and wipe the beads of sweat off my brow.

"That's super!" she says. "Well, if you need help finding anything else, just let me know. My name is Kimberly!" She points to her nametag, which says "Kimberly" and rests on top of her supple bosom like a mountain climber reaching the peak of Everest. I could probably scale that peak, I think.

Kimberly walks away, down the aisle, and I watch her go. Suddenly, I realize that I am dizzy. I lean over on a bunch of Wild Cherry Pepsi 12 packs to stabilize myself. As I take a few deep breaths and try and collect myself, I think back to another time when I was dizzy because of a girl, back in my village so many years ago.

My village was called Calyew and it was home to forty-five thousand people. It was one of the most prosperous villages in all of Kenya, featuring two telephones and a television in the town square which was always tuned to ESPN. I grew up not knowing that I lived on a continent named Africa, but I knew that in the beginning of the decade, the Lakers won three NBA championships in a row.

I had just arrived at the square and was hoping to see if another exciting episode of The World Series of Poker was on the television. As I walked up to the crowd that was gathered around the screen, I noticed two girls looking at me, then quickly looking away and giggling with each other. This seemed odd to me, as I was not doing anything funny at the time. But I decided to ignore them and began fighting for a space in front of the television. I struggled for a moment and had finally managed to find an opening, front and center. Right as I was about to reach it, I felt a finger tap me on the shoulder. I turned to see the two girls now standing right behind me.

--- Are you Bujune, asked the shorter of the two girls?

--- Yes, I am.

For some reason, this made the girls giggle again.

--- My name is Makena, said the taller girl, then gestured toward her companion. This is Tendaji. We live with your friend Akate.

--- Who?

--- Akate.

I had no idea who they were talking about.

--- Akate, she said for a third time. The girl that picked up your basket when you dropped it the other day. She said you two really hit it off.

--- Oh, right. I guess I remember that. She's the one that said "basket case."

--- Yes! She told us she said that. It was SO funny!

--- Really?

I had never considered the idea that someone else would find that line to be amusing. Tendaji stepped in front of Makena and looked at me quite seriously.

--- Okay, listen. Here's the thing. We're supposed to find out if you have a girlfriend. So do you? Do you have a girlfriend?

--- A girlfriend? No, of course I do not. I have not yet had my bride chosen for me by the village elders.

Tendaji and Makena squealed and hopped up and down. Without another word, they whirled around and scurried off down the dusty street. Feeling more than a little bit confused, I turned back towards the television, hoping for a distraction from the mysterious actions of psychotic females. Not five minutes had gone by when I was tapped on the shoulder a second time. I briefly thought about trying to ignore whoever was tapping me, but the longer I did not respond, the more forceful the tapping became. After a few moments, it actually began to hurt. I spun around and cried out in pain.

--- Ouch! Why must you poke me so painfully?!

Akate drew her finger back and blushed.

--- Oh, hello there Bujune. I did not expect to see you here at the television today.

She looked up at the sky and sighed loudly. She continued looking up for so long that I naturally assumed there was something up there to look at, so I gazed upwards, only to see the same boring cloudless sky that hovered over Kenya every single day. Akate noticed me looking up and smiled.

--- I can see that you like looking at the sky, just as I do. It is so nice to find someone that I have so much in common with. She walked several steps closer to me. I moved several steps in the opposite direction. Akate did not seem to notice.

--- One of my favorite things to do when I'm looking up at the sky is to ponder things. I ponder what is going on in my life, and what might be going on in my life if things were different, such as how life would be if I had a boyfriend.

--- That sounds very boring, staring at the sky all day. I did not mean to sound rude when I spoke to her, but I was finding it difficult to speak to her any other way. However, it did not matter in the least what my tone of voice was, because she acted as if she didn't hear anything I was saying.

--- I cannot believe I just came out and admitted to you that I do not have a boyfriend! What you must think of me! Although I am sure that you thought I DID have a boyfriend, so it must be quite a shock to you to find out that I do not.

She winked and moved towards me again. My skin began to crawl, and I started to move away when I tripped over my own feet, stumbled on a loose cobblestone and crashed hard to the ground. Akate yelped and rushed over to help me up.

--- Oh, Bujune! You poor thing! You are so flustered by the discovery that I am available that you lost your balance!

She grabbed me around the waist and hoisted me to my feet. I had hit my head quite hard when I fell, and was incredibly dizzy and seeing stars all around me. After perhaps thirty seconds, the dizziness began to fade and I noticed that Akate still had her arms around me. In fact, her face was pressed against my chest, as if she was listening to my heartbeat. She was grinning like an idiot and humming to herself. I tapped her on the top of her head.

--- You may release me now. I can stand on my own.

Akate slowly let me go, then looked at me and blushed.

--- I am sorry, Bujune. It just felt so nice to hold you so close. It felt... right. Maybe we can do it again sometime!

--- I do not fall over that much. Look, I have to go. I think my head is bleeding and I need to have it looked at by the village doctor.

--- Okay, well, I hope you are all right. Will you call me when you get back from the hospital?

--- I do not have a telephone. I do not think you have a telephone either. Why would you ask me such a silly question, you ridiculous girl?!

These words bounced off Akate's head without ever going in her ears. She ran over and gave me a huge hug, then ran off in the direction that her friends had gone. As I watched her go, I began to get a headache. I wondered if the headache was due to hitting my head in the fall. But I seriously doubted it.

III.

Glancing at my fancy digital Timex watch, I am able to see that it is almost ten in the morning. This reminds me that I have a dentist appointment at 10:45am and that I must hurry up and finish my shopping so that I can make it on time. It also reminds me that I should buy some floss. I have noticed that every time I go to the dentist, he asks me if I have been flossing lately, and when I say no, he shakes his head disapprovingly. Considering the life I have led prior to coming to this country, I consider myself fortunate to have any teeth left at all, but whenever I bring this up to the dentist, he just says "cavity this" and "root canal that," and my English is still not good enough to argue about it. But if I purchase some floss now, I can quickly floss my teeth in the parking lot before I go into the office, and he will be none the wiser.

I pick up my pace and soon find myself in the oral care aisle. I quickly find the floss and spend several minutes trying to decide on the best flavor. Do I like mint or do I prefer cinnamon? And if I choose cinnamon, do I want regular cinnamon or extreme cinnamon? What is the difference between the two? Am I really prepared to deal with an EXTREME cinnamon? I decide that it will be easier to choose mint, but my pleasure is short lived as I am suddenly presented with a whole new set of choices. Herbal mint or peppermint? Spearmint or extreme mint? It is almost too much to bear. I look away for a moment to clear my head, and my gaze falls upon the soap aisle.

Walking into the middle of the soap aisle, I am astounded by how many different options there are. Even more than with the floss. Even more than with the vegetables and the Pepsi. When I first arrived in America, I had not bathed in almost three years. There was no time. After my village was attacked by the marauders, those of us who survived spent every waking moment running away from those who were trying to kill us. None of us had even a spare moment to give to soap. And yet here, and in every supermarket in the entire country, is an entire wall devoted to nothing but soap. It boggles the mind. If my family had not been brutally slaughtered and burned to death by the marauders, they would not believe what I was seeing.

As I stare, slack jawed, at the boxes of soap, I overhear a conversation taking place near the back of the supermarket. I glance over and see an older gentleman talking to a pharmacist in a white coat, who is standing behind a counter and looking exasperated.

"With all due respect, Mr. Jones, you're incorrect," says the pharmacist, holding up a small piece of paper. "This prescription is for Motrin, not hemorrhoid medication."

"Now what sense does that make?" says Mr. Jones. "Motrin isn't going to do anything to help my hemorrhoids! I need the cream! It sooths the itching and the burning!"

"I understand that, and as soon as you give me a prescription for hemorrhoid cream, I'll be happy to give it to you. Until then, you're just going to have to buy some Preparation H."

The old man bangs his fist on the counter. "That H crap doesn't do squat for my hemmy! It's too weak. I need the good stuff!"

The pharmacist holds the little piece of paper up to Mr. Jones and points at the writing on it. "MO-TRIN! This says MOTRIN!"

Mr. Jones points at his rear end. "It feels like I'm

sitting on a papaya!"

I wince and turn back to the soap. The old man does not seem to realize how inappropriate it is to be speaking about something so personal in public. But it is not the first time I have witnessed someone do something at exactly the wrong time and place. It happened back in Calyew, and I close my eyes and think back to this very difficult memory.

None of us knew the marauders were coming. One day, everything was normal and the next day, nearly the entire village had been burned to the ground. It was incredible how quickly it happened. Even to this day, I am not sure why we were attacked. There is some sort of political reason behind it, a grudge between two groups leading to a civil war or something, but it's impossible to separate the facts from the rumors. And in any case, it's not really that important. All that has ever mattered to me is that over the course of one bloody afternoon, I lost everyone who meant anything to me, and had to run away from my home, never to return.

I was not the only one who survived the massacre. Several hundred of us were able to escape and we traveled together, hoping that there would be strength in numbers. This was probably true, but we still lost many, many people on that long journey to a place that was safe. It was very difficult to keep track of time in that situation, but perhaps I would say that it was six months into our endless walk when I heard a shrill voice calling my name.

At first I thought I was hallucinating, which was not unusual at that point. The relentless heat coupled with the starvation was taking a mental toll on me perhaps even more severe than the physical one. Also, nobody in the group did much talking, because our throats were so dry from the lack of water, so hearing ANY voice was somewhat jarring. But just when I was sure I had imagined what I had heard, I heard it one more time, and it was closer. I stopped walking and looked around, and to my complete shock, Akate was running... RUNNING... over to me.

--- Bujune! I am so glad to see you. I have missed you so!

Whereas I had lost half of my body weight and what clothes I still had were tattered and filthy, Akate did not look any different at all. She was still as plain as an unsalted cracker and full of this bubbly energy that seemed completely out of place. She gave me a gigantic hug, which I did not return, partially because I was too weak to lift my arms.

--- I am sorry I haven't been able to see you lately, but I've been spending some time with my parents. I've been thinking about you, though. Have you been thinking about me?

I attempted to respond, but all that came out of my parched throat was a low croaking noise. Akate took this to mean "yes" and clapped her hands together.

--- I knew it! Sometimes I wonder if it's a good thing that we think so alike. You know, there's that whole "opposites attract" thing. But obviously that's not true for everyone, because you and I are almost exactly the same, and we get along better than anyone else I know!

Somehow, I was able to produce enough saliva to reply to her.

--- What are you talking about? Nothing you say makes any sense! We are in the middle of the desert, walking to God knows where, trying to stay alive after being displaced from Calyew, and you're talking about how you and I get along?! It's madness!

--- I know. It's pretty crazy, isn't it? You can never tell when you're going to run into that one special person that you might spend the rest of your life with.

Over her shoulder, I saw a young boy of perhaps eleven years stagger forward several steps, then his eyes rolled back in his head and he collapsed to the ground. Before the dust had even settled, vultures were upon him. Within seconds, several of our fellow villagers were rushing towards the vultures, hoping to beat them to death so that they could eat them. Akate did not notice any of this as she was lost in her endless monologue.

--- ...I was sitting under the stars last night and I was wondering how serious you and I were getting. I thought about it for a long time, and in the end, even though I really like you, I think it's important that we take things slow. I don't want us to rush into something physical and ruin the special connection that we have.

I still wasn't completely sure I wasn't hallucinating.

--- The thing is, I was talking to Makena and Tendaji about this before they were taken away by the people that destroyed our village, and they were concerned that maybe you were just using me for... you know. You must understand, they are very protective of me. Or, I mean, they WERE, before the kidnappings. Anyways, I never believed it, because I can't imagine that someone as kind and generous as you would just take advantage of a girl, then never talk to her again. You wouldn't do that, would you?

--- You're insane, I said, and started to walk away.

--- Yeah! Exactly! It's insane! That's what I told Makena and Tendaji, but they just went on and on with their crazy theories. This is pretty much the only thing the three of us have talked about for the last six months...

As I continued walking, the volume of her voice got lower and lower until I couldn't hear her anymore. It was the most blissful silence I had ever heard. After a couple of miles, I looked over my shoulder to make sure she hadn't tried to follow me. To my dismay, she was standing about six feet behind me. When she saw me look around, she waved.

--- Don't worry, Bujune! You haven't lost me. I'm right here! And then she ran up and hugged me again. Always with the blasted hugs!

I screeched to a halt and decided that I had had enough. I was going to let her have it and really give her a piece of my mind. I spun around and pointed my bony finger in her face.

--- Now look here, I began, but she grabbed my hand and put it to her chest.

--- I just got the most wonderful idea! You should come to dinner at my parent's house tonight! Then she glanced down at my hand, which she had pressed to her bosom, then looked back up with a supposedly erotic grin on her lips, which she then licked.

--- And then maybe later, you can have some of what you want.

At that moment, everything went black, and for the first time on the entire arduous journey, I fainted.

When I came to, I was lying on a cot inside of a hut. I was covered with a single sheet, which I pushed aside so that I could sit up. The room I was in was small, but it was empty, and this was a relief to me. Maybe it had all been a dream. A horrible, horrible dream. My forehead was covered with sweat, and I wiped it off with my hand. To my left was a doorway covered with a sheet and as I stared at it, the sheet was brushed aside and Akate came sprinting into the room. She ran up to my cot, then stood there, eyes glassy, hand to her mouth. She choked back a couple of sobs, then spoke.

--- I was so worried, Bujune! I was so afraid! I didn't know if you were ever going to wake up, but I knew if you did, you would want me to be here, so I stayed. I stayed here for you!

--- Where am I?

--- You're in the spare bedroom of my parent's hut. At first, they were reluctant to let a boy stay here, but when they saw how injured you were, they said it was okay. We just have to… you know… keep ourselves under control.

Then she gave me that damned erotic grin again, which made me feel like passing right back out. The sheet behind her moved a second time, and two new figures walked into the room. Akate motioned for them to come closer.

--- Bujune, these are my parents, Silvia and Frank.

Silvia and Frank were not normal names for Kenyan people, but they seemed nice enough. The mother came over and dabbed at my cheek with a wet rag.

--- Oh, you've been through a lot, you poor boy. Would you like some water?

--- Water? You have water?

--- Oh sure. We've got orange juice too, but I don't think it's such a good idea for you to drink that, what with how chapped your lips are. It'll burn like the dickens, believe you me.

The whole thing was very strange, but the thought that I was going to be drinking water pushed the questions out of my mind temporarily. Silvia went and got me a tall glass of ice water, which I drank down greedily. It had been so long since I'd had that amount of water, so of course I vomited most of it right back up. Silvia and Akate laughed.

--- You were right, Akate. He IS funny, Silvia said, then came over and playfully rubbed my head.

Even though it made me throw up, I was grateful for

the water, but I was still completely confused. I looked over at Silvia, who seemed to be slightly more normal than her daughter.

--- How is this all possible? Didn't you lose your home and all your possessions when the marauders attacked Calyew?

Silvia seemed surprised by the question.

--- No, of course not. I mean, it was pretty obvious we were going to have to leave the village, but why would we leave a perfectly good home just sitting there to get burned to the ground? That's ridiculous. We worked hard to build this house, so we decided to bring it with us.

--- Bring it with you? How is that even possible?

But like Akate, Silvia was very good at ignoring questions and changing the subject to something completely unrelated.

--- I'm so glad we're finally getting to meet you, Bujune. Akate has been talking about you for so long, we were beginning to wonder if you even existed. It wouldn't be the first time THAT'S happened!

Silvia laughed and Akate crossed her arms and stuck out her lower lip.

--- Mo-oooo-oom!

---Oh, I can see we're embarrassing our little girl. We'd better quit while we're ahead. Let's leave these two to themselves for a little while. Come on Frank.

Silvia and Frank, who hadn't said a word the entire time and didn't even appear to be aware of what was going on, walked out of the room, leaving me alone with Akate. This was not a favorable turn of events. Akate looked to make sure her parents were gone, then sat on the edge of the cot and leaned in close to me.

--- So. I believe we were talking about how hard it can be to keep ourselves under control...

I leapt to my feet, pushed Akate to the floor and darted out of the room as fast as I could. Seconds later, I was back outside. Behind me, I thought I could hear someone calling my name, but I didn't stop running. I ran and ran until my legs ached and my lungs burned, but still I ran on. Eventually the sun went down, and with no moon in the sky, there was nothing but darkness as far as the eye could see. I could not see my hand three inches in front of my face. Even so, when I finally stopped running and went to sleep, I dug a little hole and hid in it.

IV.

I push my cart into the checkout line and grab one of those rubber sticks that acts as a dividing line between my carefully chosen items and the items of another customer. I do not know why I do this, as there is no one else in line, though perhaps it is because the little rubber stick brings me comfort. I do not know much in this adopted country of mine, but one thing I can always be certain of is that the carefully selected items on THIS side of the stick are mine, and the items on THAT side of the stick are yours. In a world full of complex grays, this is one instance where everything is always black and white.

The checkout lady smiles and asks me how I'm doing this morning. I answer that I am doing fine, although I think for a fleeting instant that I would be doing much better if the checkout lady was Kimberly and not a dumpy white haired older woman.

I quickly unload the contents of my cart - there are not many - and wait patiently for the checkout lady to ring them up. For a while, the only sounds are the hum of the conveyor belt and the repetitive beeping each time she scans an item. Soon, she has finished, and looks up at me with a crooked smile.

"That'll be $44.89, hon. Do you have any coupons?"

"I am afraid that I do not. I am confused by coupons, so I do not use them."

"I understand," she says, and I believe her. "Those darn things have got so many restrictions nowadays, you never know what you're allowed to buy half the time. Sometimes you can only buy the 8 ounce can on the first Tuesday before the second Saturday, and sometimes you don't get the 45 cent discount unless you buy eight packs of hot dogs and a specific brand of mustard." She laughs and shakes her head as if she cannot imagine that she ever would have found herself living in such a crazy world.

I do not know how to respond to her, as I have no personal stories about coupons, so I just smile and nod.

"But listen to me, just going on and on when you've probably got someplace to be. You just let me bag these groceries up for you and you can be on your way. Now, do you prefer paper or plastic, hon?"

I think about this question for a second, and instead of an answer, the only thing I see in my head is another time in my life when I had to make a choice. Perhaps the most important choice I would ever have to make. I do not deny that deciding between paper and plastic is a critical choice. I have seen marriages break apart because of it. But the choice I had to make, no more than three years ago, was even bigger.

Almost a year after leaving Calyew, those who had survived the endless march found our way into a refugee camp, just over the Ethiopian border. It was called Pinyudo and it sat on the banks of the Gilo River. Small at first, it eventually grew to house over ten thousand displaced people, just like me. Somehow, all roads led to Pinyudo once your village had been reduced to rubble.

I stayed at Pinyudo for almost four years. Through some very generous financial aid from the international community, we were able to build a school and a makeshift hospital and things of the sort. In time, Pinyudo became a decent place to live, though it never felt like a home. The dream for a refugee at Pinyudo was to be chosen for the relocation program, in which you would be sent to another country to start a new life. Everyone applied for the program, but when ten thousand people are vying for something that is only available for twenty-five or thirty people a year, there is bound to be disappointment.

Every day, before I went to school or work, I would walk to the relocation office and see if my name had been posted on the bulletin board. If it had, it meant I had been picked, and my dream of leaving Pinyudo would be coming true. After four years, I had gotten to the point where I never actually expected to see my name on the board, but that tiny shred of hope kept me going back day after day.

So imagine my surprise when I walked up to the bulletin board one morning and saw the name "Bujune" posted there. I did not believe it at first. I closed my eyes and rubbed them, and when I reopened them, my name was still there. It was true. I was going to be relocated. I did a little dance and pumped my fist in the air. It was perhaps the first time I was truly happy since Calyew had been attacked.

--- Congratulations, Bujune! I am so happy for you!

My blood ran cold. I knew that voice. I knew it instantly, even though I had not heard it since I escaped from the hut of Frank and Silvia. It was Akate. I turned around and my fears were confirmed. Akate stood there, beaming. She opened her arms and walked towards me, as if

to embrace me. I shoved her backwards with both hands.
--- You! How did you find me? It has been years. Years!
--- You're so cute. I think it's so sweet you've been worried about me. I've been worried about you too. Did you hear that my parents got eaten by lions?

It was an odd question, because she said it in the same tone of voice one would use if they were asking "Did you hear that it's going to rain on Tuesday?"
--- I... that is terrible. I am sorry for your loss.
--- I wrote you a song.

This was perhaps the last thing I expected her to say after telling me that her parents were gone. But I did not have much time to be surprised by what she said, because she quickly topped herself and surprised me even MORE with what she did. She reached down and picked up an acoustic guitar that was lying at her feet and began strumming it softly.
--- I'm not the kind of girl who gets all mushy over a guy, but the way you make me feel... I couldn't NOT write this song about you.

And then, as the sun beat down on the refugee camp, she looked into my eyes and began singing.

Dear, won't you place some of your love inside a jar?
I'll wrap it up and store it in my heart.
There it will be warm and there it will be safe.
I'll hold it close each time that we're apart.

But I don't really think that we should ever be apart.
I don't ever want you ever out of my sight.
And if I don't know where you are, I'll just pull out the
jar,
Because I know your love will give me light.

I can't wait to sing our kids this song.
We'll play it for them here on this guitar.
They will love, to hear the story of,
The time you gave me love inside a jar.
Oh, Bujune, won't you put some love inside a jar?

When she finished playing her agonizing music, tears were streaming down her face. I will not lie. I was crying too, but for completely different reasons. Akate let go of the guitar and it fell to the ground, where it shattered, something she didn't appear to care about or even notice. She ran at me again for a hug and this time, when I shoved her backwards, she lost her footing and fell down.

--- I am sorry. I have been taught never to strike a female, but you have forced my hand. You must leave me alone. Your torment must end now!

--- It's fun when a couple playfully wrestles, she said, getting back to her feet. It is kind of a turn on, if you know what I mean.

--- I am being relocated. Do you see? Do you see? I pointed at the bulletin board.

--- I know! That is why I am so happy for you. Well, what I really mean is that I am happy for US. I am being relocated as well. We get to relocate together!

This was madness, of course. Due to budget constraints, only one refugee was able to be relocated at any given time, and I was just about to tell her this when out of the corner of my eye, I saw a new piece of paper on the bulletin board. I turned to look and there, underneath the name "Bujune" was the name "Akate." I could not help myself. I screamed.

--- Isn't it exciting? Where do you suppose we are going to

live? England, maybe? Or Canada? Or maybe we'll get lucky and be moved to America? Wouldn't that be incredible, to spend the rest of our lives together in the United States?

I was on the verge of hysterics as I tried to figure out exactly what was going on.

--- This is impossible! Your name was not there two minutes ago!

--- I brought you a present to celebrate our future.

Akate reached into her pocket and pulled out a watch. She blew hot air on it, then polished it on her shirt. She looked up at me and smiled.

--- This watch belonged to my grandfather's grandfather.

I found this difficult to believe, as it was a digital Timex watch, but I was too freaked out to say anything.

--- When my grandfather gave it to my dad, he said to him, "Frank, give this to your daughter, and when she finds her soul mate, tell her to give it to him. And after she gives him the watch, tell her to tell him that he needs to take her behind the building and freak her crazy style."

She held out the watch and I recoiled from it as if it were a scorpion. She started walking towards me again, waving the watch around and puckering her lips. I began swinging my arms around to protect myself and managed to swat the watch out of her hands. She yelped.

--- Frank's watch!

We both stared at the watch as it soared through the air. Eventually gravity kicked in and it crashed to the ground. Neither one of us said anything right away. When Akate finally looked at me, I saw something I had never seen before. Anger. She was actually mad at me. It was a wonderful moment, because it meant she might finally leave me alone. But wonderful moments never last. The anger faded as quickly as it had appeared and was replaced by a sly smirk. I could tell she was about to make a joke.

--- I guess you could say that sometimes... TIME FLIES!!

And she laughed. And as her excruciating laugh stabbed my ears, I made a decision. We were going to leave Pinyudo together, she and I. We were going to get on that plane and put on our seatbelts. And as that plane taxied down the runway, I was going to take off my seatbelt, run down the aisle, throw open the door, and jump right out of that plane, even if we were going several hundred miles per hour. This is exactly what I ended up doing.

I do not know where Akate is today, except that she is not in America. As soon as I made it to this country, I contacted the government and informed them that she was a terrorist, so that she would not be able to enter the United States. But this does not mean I do not fear. I will probably never feel truly safe. Every time I leave my house to go to the gym or the post office or the grocery store, I remain on full alert. She could be anywhere. Behind that bush or inside that Christmas present. It is not an easy life, but it is one I must attempt to live. I wear Frank's watch on my wrist to this very day, because it forces me to remember. To remember the way things could be if I was ever to forget. To forget that time. The time time flew.

The following True-Life Tale is being brought to you by...

More Than Dairy

A recent study announced that the average person does not get enough calcium. This is a troubling development because without calcium, your bones will shatter and your teeth will fall out of your head. But where does one get calcium? Sure, you can take calcium pills, but they're so expensive. That pretty much just leaves drinking milk. However, a lot of people don't like milk. Some of the common reasons are "It doesn't taste good," "For Pete's sake, look what it comes out of!" and "I'm allergic. If I drink it, I will die." That's where we come in. Hi, I'm J.C. Finn, and I'm the creator of Milk 'N Chunks®.

Milk 'N Chunks® is like no other product on the market. We cater to a different kind of customer. The kind of person who enjoys a few cookies and some chewy milk. Our Milk 'N Chunks® process is patented by a website on the internet, so you KNOW it's legit. We take normal milk, dump it in a barrel, and then add chunks of stuff. What kinds of stuff, you wonder? Sorry, that's top secret, but you can rest assured that every carton of Milk 'N Chunks® is unique. You may find mashed potatoes and Jell-O® in one carton, but chances are the next batch will be full of margarita mix and splinters from the barrel. It's like a lottery in every bottle!

Milk 'N Chunks® is the calcium-providing product for the 21st century. We've only heard good things so far, but we're still listening. If you have an idea about Milk 'N Chunks®, for instance, "more chicken," "less chicken," or "Can you at least pluck the feathers off the chicken?" then you can simply drop us a line and we'll be glad to hop right to it. So the next time you go to the dairy case, don't reach for no sissy milk. Reach for the milk that's got lots of different colored things floating in it. And remember, to avoid choking you should always chew your milk at least twenty-two times before swallowing!

Milk 'N Chunks®

From the makers of Ketchup 'N Spinach®, Sprite 'N Motor Oil®, and New Improved Milk 'N Chunks® - Now with more chunks!

A Story About Fruitcake

November

While on one of our many breaks from work, my co-worker Steve and I rolled into the AmPm to get some snacks. As usual, I made a beeline for the Hostess rack and it was there that I noticed something I'd never seen before. It was an item called the Hostess Holiday Fruitcake, a shrink wrapped, one pound dense brick of something that sort of resembled fruitcake if you squinted just right. I guess Hostess makes these for the Christmas season, but Steve and I thought the whole concept was laughable. I picked up the fruitcake, banged it on the table, and was amused by the loud thudding noise it made. The Hostess Holiday Fruitcake was "chock full of nature's finest fruits and nuts" according to the label, but the idea of Hostess making this thing and selling it in an AmPm was absurd. Who would walk into an AmPm, see this thing and think to themselves, "Hey! Fruitcake! That would hit the SPOT right now!"? On top of that, it cost $3.59, so it wasn't even cheap enough to be an impulse purchase. Steve and I mocked this fruitcake, called it names, and questioned the intelligence of the poor fool that would one day buy it.

December

Every day, with every trip into the AmPm, the fruitcake was a never ending supply of humor. Nobody bought it, of course, so it just sat there between the Cupcakes and the Ding Dongs looking sad and pathetic. We'd pick it up and squeeze it and toss it back and forth, which didn't matter because you couldn't really make a dent in the thing. As Christmas neared, there was some point when Steve said, "You know, I'd give someone ten bucks if they ate that whole fruitcake at one sitting."

"The dumb fool!" said I. "The poor moron! I'd sure like to see THAT!"

There was much laughter. The notion, the fantastical notion, of someone eating this log of fruits and nuts, was way funnier than, say, The Love Guru.

Christmas Day

No one had purchased the Hostess Holiday Fruitcake. It sat on the shelf, same as it ever was.

January 4th (4:30 PM)

So we were outside the workplace, hanging on Steve's truck, when conversation turned once again to the Hostess Holiday Fruitcake. It is truly shameful how much of our time this fruitcake ate up. It just had this grip on us. After a couple of minutes, Steve repeated his offer. "I tell you, I would give someone ten bucks if they ate that thing."

I do not know what came over me in that moment. I'm not the most daring food eater in the world, but for some reason I decided that I was all man, and I knew exactly how to prove it.

I looked at him and said, "You know what? I'm feeling froggy. I'll eat the fruitcake."

"The whole thing?" he asks. "At one sitting?"

"Just show me the ten bucks," said I.

January 4th (7:30 PM)

It was almost fruitcake time, and the entire workplace was abuzz. They all knew of the fruitcake, and they were all excited about watching the skinny kid devour it. I said to Steve, "Look, I don't want that fruitcake to be all I eat, so let's get lunch first. I need something else on my stomach." The logic of the damned, I guess. So we headed off to Subway, where I proceeded (in a moment of temporary amnesia) to order a foot-long roast beef sub, which is what I always order because it fills me up. The problem was that I still had this fruitcake to eat afterwards, something I didn't remember until I was shoving the last bite in my mouth. Oh well. I'd accepted the bet, and I couldn't back out, because I had to prove to everyone that I am significantly macho.

We drove over to the AmPm and Steve gave me the money to buy the fruitcake and a drink to help me wash it down. When I got to the register, the lady ringing me up gave me a confused look and asked, "Fruitcake?"

"I don't want to talk about it," I replied. Because if I started talking about it, I just KNEW the lady was going to point out that this thing had been sitting in the store since November. And I REALLY didn't want to hear that.

Not long after, we were back at work and I was staring at this solid brick of "nature's finest fruits and nuts" and wondering why I was about to do this. For ten dollars, no less. Steve insisted that we have an official Pre-Fruitcake Weigh-In, so we walked over to the scale and I stepped on it.

"One hundred and thirty seven pounds," he

announced, which kind of surprised me because that's the most I'd ever weighed at that point. Keep that number in mind. 137. It will play into the rest of the tale.

January 4th (8:00 PM)

With a plastic fork in hand and a crowd of six anxiously watching, I peeled off the wrapper and took my first tentative bite.

It was not delicious.

This was going to make the whole thing about ten times harder. If it was good, then at least I wouldn't have to dread putting every bite in my mouth. But this… THING… it was the foulest thing the devil ever made. Aside from the flavor, which was generally just unpleasant, sitting in the sun for the previous two months had pretty much completely dried it out. And it was the consistency of a sponge. It was very difficult to enjoy nature's finest fruits and nuts. And I still had a pound to go. At that point, my eye fell upon the nutrition facts printed on the back of the wrapper. It was there that I saw the following helpful information: "Servings per package: 4." Four servings… and there I was attempting to eat it all at once… already full from a foot-long sub. The thought occurred to me that this was not my finest hour.

So there I was with a bunch of people gathered around, cheering me on as I slowly worked my way through the Hostess Holiday Fruitcake. After two bites, I could no longer swallow it plain, so from that point on, every bite was chewed into mush then washed down with a great swig of Pepsi, which eventually gave way to Cherry Pepsi and then bottled water. I was going through drinks much faster than I was going through fruitcake. Halfway through, I stuck the fork in and twisted my wrist, hearing this SNAP as the fork broke in half, leaving little plastic tines buried in the fruitcake. Again, this horrible thing was dense. Nevertheless, I kept going. Time passed and Steve and the guys kept saying helpful things like, "There's only fifteen bites left!", "Look at him in the light. Is he starting to look pale?" and "Come on. It's not THAT hard". About 3/4 of the way through, Steve upped the bet to $20 in an attempt to keep me motivated. Nice guy, that Steve.

January 4th (8:57 PM)

I crammed the last god-awful bite into my mouth, washed it down, and plopped my forehead onto the table. A great cheer rose up, for the skinny kid defeated the Hostess Holiday Fruitcake. There was much high-fiving, but I want nothing to do with it. Steve handed me my twenty dollars which I weakly grabbed, and they all herded me toward the scale for the Post-Fruitcake Weigh-In. I felt absolutely awful. The walk over to the scale was brutal. It felt very much like what was in my stomach was a Hostess Holiday bowling ball. I staggered over to the scale, stepped on it, and waited sluggishly for the verdict. At that moment, I heard several voices all say, independently of each other, "No WAY!!"

"What?" I grunted, barely able to summon the strength to speak. "What is it?"

Steve stepped forward, looking entertained but slightly shocked. "You weigh 140 pounds," he said. And my jaw dropped. I'd gained three pounds while eating this one pound fruitcake. This news made me feel worse somehow, and I stumbled away as everyone else discussed this great feat. Nobody really noticed me leaving.

I had not thrown up for at least five years. It's just not something I did. But as I walked toward the door, I knew exactly what the feeling in my stomach meant. I made it outside, stumbled over to the parking lot, dropped to one knee and said, "Blarrrrrrrgh!" I tried to stand back up but my legs buckled. I went down on all fours and repeated the sentiment, "Blarrrrrrgh!" I fell over to my side, then rolled over onto my back, on the ground, and stared at the beautiful night sky. When I had woken up that morning, this was not exactly how I saw my day turning out.

I threw up three more times in the next ten minutes, pretty much every time I tried to move, and in the end they sent my stupid ass home a couple of hours early, because at that point I was basically useless. But I'd made $20, dammit, which just about made up for the couple of hours that I wasn't getting paid for, so one might say that I almost broke even. The success of this endeavor made me realize it was about time to retire from the business of eating things for money. After all, there are so many better ways to humiliate myself in front of people that do not involve vomiting.

In the years that have followed, there have been many Christmas seasons that have come and gone, but I have never again seen the Hostess Holiday Fruitcake. I kind of miss it. Except that I do not miss it at all, and every time I think about the wretched thing, my stomach twists into knots. I only tell this story in hopes that the Hostess Corporation will read it and feel compelled to send me a large cash settlement for my pain and suffering. That IS how this sort of thing works, right?

Right?!

Shadows of the Invisible
(a tale told in "real-time")

Week Seven: Stalling Until Week Eight

"Last week, an assassin attempted to assassinate the president of Antarctica for the second time. It appears that people that I work with may be involved. My name is Librarian of Congress Jacques Vargas, and these... are the longest eight weeks of my life..."

FRIDAY, DECEMBER 27th, 2002

1:15pm - Andes Mountains, Bolivia

After tumbling head over heels down the side of a mountain for the better part of a minute, Jacques Vargas skids to a stop. He lies very still for a moment, breathing heavily, then with a great effort, gets back to his feet. He glares at the mountain, gives it the finger, and spits on the ground. "Up yours, Andes! You need me WAY more than I need you!" Satisfied that he has said his piece, he reaches into his backpack and pulls out a cell phone. He presses a button and holds it to his ear.

"L.O.C. This is Damole."

"Irma! It's Jacques. Listen, I'm following this lead in Bolivia, and so far as I can tell, nobody here has ever heard of Vlad Umpire or running water. We're just not getting any solid information off any of the people we've shot. Are you having any luck back in the States?"

"Not really. Chuck and Todd are knocking on

random people's doors, but it doesn't seem to be doing much good. How's Bolivia, anyway?"

Jacques swats a gigantic horsefly on his arm and wipes the dripping sweat off his forehead. "It's peachy, Irma. I'm so glad I got to spend my Christmas here, talking to foreigners about vampire terrorists. But on the plus side, at least I can't digest the food."

"I think it's about time you came home. You're a better asset here than in Central America, fending off tsetse flies with a machete."

"I had to sell my machete so that I could afford to bribe my way out of the Peruvian prison. It's a long story, but I don't ever, ever want to tell it." He rubs his eyes and sighs. "I feel like a failure, Irma. We've been tracking down this assassin for seven weeks now, and I don't think we're any closer now than we were at the beginning. We've exhausted every obscure lead, every illogical possibility. And the only thing we've come up with is that this thing isn't political or based on revenge or being orchestrated by some jilted lover. That's the problem. There is NO LOGICAL REASON why anybody would want to kill the President of Antarctica. I'm not sure what to do next, Irma. We've hit a dead-end. We don't even know who the mole is inside the Library!"

"I thought we'd decided that it was Todd."

"Todd shot and killed the guy that was trying to shoot and kill the President. If he's the mole, he's the worst mole ever."

Irma speaks, sounding unconvinced. "What about the day we caught him taping our conversations? That was more than a little bit creepy and mole-like."

Jacques begins to walk as he talks, towards a particularly colorful mirage. "I asked him about that. He said that the only reason he was taping us was because he takes the tapes home and listens to them over and over. Something about "drawing wisdom and knowledge from our method of investigation". That kid is really into his job." He begins to wave at the topless woman that isn't really there. "I dunno. Maybe there isn't a dirty agent at all. There are lots of ways that highly classified information could be leaking to our enemies. Carrier pigeons maybe."

"I'll put the local law enforcement on high bird alert." There's a brief pause, then from the other end of the line, Jacques hears Irma snap her fingers. "Oh! I almost totally forgot to tell you. The killer called here earlier this morning. I can't believe that slipped my mind."

Stopping dead in his tracks, and motioning towards the woman to hold off on mixing the daiquiris just yet, Jacques makes a low guttural noise in the back of his throat. Eventually, it turns into words. "The killer called there... and you didn't think that maybe I'd be interested in that? Here I am, traipsing around the middle of the desert looking for clues, and the biggest possible clue called you on the phone?"

"Jacques, just relax. I've got a lot of things on my mind. You're not the only one that's being completely inconvenienced by this assassination madness."

"I'M IN BOLIVIA!!" Jacques shouts in a voice so loud, it causes the entire mirage to melt away. He pulls the phone away from his ear and makes as if to throw it, but he comes to his senses. Suppressing a truly impressive amount of rage, he hisses into the phone. "Well... what did the killer say, I wonder? Perhaps you could tell me true?"

"Well, first of all, we were able to confirm that it's William Williams."

"How? Satellite call tracing? Voice mapping

recognition?"

"Uh... no. When I picked up the phone, he said, "Hi, this is William Williams, the guy who's been trying to assassinate President Kemo." It made it kind of hard to miss."

Jacques grabs his canteen and puts it to his lips. Empty. He looks around, wondering how many miles away he is from civilization. Ten. Maybe fifteen. He decides this is Problem B, and he will deal with it after he works on Problem A. "Okay, so why would Williams just up and call us when he knows we're trying to find him?"

"He wanted to inform us that he'll stop trying to kill the President if we pay him 25% more than he's being paid to kill the president. He's a businessman, he says, and he's happy to go where the money is."

"Yeah, well, it's not like he's doing a very good job. His "killing the President" skills are sub-par at best. How much is this payoff supposed to be anyway?"

Jacques hears Irma rustling some papers around. "He wants, lemme see here... okay. He wants $1,250,000. He realizes it's a large amount of money, so he's giving us a week to get it. As long as it's in his hands by midnight on January 3rd, no harm will come to anyone. If we refuse, he promises that President Kemo will be, and I quote, "President Alive-No-Mo"."

"He's out of his mind. So far, both of his assassination attempts have failed. Does he really expect us to think that he's EVER going to be able to finish the job?"

Irma lowers her voice. "Normally, I'd agree with you wholeheartedly, Jacques, but this time I've got a real bad feeling. He sounds disturbingly confident. I'm beginning to suspect he's got somebody working for him within President Kemo's inner circle. A mole, if you will."

"ANOTHER mole? Is EVERYBODY a mole?"

"I'm certainly working under that assumption. You and I are the only people I can trust. And Dr. Phil too. He really tells it like it is."

Very thirsty and growing dizzier by the moment, Jacques finds shelter under a shade tree. It's a mirage, of course, but he has little time for sanity. "Let's assume we decide to pay this madman. Will he tell us who hired him and why?"

"He didn't say, but I'm sure a few extra dollars will loosen his tongue."

"My tongue is very dry, mommy."

"What did you just say?"

"Nothing. It's the phone. Can you hear me now? Good."

"I guess it's good. Look, all Williams wants is for us to drop the money off at the Kaffa House next Friday. I think it might be in our best interest to do what he asks. There's certainly no way we're going to be able to solve this case on our own."

"The Kaffa House? That's the same place they wanted me to go when they kidnapped Lily. What is so important about that stupid restaurant?"

"It's got good seafood, and cocktails are cheap."

"Yes. Drinks. Drinks are very important. Especially when you're so, so thirsty." Jacques' mouth begins to water, but not THAT much. "I'll tell you what, Irma. Get in contact with President Kemo's people and tell them what you've just told me. Then get on the phone with the Kaffa House and make a reservation for next Friday. We might not bring the money, but we're most certainly going to be paying Mr. Williams a visit."

"Consider it done. What about you? Does that mean

you're coming back to DC?"

Jacques laughs a strange demented laugh. "I most certainly am, mommy. In fact, my private plane has just landed. First class all the way." And with that Jacques begins to flap his arms and make an airplane noise as he runs in circles. Irma starts to say something else, but the phone goes dead in her ear.

1:27pm - Kaffa House Restaurant, Washington DC

Sitting at his usual table in the back, William Williams chatters into a cell phone. He's moving his arms with big sweeping gestures, and seems to be very excited. "I'm telling you, they're going to get me the money! That's the best part. We're going to get the entire ransom, PLUS, you're still going to be able to kill Kemo and Vargas. We're all going to end up winners here. I can feel it. It may take a little longer than I meant it to, but William Williams never fails to complete a job." He listens to the voice on the other end and shakes his head. "No, not yet. I'm expecting the call any minute, though. I really thought you were going to be here so we could both hear the good news, but I got the times mixed up."

The person on the other end talks for a few more seconds, then Williams speaks up. "Hold on. My call waiting is going off. I think it's time. We're about to get conformation." He presses the flash button and speaks in a slightly disguised voice. "Hello and good morning. You have called the Stop 'N Buy N' Leave! This is me to say how can I help you?"

"William. It's me."

Williams reverts back to his normal voice. "I was

getting a little concerned. What's the story? Have your sources told you what we want to hear?"

"They have. The reservations have been made. It's all set for next week, and everything is going to go exactly according to Plan C. I'll make sure of it."

With a relived sigh, Williams smiles and leans back in his chair. "I knew you'd come through. Excellent work, Irma. We couldn't do this without you."

To Be Concluded...

The following True-Life Tale is being brought to you by...

Two Hearts Beating As One

Hello, American male. My name is Katya and I am look for love. I wish to be wife of big, strong American male. Maybe it is you for me? You want to know more about me, yes? This is fine. I am 18 year old girl of much hotness. I like to go to movies, and watch sports, and cook and clean for American male who is also my husband. Whatever you like is what I like. We are meant for each other, yes?

I believe in love and romance. I think that somewhere out there is American male who can get me out of this horrible country. I do not speak much English, but I am smiles to try learning! If you choose me to be your wife, I will be delivered by Federal Express. Overnight. This is good enough for you, yes? Please choose me. There are so many of us, and the one-room shack is so small. I am ready to make happy Hollywood story ending. I look forward to hearing from you.

Take care, with warmest thoughts...

--Katya

MESSAGE FROM AGENCY - You like girl, yes? Maybe you want to marry girl? Girl is client number A1038. For only 75 dollars American money, you can have more letters from girl. If you decide you do not like girl anymore, she will be severely disciplined, and you will soon have new girl what you will like more. You may call girl, if you wish. The cost is 1 dollar American money per minute. You not understand a word girl says, but love is stronger than language. When you marry girl, you will pay monthly fee to us, the Agency. If you neglect to pay fee, black car will

pull up in front of your American house, and large men in masks will take girl. Do not test us, American male. Girl must find love and romance, and we will allow nothing to get in our way. Client A1038 is lovely, yes? YES!! Marry girl now or suffer the consequences!!

Best regards...

--The Agency

The Agency

Bringing Girl Together With American Male Is What We Do

Employee Of The Month

Eight hours a day, I am surrounded by incompetence.

Well, to be fair, this isn't really the case anymore. The people I currently work with are relatively functional co-workers, but for a long time there was what felt like an endless stream of bumbling, hopeless lunatics who I kept getting stuck with. They never seemed to stay employed for very long. In fact, I could never understand how most of these people got hired in the first place. But they'd always be on the job juuuuuust long enough to drive me up the wall.

For the most part, these people are completely interchangeable. One faceless random guy I worked with for six weeks isn't going to stick out in my mind any more than some other anonymous idiot who barely made it through a month before getting canned. Especially not when I have so many other important things taking up space in my brain, such as the name of that little plastic thing on the end of a shoelace (it is called an 'aglet') or the kid in 5th grade who used to fall asleep in class every single day (his name was Pablo). But once in a while, like a diamond in the rough, one of these short-timers would manage to be just nutty enough to carve themselves a place on my own mental Mount Rushmore.

A good example of this would be Wally, who briefly drove a semi-truck for the company. We all thought Wally was pretty weird right from the beginning when he walked in on his first day dressed in full cowboy gear and it wasn't even Halloween. He had the hat, the vest, the belt buckle, the Wranglers, the boots. The only thing he was missing was the spurs and a herd of cattle. Just playing cowboy dress-up was bad enough, but as we got to know him, we came to discover that Wally was extremely ornery. If things were not done exactly to his specifications, he'd start hootin' and hollerin', and as far as I could tell, we were NEVER able to do anything to his specifications, because he was ALWAYS hootin' and hollerin'. He always made me think a little of Yosemite Sam, just four feet taller.

He might have been great on horseback, but Wally wasn't so hot behind the wheel. Within the first two weeks he was on the job, he had three accidents. Never in traffic or anything, but he was always backing into stuff, including one glorious afternoon when he was out on a delivery and backed over a fire hydrant. The next day I had the opportunity to ask him, "What happened yesterday with the fire hydrant?"

Wally's reply? "That hydrant shouldn't have been there… and also, I HATES rabbits!" Okay, he didn't say the second part, but I swear he said the first.

My very favorite Wally activity was something he did every single day before work. He would show up thirty to forty-five minutes early, park his white truck (which would occasionally have bales of hay in it) in the furthest corner of the parking lot, away from everything and everyone else but near a blue trash can that was out there, and then he would grab a rope, walk several feet away, and spend a good half-hour trying to lasso the trash can. Yes, you read that right. I remember the first time I stumbled upon him doing this little activity, I quickly ran inside, grabbed a co-worker, and made him confirm to me that what I thought I was seeing was actually happening. The interesting thing about it was that although he would practice lassoing the trash can every day, he wasn't very good at it and never seemed to get any better. I began to wonder if maybe that's why they kicked him off of whatever ranch he came from.

Wally lasted a few months before moseying along to parts unknown, but there was another driver who was able to make just as deep of an impression even though he was only with the company for two weeks. The first day I worked with him was actually his second day on the job, so I politely asked him how his first day had gone. He told me that he'd already gotten in trouble because he hadn't done something or other, then finished his rant by saying, "So, you know, they can ask me to do whatever they want me to do, but I can only do what I can do, cause I ain't Jesus, you know what I mean?"

Of course I nodded, because he most certainly was not Jesus. The thought hadn't even really crossed my mind. I hadn't taken anyone aside, pointed across the warehouse and whispered, "Hey, man. Look over there. Do you think... naaaaw... it can't be... working HERE? That's crazy! But maybe..."

The next day, while regaling us with another story of how he'd been wronged by management, he said it again. "So they asked me why I didn't finish taking the load, but man, I ain't Jesus!" And again I agreed with him, because there's no way Jesus would be so lazy.

It wasn't just at work, either. If he was telling you about his day off, at some point he would explain to you how he had to let someone know he wasn't Jesus as if he was getting autograph requests all the time. It must be a hard life being constantly confused with the son of our Lord, especially when you're just a simple truck driver. And not a very good truck driver, considering how fast he got fired. I thought maybe he would return to work three days after he was canned, but he never did.

You will notice that I don't use his real name. That is because I have absolutely no idea what it was. In fact, to this day, nobody I work with remembers his name. We all just refer to him as the guy who wasn't Jesus.

But for me, neither Wally or Ain't Jesus is the one I remember the most. No, that honor goes to a young man named Edwin. Edwin had a terrible issue with attendance. The dude could never work more than three or four days in a row without calling off. It was a constant problem, and it drove me batty because when Edwin wouldn't show up, I would get stuck doing his job.

Edwin would call off with the regular list of excuses: "I'm sick," "My car won't start," "I didn't get any sleep," "I was totally on my way to work just now, but I got a flat tire so I'm just going to go home." Occasionally, just to mix things up, he would show up and work for ten minutes, then tell me all of a sudden he had the flu or some such nonsense. But one day, he forever earned a place in the Hall of Fame, when he called me with the single greatest excuse I've ever heard.

I was just getting settled in at work when the phone rang, and without even picking it up, I already knew it was going to be Edwin calling off for some reason or another. So I was less than surprised when I heard his voice on the other end of the phone. But what his voice SAID threw me completely off.

> **Edwin** - Hey Matt, it's Edwin.
> **Matt** - Uh-huh.
> **Edwin** - Hey listen, I don't think I'm going to be able to make it into work tonight.
> **Matt** - Again? Why this time?

Edwin - Well, it's cause I was driving to work, y'know, trying not to be late and all...

Matt - Right...

Edwin - And then I got shot in the head, so I think I have to go to the hospital.

Matt - Look man, the thing is, when you don't come in... wait, what did you just say?

Edwin – I was driving to work and I got shot in the head.

Matt - You got shot... in the head... just now?

Edwin - Well, like 15 minutes ago. I had to call the cops first before I called you.

Matt - (longish pause) Okay, so... you got shot in the head...

Edwin - Right.

Matt - And this happened how, exactly?

Edwin - Okay, check this out. So I'm driving to work and these homies pull up alongside my car and they're all mad-dogging me, you know. So I'm like "What's up?" and they start chasing me!

Matt - Um...

Edwin - So they follow me for a while and I'm trying to get away from them but still trying to get to work, you know, and then they pull back up to my driver's side and one of them's got a gun. So I'm like, "DAMN!" and then I heard a pop and I felt like I'd gotten punched in the forehead, so I pulled over to the side of the road and the homies drove away. I'm lucky I had my window down, though, or I'd have shattered glass all over me!

Matt - And instead, you just have a gunshot wound to your head.

Edwin - Yeah. Hey, you wanna talk to the cop?

Matt - The cop? What cop?

Edwin - The cop that came out when I called the police. Hold on a second!

At this point, Edwin put me on the phone with a guy who identified himself as Officer Something-or-other from the Fontana Police Department who told me that he was advising the victim to seek medical attention and that in his professional opinion, Edwin probably shouldn't come to work today. The entire time I was on the phone with the "Officer," I kept thinking the same two thoughts over and over:

1) I do not believe I am speaking to an actual law enforcement official
2) The head? Really? He got shot in the HEAD?

So when Edwin got back on the phone, I decided to ask him what I thought was the most important question at that moment.

Matt - So do you think you'll be coming

to work tomorrow at least?

Edwin - Oh yeah! I'm just gonna go to the emergency room and get patched up and I should be there tomorrow no problem.

True to his word, Edwin did in fact show up to work the next day, sporting a small band-aid on his forehead. When I asked him how he was feeling, he was surprisingly upbeat for someone who'd been gunned down in a hail of bullets less than 24 hours earlier. He said that aside from a slight headache, he was feeling pretty well.

I pointed at his forehead. "I would have expected a bigger band-aid."

"Yeah," he said. "The emergency room people think that maybe I only got hit with a bullet fragment instead of an entire bullet. They kept telling me how lucky I was."

I was having a hard time imagining how the homies went about firing PIECES of bullets out of a gun. Maybe they only had one bullet left and they were trying to make it last as long as possible. It probably wasn't all that important. Edwin still called off of work on a fairly regular basis until the time he finally just stopped showing up completely, but it was never the same. How do you top "I got shot in the head?" "I was abducted by aliens," maybe? I've never been able to figure it out.

So I guess I should be grateful that my current co-workers are consistently reliable. They could easily be worse. Together, we are able to stand as a team, putting forth the maximum effort to achieve our shared goals in a timely and efficient manner. I'm really quite lucky!

I wonder how things are looking on Monster.com.

Lounging

I sit on my front porch in a lounge chair with a glass of water on a small table to the right. As I reach over and take a sip, I see my neighbor pull into his driveway directly across the street. He works hard all day at some sort of office job. He's always complaining about how stressed out he is and how hard he works. It's very entertaining. And now, as I watch him throw open the door to his car and pull himself out, I can see that today has been particularly strenuous.

His tie is half undone and his shirt is half in, half out of his slacks. His smartly cut brown hair is ruffled, and the lines on his face seem especially deep. His face has a pained expression that I have seen before. It's the look of the unappreciated working man. He reminds me of Dilbert, but without the humor and the talking dog.

He grabs his briefcase from his backseat and shuts the car door. He now begins to walk toward his front door. Each step is more labored than the last. He is lost in his thoughts, most likely thoughts of deadlines and forms. He absentmindedly reaches into his pocket and pulls out his keys. At this point, I shift in my chair to get a better view.

He looks at his key ring for a second, and an odd expression comes over his face. It is the look of mild confusion. He puts the briefcase down and grabs the ring with both hands, madly looking for his house key. But it is not there. Now the look on his face is true exasperation. It's that look that says "How can things get any worse?" His house key is missing, and living in Los Angeles, he always locks his doors and windows. Now he puts his keys back in his pockets and puts his head in his hands. He stays in that position for a moment and then loudly utters a very naughty word.

I grab my glass of water and take a small drink. It is fascinating to watch this man, my neighbor, as he realizes that after a terrible day at work, he is now locked out of his house. At least the weather is nice, I suppose. But then, all of a sudden, his eyes light up as he remembers something. From my vantage point, I can see a small smile creep onto his tired face. I know what he is thinking. He is thinking about the spare key he has hidden for just such an emergency. He is not going to let this day beat him. He walks toward the back gate where the key is hidden under the third brick from the left. He nudges the brick to the side with his foot and looks down.

The look on his face is priceless. It is true shock and defeat. The key is not there. He drops to his knees, not worried about ruining his good slacks, and begins to madly look around for where the spare key may have gone. But it proves useless. The key has vanished. He stands back up and walks over to his car. He then lets loose with a profanity and gives the left front tire a good swift kick. I have not seen him this angry in years. And then, from deep inside his house, the phone beings to ring. He looks up quickly and a look of panic fills his face. It might be his boss on the phone. He was supposed to call today, right about now. And he'd guaranteed his boss that would be home to take the call. I know this because he told me so last week. He told me how this call was crucial to his career. It could mean a big promotion or the end of it all.

He runs to the front door and begins to madly pull the knob, hoping beyond hope that it will just pop open. But it is to no avail. The phone continues to ring. He kicks the front door, and screams to the caller to not hang up, to please, please not hang up. And then his eyes happen upon the briefcase, which is right near his feet. He stops kicking the door and picks it up. Then he looks at his front window. A determined look comes over his face as he winds up and does the last thing he can do. He hurls the briefcase through his front window. The glass shatters in a fantastic explosion as his house alarm goes off. He seems to not hear it as he jumps in the window and rushes out of sight to answer the call.

In my ear, I hear an out of breath and panicked voice yell, "Hello!! This is Edwards!!" I wait a moment and then hang up the phone and place it back down near my glass of water. A smile creeps over my face as I reach into my pocket and pull out a small key with the word "spare" written on it in tiny letters. I examine it for a second and then place it back in my pocket. I get up out of my chair and grab my water and my phone and walk back into the house, where Wheel of Fortune is just about to begin.

END

The following True-Life Tale is being brought to you by…

I Sell Beanbags

You want some beanbags? I sell beanbags. Got lots of beanbags. My store is called The Beanbag Place®. It's where all the beanbags I'm selling are. Got beanbags in every shape, size and color. Don't got chairs. Don't got pillows. Don't got french fries. I got beanbags. You want some? Then let's talk. You want a pair of shoes? Get out of my sight!

People like beanbags, and I sell beanbags. You don't want a beanbag? That's fine. You're dead to me. You wake up one morning and decide you're serious about having a beanbag, you're back to life in my eyes. I don't haggle on the prices of my beanbags. If the tag says $59, that's how much that beanbag costs. You want a $20 beanbag for $19.99? Get out of my sight!!

So what are you waiting for? You either want a beanbag or you don't. I can help you with one of those options. It's the beanbag one. And hey, once you buy your beanbag, get out of my sight! You're dead to me! …until such time as your beanbag desires bring you back to The Beanbag Place®. That's all I got to say.

The Beanbag Place®
Bags Full Of Beans… For A Price

It's Like Looking In A Mirror

"You look like Jerry Seinfeld."

This coming from the mouth of the extremely cute girl taking my order at the In-N-Out Burger a few days ago. I saw it coming, because she kept sneaking glances at me as she was punching buttons on the register the same way I keep sneaking glances at heaving cleavage. "Those bosoms look like Jerry Seinfeld's!" is something that I would like to be able to say when I get caught doing that, but it never seems to work out.

Once she made this incredible revelation, I laughed and thanked her for noticing, and she seemed relieved. "I thought maybe you'd be offended..." she said. I don't know why. Seinfeld's not a bad looking dude. It's not like she told me I looked like a white Al Roker or something.

I've been hearing about my resemblance to Jerry Seinfeld since the mid 90's, when his show was in its heyday. For me, Jerry is a good celebrity to sort of look like, because I love his work, so I don't have to grimace every time it gets brought up. People almost always say it with a smile. It would be quite different if, say, I looked like Hitler. Every trip out of the house would be an unpleasant experience. I'd be standing in the checkout line at the supermarket, people behind me whispering and pointing. The lady ringing me up won't look me in the eye. The rabbi in the aisle next to mine has tears in his eyes as he clutches his copy of the Torah. I try and make a joke with the checkout lady to ease the tension:

Matt - Hey, I kind of look like Seinfeld, don't I? What IS the deal! Ha-ha-ha!

Checkout Lady - (mutters under breath) Actually, you remind me more of Hitler…
Man in Suit and Sunglasses with Earpiece - Sir, I'm Agent Collins, FBI. Why don't you come with me so we can have a little talk and why don't you not make any sudden moves, m'kay?
Rabbi In Next Aisle - Oy, why don't you at least shave off the mustache?

I get the Seinfeld thing a lot, but to be honest, our physical similarities are minor at best. I look like Jerry Seinfeld the way that Sunny Delight tastes like orange juice. It's the same color and it is a liquid, but once you get that out of the way, the whole comparison starts to fall apart.

Pre-Seinfeld, what I always used to hear was, "Hey, you look like Paul from The Wonder Years!" which was not my favorite thing in the world. Paul was not exactly a studly dreamboat, nor was he the Fonzie of cool. One time, I was told that I looked "exactly like" Tom Cruise, which is nowhere near the vicinity of reality. The only thing I can figure is that this was said right around the time Tom Cruise started going insane, so maybe it was more a personality thing than a mirror-image sort of thing.

The main thing I've noticed about looking like a big-time Hollywood superstar is that I get absolutely no benefits from it. I never get my drinks taken care of at the bar. I don't get free DVD's when I'm in Best Buy. It's never like, "Gee, guy-who-kind-of-looks-like-Seinfeld-if-I-squint-and-the-lighting-is-bad, here's a Porsche, on the house!" And do hot chicks ever tackle me in public, all the while tearing off their clothes and moaning, "Take me, Faux-feld!"? Yes, of course they do, but it doesn't happen nearly enough. I mean, what's the use of having this power if it doesn't help me out in any way?

So I guess being Seinfeld's twin will remain nothing more than a novelty in my life. A conversation starter, at best. And that's okay, because judging people on their looks is a shallow way to live. It's not who you look like on the outside that matters, but who you are on the inside.

And on the inside, I just happen to look exactly like Brad Pitt.

The following True-Life Tale is being brought to you by...

Mr. Cran-Man, Bring Me A Dream

Ah, there's nothing like a cool glass of Ocean Spray cranberry juice. It's not just good, it's good for you. Ocean Spray is proud to make the very best cranberry juice and our world famous cranberry blends. With choices like Cran-Grape, Cran-Strawberry, and our newest flavor, Cran-Mercury, there's always an Ocean Spray beverage for any occasion.

We got a lot of letters and e-mails here at Ocean Spray, from people of all ages that were white, and they all asked us the same question: When are you going to introduce a Cran-flavor that's crisp, refreshing and a powerful neurotoxin? As of last month, you don't have to wonder anymore. We're proud to say that Cran-Mercury is the only drink on the market with great cranberry taste and trace amounts of mercury in every bottle. No, no. Not the planet. That's just silly! We're talking about the toxic metal that you find inside thermometers and condemned housing tracts. Mmm-mmm! That's good drinkin'!

Cran-Mercury is an excellent source of Vitamin C, not to mention naturally fat-free, cholesterol-free and very low in sodium. Also, it's chock-full of mercury, right to the brim! Can RC Cola say that? Not since the 40's. Now, we get lots of letters and e-mails from people who love Cran-Mercury, or at least their lawyers. Here's a sampling:

"(dead)"

Janice L. - Jefferson City

"(dead)"

Abby D. - Chicago

"My client didn't even drink your devil drink. All she did was inhale the vapors, and the mercury got absorbed into her bloodstream! Sure, her urinary tract isn't infected anymore, but she's suffering from dementia! ... No, wait. She's dead. Never mind."

Dylan M. - Boston

Yes, the drink you've been seeing on the news for the last four weeks is available to buy in your local supermarket. Ocean Spray knows you're gonna love Cran-Mercury. The cranberry goodness goes straight to your taste buds, and the mercury goes straight to your nervous system! (Also available in juice-boxes)

Cran-Mercury

Coming soon from Ocean Spray: Cran-Uranium, Cran-Thrax and Cran-Peach

Powerless

Here is something that happened to me when I was living by myself that always does an excellent job of reminding me why I have no business living alone ever again.

One of the problems with my old apartment (or more accurately, 'twas a duplex in which I occupied the left side) was that the main electrical breaker was somewhat temperamental. If I was to run too many things at once, it would trip the breaker and plunge me into darkness. I had to learn this the hard way and after it happened several times, I had a pretty good idea of the combination of things I had to be running to make the power go out. Computer, TV, microwave... okay. Microwave, washer-dryer, DVD player... power outage. And oddly enough, every time I used the dinky little toaster, I had to be sure that everything else was turned off, because that damn thing would ALWAYS blow the lights when it would eject my Pop-Tarts. No, seriously.

Whenever the power would go out, I always had to go through the same routine to get it back on, which was as follows:

1) Go into backyard
2) Find box along back of house containing all electrical breakers
3) Manually flip all switches to the "down" position
4) Manually flip all switches back to "up" position
5) Return indoors and reset all clocks while muttering profanities under breath

I went through a brief stretch early in my stay there where I was doing this every few weeks, but over time, I figured out the secrets and when January 2005 rolled around, it probably hadn't happened for nine or ten months. Now, the other interesting quirk when the power would go out is that the only breaker that would trip was the one that controlled the electrical outlets. This means that anything that was plugged in would lose power, but the room lights would always stay on, which means that the thing earlier when I said I would be "plunged into darkness" was a bald-faced lie. It's called setting the mood, people. You're going to have to cut me some slack.

By the way, before I go any further, can we just overlook the very obvious fact that someone as accident prone as myself shouldn't be going anywhere near a box containing high voltage? I understand that, but my stubborn side will always (ALWAYS) defeat my common sense side, mostly because my common sense side is the size of a Tic-Tac and, like a Tic-Tac, it occasionally gets stuck in my ear.

So it was around 1:00 am on that fateful January morning and I was enjoying some of the extras on my newly purchased Anchorman DVD when I was struck by the urge to "nosh" on some "munchies." I got up and wandered into the kitchen, where I found a delicious plate of leftovers resting comfortably in my fridge.

"Ah-ha," I exclaimed. "These munchies will be highly suitable for noshing! But first, I will need to reheat them in my microwave, or as I call it, the Nosherator!" This is the sort of gibberish you find yourself speaking out loud when you live alone for too long.

I put the plate into the Nosherator, set the timer to two minutes, turned it on, and headed back towards the living room. I sat there for roughly a minute and 59 seconds when all of a sudden, the power went out. Not the lights, mind you, but the microwave, the TV, the DVD player, the computer... everything that was plugged in. I put my head back and groaned, "Oh, come ON!" and glared at the wall, because I knew that I had to go outside in the cold and the dark to reset the power so that I could continue to watch Will Ferrell act like a spaz. Let this be a lesson: When you refer to eating as "noshing," terrible things will happen to you.

I went in my room, grabbed my lame little flashlight, and then went out into the backyard and up to the wall where the breaker box was located. But to my surprise, I did not see the breaker box. All I saw was thick Wrigley Field-esque ivy, which had grown from the ground all the way up the wall. I hadn't noticed this before, as I almost never went into the backyard, and now was certainly not the best time to discover it. My flashlight was not exactly the greatest flashlight in the land. It was largely decorative, like those little seashell shaped soaps in the bathroom that you are not allowed to use. As far as producing light, I would have had more success if I had taken a match and set the flashlight on fire.

So anyway, I'm squinting at the wall in the middle of the night, trying to find the box through the ivy, wondering if perhaps the Indiglo on my watch would throw off more illumination than the Fisher-Price flashlight in my right hand, when I caught a brief glimpse of the breaker box. I walked over to it, brushed the ivy aside, and to my delight, there it was. My own personal Holy Grail. Relieved that DVD's were still in my future, I flicked all the switches down, then back up, thereby resetting the whole works. I briefly congratulated myself on a job well done, then walked back into the house with my head held high... only to find that everything was still off.

Surprised, but not really bent out of shape, I turned

on my heels and walked back outside, shivering a little against the bitter Southern California cold. I headed back over to the ivy wall, felt around again until I found the box, flicked the switches back down, counted to ten, then back up. I returned to the house and… nothing.

At this point, I started to get somewhat concerned. I thought that perhaps I'd finally blown the breaker to the point where I was going to have to get a new one. This thought bothered me not so much because I wouldn't have the use of any of my electronics for a while, but because it would require calling my landlord, a person who could be somewhat intimidating to say the least. Also, the power to the refrigerator was off, and it contained much tasty food which would probably spoil by the time I was able to make that unpleasant phone call and get the problem fixed. I was going to have to wait until normal business hours, as I didn't think my landlord was going to be a huggy teddy bear if I tried to call him at 1:15 in the morning.

I paced back and forth for a few minutes, trying to figure out what my options were, something I often do in situations like this, when my gaze went to the shining light over my head (I know, I know. There's that whole corny "light bulb over the head/I got an idea" thing going on here, but it's unavoidable, because it's what actually happened). I stopped pacing, looked at the light for a second, then began to wonder why it was that only my plugged-in stuff lost power, which led to the nagging thought, "When I flip all the breakers off, are the lights going off too, and if they aren't, why not?" I walked back into my bedroom and flipped on the lights, which I would be able to see from the breaker box outside, then trotted back out to the backyard, over to the box, flipped the switches down, which should've, in theory, cut ALL the power to the entire place. But that is not what happened. No, the lights stayed on.

Now I was REALLY confused. "Why in the hell isn't this working?" I thought. "There shouldn't be any light! I've turned the power completely off! This doesn't make any sense!"

I looked back at the breaker box, then happened to look about five feet to the right. It was there that, poking out through the ivy, I saw another breaker box. MY breaker box. As opposed to the breaker box of my neighbor, which I had been flicking on and off for the last half-hour. The thing that I said was, "Ooooooooh... OH-NO!"

So I reset my breakers, then restored my neighbors power and bolted back into the house, where I proceeded to get a real stupid case of the giggles, brought on by the image of my poor neighbor, sitting in her house, wondering why the power kept going off, then back on, then off, then back on, and perhaps calling an exorcist. I was pretty sure she was asleep, but I took a wild guess that her alarm clock probably wasn't going to be going off in the morning, and that got me laughing as well. But at the heart of it, I just felt stupid, which is when I knew everything had gone back to normal.

I have no witty ending for this, so I take a small bow.

Cell Phone

1.

"You don't understand," Ryan said as he stepped on the gas and turned onto the on-ramp. "It wasn't my fault. I didn't build the display and if I had, I certainly wouldn't have made it so rickety."

Ryan's friend Henry, seated in the passenger seat, rolled his eyes. "So you're blaming it on the guy who built the display? The box boy working for minimum wage who came into work one day and was told by the manager to stack a bunch of cans of Planters at the end of the aisle. It's his fault. This is what you're saying?"

"If not one hundred percent, at least fifty. If that display had been even slightly sturdier, I wouldn't have knocked it over. People need to take pride in their work."

"People also need to watch where they're going, not that I'm pointing any fingers," Henry turned to Ryan and pointed his finger directly at him.

Ryan shook his head in mock disgust, then grinned as he steered the car into the fast lane. "I'll bet Mr. Peanut is really pissed at me."

"I'd be more worried about Mr. Store Manager. You keep knocking stuff over, you're gonna have to do all your grocery shopping at Le Dumpster Behind Le Supermarket."

"Okay, okay. So I have a small clumsy streak. What do you want from me?"

They drove on down the freeway, doing about eighty. Traffic was light at this point in the afternoon, and they were making pretty good time to the movie theater. Ryan glanced at the clock on the radio.

"2:45." he said. "You think we have enough time to stop off at the Best Buy?"

Henry shrugged. "Probably. As long as you don't get hypnotized by all the pretty colors and flashing lights. It'll have to be one of those in-and-out trips, as opposed to your typical nine hour browse-fest."

"I can do that." Ryan said as he looked down briefly to fiddle with the radio. "I already know exactly what I want to get." He looked back up and noticed a shiny new Lexus in the lane ahead of him. The Lexus was driving along, but not nearly as fast as Ryan's car. He grimaced, and began to apply the brakes. As his car slowed, he decided just to pass the Lexus on the right, but a truck blocked his way. He lightly tapped the steering wheel with his fist as he pressed down harder on the brakes. "I hate when these people go slow in the fast lane. Hello! Fast lane!"

Henry looked at the speedometer. "Well, you WERE driving a little over the speed limit. Maybe Lexus guy is just obeying the law."

"Yeah, because people who buy brand-new Lexus's care about laws. I mean, that car can do 125 and not even break a sweat. Why spend all that money on a prestige vehicle, then take it out on the freeway and keep it in first gear? It doesn't make any sense!"

Henry shook his head, grabbed a CD case that was lying on the floor and began flipping through the booklet. He spoke without looking up. "I like how you don't get worked up about war. You don't get worked up about pollution. You don't get worked up about murder or famine or incurable disease. No, you save YOUR rage for the people who drive 65 in the 65 mile-an-hour zone." Henry held up his fist. "Power to the people, brother!"

Ryan frowned and continued to glare at the Lexus,

which he was now tailgating. He began to mutter softly. "Move. Move. Move. Come on, you can do it. You're interrupting the flow of traffic, you moron. Get out of the way." Suddenly, Ryan craned his neck forward and he squinted in the direction of the Lexus' tinted back window. "AH-HA!!" he shouted, causing Henry to jump slightly. "You see! There's the problem right there. Mr. Lexus is on a cell phone! That's why he's driving so slow."

He turned to Henry, smiling and nodding, and Henry gave him a weak thumbs-up. "Well done, Sherlock. We're all very impressed."

"These people! And the cell phones! What is up with the cell phones? What kind of world is this where suddenly everybody has to have a phone with them at all times?" He backed off the Lexus's bumper slightly and put on his right-turn blinker. "I mean, what in the hell is so important that it can't wait until you get home?"

"Well, maybe he's talking to his business partners. Maybe he's ordering takeout from a Chinese food place. Maybe his wife is in labor and he's talking her through the delivery. What does it matter? He's got a cell phone and he uses it. Good for him."

"But his stupid cell phone is directly responsible for me not having time to go to the Best Buy!"

"You mean the same way that the box boy was responsible for you tripping over your feet and diving headfirst into the Planters display?"

Ryan grinned weakly and moved into the right lane. He stepped on the gas and sped past the Lexus, then cut back into the fast lane. He laughed and pumped his fist. "Sorry, Phone Dude, but I win! One to nothing!" He continued driving on, with no other traffic to impede his progress.

2.

The movie theater wasn't completely full, but it was opening day for the film, so most of the seats were occupied. Even so, Ryan and Henry were able to get decent seats, and they sat down just as the lights dimmed. Ryan had read several reviews of the movie, all very positive, and he was ready to sit back, relax, and enjoy himself. And for the first forty-five minutes, that's exactly what he did.

It was right in the middle of a very emotional scene between the father and son when Ryan heard the noise. At first, he assumed it was just part of the movie, but as it continued, he knew that couldn't be right. He couldn't put his finger on what the noise was, but it almost sounded like a melody. He turned his head and looked behind him at where the noise seemed to be coming from and saw a teenage girl reach into her purse and pull out her cell phone. Now that the sound wasn't being muffled, he recognized it as the theme from Friends. The girl held the phone to her ear and spoke softly into it.

"Hello. Oh, hey! Yeah, I'm good. No, I'm just sitting here watching that new Mel Gibson movie. It's so boring. Nothing's happened for like, three hours!" There was a pause, then she giggled at the response on the other end of the line. "I KNOW! You don't even have to tell me!" She continued talking into the phone, voice growing steadily louder, until she was almost speaking at a normal level. Ryan continued to stare at her, brow furrowed, scowling. If it was possible to shoot knives out of his eyes and have them strike someone dead, Phone Girl would have been stabbed six thousand times.

After a moment, she looked up and noticed Ryan staring at her. She kept talking for a second, then glared at Ryan and said to the caller, "Hey, Kelly, can you hold on for just a second?" She lowered the phone and leaned forward towards Ryan. "Do you MIND?" she hissed.

Ryan furiously pointed at the girl. "Do YOU mind?!" he snapped and made a sweeping arm gesture towards the screen.

The girl held out her hand, extended her middle finger, than sat back in the chair and continued her conversation. Ryan's jaw dropped and he drew in a sharp breath. Hair falling over his eyes, he forcefully said, "Excuse me? Excuse the hell out of me! I'm trying to watch this movie! Can't your stupid phone call wait, you rude cell phone lunatic?!"

The girl flipped him off with her other hand, then began telling Kelly all about "this jerk sitting in front of me." They shared a chipper laugh, and Ryan turned back around with disbelief. "I don't understand this," he said to no one in particular. "What is going on in the world today where something like THAT is acceptable? In a movie theater no less. DURING the movie!"

A voice came out of the darkness. "Hey, dipwad! How about shutting the hell up?"

Ryan didn't say another word for the rest of the movie, but he found it impossible to pay any attention.

3.

As Ryan and Henry briskly walked from the theater to the local coffeehouse, Henry couldn't help but notice the faraway look in Ryan's eyes. He snapped his fingers in front of Ryan's face and, after a very long moment, Ryan blinked and looked over at his friend.

"What is UP with you, man?" Henry asked. "You're more out of it than usual tonight."

Ryan opened his mouth to speak, then his eyes fell upon an attractive young woman leaning against the side of a building, chattering away on her cell phone. He found himself struck with a sudden, uncharacteristic flash of anger. With an effort, he was able to repress this feeling, then he turned to Henry and shrugged. "I dunno. I've just got a lot on my mind, I guess. But I'm fine. I'm sure an overpriced flavorless coffee drink will take the edge off."

"And that happens to be the specialty of Fair Grounds." They had reached the entrance to the coffeehouse, and Henry opened the door. "After you, madam."

Ryan walked in and up to the counter where he ordered his usual. Fair Grounds was surprisingly populated for the time of the evening. It typically didn't start hopping until after nine. Even with the crowd, Ryan was able to find a table pretty quickly and he sat down, coffee in hand. A few moments later, Henry plopped down beside him and beckoned towards a pretty girl sitting by herself in the corner.

"You ever notice she's always in here, always at the same table, always alone, and always reading the same book?"

Ryan glanced in the girl's direction and took a small sip of his coffee. "She's getting pretty near the end, from the looks of it. I wonder what she's gonna do when she finishes the book."

"She'll probably close it, sit there for a moment, then open it again and start from the beginning. One of those 'a book is better than a movie, and easier to rewind' kind of chicks."

"I think you underestimate her," Ryan said. "I'll bet she's got that book on audiotape. I'm sure that's her next move."

"She may have the book on audiotape, but ten bucks says it's her voice reading it."

They both grinned, and at nearly the same time, they both took drinks of their coffees. Ryan looked out the window. "I like how we've got nothing better to do than to analyze the potential reading habits of girls we don't even know." He scanned the sidewalk for a minute, and noticed the woman on the cell phone, still yakking away. *But no... that's not the same girl*, he thought. *Cell phone girl was wearing a skirt, and that lady is wearing jeans.* His eyes narrowed. They sure looked the same. *Maybe they're related. Or maybe the one in jeans is on the phone with the skirt. What sense does that make? They can't be more than twenty feet away from each other.* His mind began racing with a growing anger. *Just because you HAVE a cell phone doesn't mean you always have to be talking into it! Just hang up the phone! She's right there! You can see her!*

"...you can friggin' see her!!"

Henry looked up from his coffee and gave Ryan a puzzled look. "What's that, Ryan? I can see who?"

Ryan turned back to Henry and for a moment could not understand what he had been asked. Slowly, it clicked, and he shook his head. "No, not you. Sorry." He waved his hand toward the window. "It's just... these people out there. You know, people and their cell phones. It's nothing."

Henry put his coffee down and leaned in. When he spoke, it was very quiet. "Are you SURE you're okay? You're really acting strange, even for you."

"I'm fine." Ryan said, and he made a special effort to

look Henry in the eye as he said this. This proved to be very difficult, as he desperately wanted to watch the lady on the cell phone to see what she was going to do next. "It's this coffee. Too much caffeine. Makes me jumpy. Try not to worry about it."

"I'm not worried. I'd just like to be sure that you aren't going to drive us off an overpass later on." The lady in the jeans finished her conversation and put the phone in her purse. Ryan felt the strangest sense of relief. He also felt Henry staring at him. Before he could reply to Henry's comment, there were fingers in his face, snapping. "I'm serious, man." Henry said as he withdrew his arm. "I got too many things to do next week to have you freak out and go on a shooting rampage or something."

"I'm fine," Ryan said for the third time in ten minutes. "Honest. Cross my heart and hope to die. Stick a needle in my phone. Eye. I meant eye." He giggled. "Can you believe I said phone? I really meant to say eye. What a goof!"

Henry pushed back his chair and stood up. He pointed at Ryan, who was still letting out unnatural giggles. "You need to get on drugs or something, because this clean and sober thing just isn't working out for you at all. I'm gonna go to the bathroom real quick. Just sit there. Don't do anything... weird."

As Henry turned and walked off, Ryan sat back in his chair and took a deep breath. He closed his eyes and sat very still. *Henry's right,* he thought. *I am acting a little weird. I've just got to relax. Nothing's worth getting this worked up about. Especially not a bunch of whores and yuppies on cell phones.* Feeling slightly better, at least in theory, Ryan slowly opened his eyes and took a long look around the coffeehouse. The very first thing he saw, sitting alone on a table not far away, was a cell phone. There was nobody standing near it, and no one else even seemed to notice it was there. Ryan stared at it, unblinking, until a tinny ringing noise made him jump in his seat. *The cell phone is ringing,* he thought, but that wasn't right. The cell phone WASN'T ringing. That noise was coming from his left. He craned his neck in that direction just in time to see a man reach into his pocket and pull out a cell phone of his own. The man punched a button and began speaking into it. Ryan's head snapped back toward the phone on the table, still sitting there. Somehow, it was impossible not to look at it, even as the man's conversation echoed in his ear. Something inane about the Lakers game. *Who cares what the final score was? And why NOW? Why is it so important right now? That's what SportsCenter is for!*

Ryan wanted very badly to shout at the man, to tell him what a fool he was, but he saw movement over to his right and shot a glance in that direction. It was a younger girl, not more than 15, and damned if she didn't have a cell phone shoved against the side of her face. And she was laughing! Talking into the phone and laughing! Had she no idea? No concept of how wrong she was? *Has to be peer pressure. HAS to be!* Ryan's head began to throb, even as another ringing sound came out of nowhere. This one from behind him. He turned around so fast that two legs of his chair came off the ground briefly. Someone else answering a cell phone. Sitting next to her, a younger guy. A younger guy DIALING on a cell phone. Calling out! And to talk about what? The coffee? Maybe what kind of coffee the Lakers would drink? Ryan clenched his fists without realizing it. Back to his right, the door to Fair Grounds opened and Skirt Lady walked in, still heavily engrossed in her phone call. As he watched her walk to the counter, beads of sweat began to form on Ryan's forehead. No, this was all wrong. All of it. More customers began to funnel into the coffeehouse, every one of them, every last one of them either holding a cell phone or talking on a cell phone. And even the ones that weren't still had them. Ryan knew this for a fact. He knew this with stunning clarity. They might not have their cell phones out in the open, no doubt in an attempt to hide them from Ryan, but Ryan was onto them. He wasn't stupid, and he wasn't going to let these people, these cell phone zombies, try to trick him.

And yet, he felt his grasp on reality slipping. He knew he had to be strong, not let them see his weaknesses. They could smell fear, and he tried hard to suppress it, but it wasn't easy. Not with all the chattering. The chattering and the ringing and the dialing and the talking. It was all around him. It was inside of him. There was nothing he could do to keep it out. The noises…

"…and then Kobe just STUFFED that ball, man! Just stuffed it!"

"I think the movie starts at 7:30, so why don't you just meet me here at 7:00?"

"RIIINNNNNGG! RIIIIINNNG!!!"

"…Oh, he was SO looking at me. You know he was! And then I heard Ashley say that he…"

"…no honey, I'm working late. I probably won't be home until 11:00 or 12:00. The boss is on me to finish these reports and he won't let up. That sound? That's just the Xerox machine, dear. I've really got to run."

"…expect them to play all forty-eight minutes. It's not the playoffs or anything!"

"RIINNNNGG!! RIIIINNNGG!!"

"Of course it's gonna be good. It's got…"

"…only if my mom stops being such a psycho. I

swear she hates me. She never lets me do ANYTHING!"

"...don't know anything about defense, but it doesn't matter when the offense can score at will. It's like..."

"...ask him out..."

"...don't call the office..."

"...championship caliber..."

"RIIIINNNNG! RIIINNNG!!!"

Ryan put his hands to his ears and moaned, but the sounds only continued to grow ever louder. Eyes darting wildly all around the coffeehouse, he set his sights on the girl reading the book. He fixated on her. The only one in the entire building who hadn't fallen into the trap. *You're just like me,* he thought. *You're another lone boat on the ocean, trying to find land! We can help each other! We can help each other!* As if she heard his thought, she looked up and stared directly at him for a split second. Then she glimpsed at the table, saw the lone cell phone and jumped up. Her book fell to the ground. She grabbed the phone, which really HAD been ringing the whole time, and answered it.

"Hello? Oh, hi Mike! Sorry I didn't pick up right away. I was really into my book."

With the only person who understood now a willing victim of the plague, Ryan grabbed his coffee, crushed the cup and slammed it down on the table. Brownish liquid and frothy milk dripped onto the ground, forming a quickly growing puddle. He got up and stumbled out the door, pushing several people out of the way. He bumped Skirt Lady and when he saw who he had touched and what she was holding, he hissed and recoiled. He forcefully burst out the door, lost his footing and fell onto his knees. He stayed in that position for a minute, breathing heavily. He could still hear the ringing and see the cell phones when he closed his eyes, but his head was beginning to clear, and for that he was grateful.

When Henry emerged from the coffeehouse a couple of minutes later, he looked down at his friend on all fours in the middle of the sidewalk, sweating slightly and muttering to himself. He looked around, took a long drink of his coffee and cleared his throat. When he got no response, he cleared his throat louder and softly tapped Ryan in the ribs with his foot. Ryan grunted and looked up without saying anything. Henry took another drink and scratched his head.

"I know you're fine," Henry said, bookmarking the last word with quote marks. "So I'm not even going to ask if you're okay. However, I'm afraid I'm going to have to ask you if you've lost your mind, which is all right, because that's not really the same question."

Ryan didn't say anything at first. Only shifted his position until he was sitting on his rump, though still using one arm to keep himself steady. Finally he looked up towards Henry, without making eye contact. "I think I need to go home."

Henry nodded.

4.

Three weeks passed. The incident at the coffeehouse was not spoken of again, and that was exactly how Ryan wanted it. Looking back on it, he felt extraordinarily foolish, and he was quite content to put it in the back of his mind, never to be remembered. It was an embarrassing moment, but it was only a moment. A moment unrelated to anything else, and a moment which didn't affect his life in any way. Knowing that made it all even easier to forget.

Although...

...after the night at the coffeehouse, Ryan began to find excuses not to go out with the guys. An invitation to the movies was met with "I've got to work tomorrow." An offer to go hang out at a party was shot down with "I've had a long day. I just need my rest." And simple requests to get a burger and fries always seemed to be badly timed because "I just ate. Really sorry, guys. Maybe next time." Ryan was not unpopular. He had a lot of friends and many more acquaintances. Separately, these excuses didn't seem odd, but they started to add up. Fast.

Although...

... Ryan began to watch television with the remote control always in hand. He was never a channel surfer and was usually content to find a show and watch it until it ended. But suddenly he became very picky about shows and commercials. If the main character of the sitcom took a call on a cell phone, Ryan would change the channel. If a Verizon commercial came on, Ryan would change the channel. Even watching Larry King became a challenge, as every time Larry took a call, Ryan would be overcome with the thought, *Where's that guy calling from?* Sometimes, Ryan's skin would break out in goose bumps, something he attributed to the approaching winter.

Although...

... the phone in Ryan's house simply had to be replaced. It was a portable phone, he'd had it for many years, but it had never occurred to him how uncomfortable that phone made him feel. "I just feel more secure when my phone is attached to the wall," he told the checker at the Wal-Mart as he purchased his new ground-line phone. The checker smiled. Ryan smiled. And when Ryan got home, he took his portable phone, placed it under his back tire, and threw the car into reverse. The goose bumps went away. His mind cleared. The sun seemed to shine a little bit brighter. The smile never left his face.

5.

December rolled around, and one Saturday found Ryan sleeping soundly in his bed. He heard the knock on his door, but didn't connect it to a meaning. It was all just another part of his dream. The cell phones were attacking him, just as they did nearly every night. But as time passed, Ryan happily noted when he'd awaken, there were fewer and fewer. He was winning this battle. No wonder he smiled all the time.

Still, the knocking continued, and after enough time, it jarred him awake. He sat up, looked around and leapt out of bed, wiping the sweat off his forehead. By the time he reached his front door, the knocking had gotten louder and more violent. He heard a familiar voice on the other side.

"Ryan, you know I'm not going to stop knocking until you come to the door, so would you just open it before my knuckles start to bleed?"

Ryan fiddled with the chain, unlocked the deadbolt, and threw open the door. Henry stood there, holding a small package. He grinned. "Ah-ha! You ARE alive. Looks like I just won twenty bucks. Can I come in?"

"Um… yeah. Sure. No problem." Ryan stood aside, wiping the sleep out of his eyes as Henry walked in.

"Were you still in bed? It's like two in the afternoon, man."

"Is it really?" Ryan looked at his watch. "Huh. Look at that. I guess time got away from me. I've just been really tired lately."

"I'm sure it's just the first stage of inoperable brain cancer." He chuckled and looked over at the front door. "Hey, when did you get the chain?"

Ryan's eyes darted to the door, then back to Henry. He shrugged. "I uh… I had it installed. You can never be too careful. Safety first."

"I guess. I mean, I for one have always said that nothing keeps a chainsaw wielding maniac out of your house like a dinky gold plated chain on the front door. Well done." Henry shifted the package from his right hand to his left and then pointed at Ryan. "Where have you BEEN? You realize it's been over a month since I've seen you. You can't be THAT busy."

"My schedule has been… um… a real mess these days. Just don't have time to go out, you know?"

"I hear you. And that's what I've been telling everyone. But when there hasn't been a confirmed Ryan sighting in five weeks, people start to talk. Which would be why I'm here." Henry glanced over Ryan's shoulder and furrowed his brow. "Where's your TV? Did you move it into your room?"

A cold sweat, slight but definitely there, broke out on Ryan's forehead. And the goose bumps were coming back. Damn the goose bumps. His heart began to speed up. When he spoke, he spoke sharply. "Look, the TV broke. Why're you giving me the fifth degree?" He put his hand to his head and took a deep breath. When he looked back up at Henry, he sighed. "I'm sorry, Henry. That was out of line. It's been a rough few weeks, that's all. I'm not feeling like myself."

Henry nodded, as if Ryan had said what he'd been thinking. "I've noticed, and I started thinking about what might've sparked this. I couldn't figure anything out for a long time, but it suddenly hit me." He snapped his fingers.

"You're depressed about your birthday!"

"My birthday? But my birthday isn't for two more weeks."

"Yeah, but you've been thinking about it. I can tell. Internally bemoaning this change in age. Thinking too much about what it means. What have I accomplished? Where am I in life? Getting too old too fast, with nothing to show for it. I've been there, man, and I know how it can get you down."

Ryan plopped down on his couch and ran his fingers back through his hair. "I guess that might have something to do with it." He absentmindedly popped a knuckle. "It's certainly possible."

"Exactly!" said Henry, obviously just getting warmed up. "The PROBLEM is that you've chosen the wrong way to go about this crisis of yours. You're trying to keep it all bottled up, when the only way to get through something like this is to talk it out. That's what your trusted friends..." he pointed at himself. "...are for. You've been soaking in your misery, all by yourself, and it's turned you into a mental case. And that's sad, because the solution is so simple. All you gotta do is talk."

"Talk?" It was a question, but barely.

"Hell yes, talk. And THAT is what this little gift is all about." He handed Ryan the package, which was hastily wrapped in Happy Anniversary paper. "Think of it as an early birthday present. I got the idea from that night you freaked out at the coffeehouse."

The reminder of his actions caused Ryan's stomach to turn, but only briefly. He studied the package, which was quite light, and fairly small. He squeezed it and shook it, then looked up at his friend.

"Don't stare at me. Open the gift. THEN stare at me, if you're so inclined."

Ryan looked back down, and with a flourish and a burst of quick energy he hadn't exerted in several weeks, he tore the package in half. A cellular phone fell out of the box and landed on the carpet with a slight thump. He looked down at the phone and braced himself for the horror which he knew was about to overtake him. Here it was, his unspoken nemesis, in his home. Surely this was going to cause him to freak out, and he was about to do something even worse than throwing the remote control through the TV. He was ready for whatever it was... but it never came.

Looking down at this small phone, he felt a clarity in his head he hadn't felt for ages. It was as if the sun had finally broken through the dark clouds. A grin began to spread on his face. A legitimate grin. He reached down and grabbed the cell phone, and as he picked it up, a massive weight lifted off his shoulders. He stared at it, almost in a trance, and flipped the faceplate open. The screen glowed green and the words "HELLO RYAN" appeared.

"Hello cell phone..." Ryan whispered.

Henry clapped his hands twice and then pointed at Ryan. "So, do you like it or not? You've got me in total suspense here."

"I love it..." Ryan said, still speaking in a whisper as he gazed at the phone.

"Good. I'm glad. I figured you were so jealous of that guy with the cell phone in the Lexus that I might as well see if I couldn't get you a taste of the good life. Me and a bunch of the guys chipped in and got you a great deal. 3000 night and weekend minutes. 600 anytime minutes. Roaming and instant messaging and all that junk. You won't be able to use all those minutes no matter how hard you try. Plus I think all your incoming calls are free."

"Incoming calls?" Ryan asked, speaking in a normal,

though wobbly, voice. "As in, people calling me?"

Henry nodded. "Yep. And the phone's a Nokia, too, which I think is pretty good. It plays games and gets stock quotes and stuff. You know how cell phones are these days. They're almost TOO advanced."

Ryan closed the faceplate and held the phone up to his nose. He inhaled sharply. Without opening his eyes, he said, "Ah… it smells so good. Like sanity." His eyes popped open and he quickly looked at Henry, who was smiling widely. "I meant like… um… it just smells good. Got a new car smell… but like a phone."

Henry held up his hands. "Whatever, man. I'm not here to judge your steamy love affair with the cell phone. I'm just happy I could bring you two together. But seriously, you do like it, right? Cause I can always take it back if…"

"NO!!" Ryan shouted, rising up a little out of his seat. Henry jumped a little and stopped talking. Ryan clutched the phone to his chest and sank back onto the couch. "It's really nice, I mean. There's no reason to take it anywhere. It needs to stay here… with me…so I can get the incoming calls." He smiled. It was a big smile. Although if you asked Henry later, he would have told you that Ryan's smile was almost a little TOO big.

6.

That night, Ryan slept like a baby. No fevered nightmares whatsoever. He woke up feeling rested and refreshed. As soon as his eyes popped open, he looked for the cell phone. There it was, lying on his dresser. He smiled and hopped out of bed.

"Good morning, cell phone! You're looking lovely

today!"

He picked it up and stared at his reflection in the face plate. He never thought of himself as a good looking man, but something about the man he saw in the cell phone was highly attractive. He made his hand into a gun shape, and fired an imaginary shot at the reflection.

"What's up, stud? Yeah, you looking good. You know it!"

Phone in hand, he strutted into the bathroom and took a shower. Although the phone didn't go into the shower with him, he left the curtain open just enough so that it never left his sight. The phone comforted him, and after several weeks of being a depressed lunatic, he was happy to have something concrete which kept him sane. Besides, it just looked so good. So right.

Two hours later, Ryan sat in a chair in the middle of his living room. The phone's user manual sat on his lap, and he was intently programming names and numbers into the phone. His whole life had been incomplete, but he'd finally found the final piece of the puzzle. He was whole, and he liked the way it felt.

"You know the best part?" he asked the phone. "I'm not lagging behind in the technological revolution anymore. I'm just like everybody else. Thanks to you, I can keep in touch with anybody, anytime. It's so liberating." He paused and got a dreamy, faraway look on his face. "And I can receive incoming phone calls. That's going to be... just the best..."

Finally, he finished programming numbers into the phone, and flipped to the next page of the manual. Glancing down at what was written, he furrowed his brow.

"Voicemail. Huh... Why would I need voicemail? I'm always going to ANSWER my phone." Then he barked out a highly unnatural laugh and smacked himself on the forehead, leaving a red mark. "Oh! It's for when I get an incoming call, then get ANOTHER incoming call while I'm still on the phone! That's BRILLIANT!!"

The thought of these endless incoming calls threw him into a joyous fury, and as he recorded his voicemail message, he was on his feet, jumping in place.

The prerecorded woman spoke into his ear. "Please record your outgoing message at the beep, and then press one. BEEP!"

Ryan sucked in a deep breath. He wanted to get this one right. He didn't want to sound like a dolt to all the people that were calling him. "Hi there!" he said with too much force. "This is Ryan, and I'm not available right now! I'm on the phone with someone else that called me, but I can't wait to talk to you. Please leave a message or even... call me back. You can call me back if you want. I take my cell phone everywhere." He paused, then spoke. "It's a Nokia!" He paused again. *Why did I say that?* He wondered. *Does it matter that it's a Nokia? Yeah, it probably does.* "Nokia!" *I should tell them that it doesn't matter what time they call me, because my cell phone sits in its charger at night, and the charger is right by my bed.* "Incoming calls can happen twenty-four hours a day!" Had he just spoken that, or had he only thought it? He wasn't sure. And was the message going on too long? Ryan's mind began to spin. *You're blowing it! You're blowing it! Finish off the message! Press one, you fool! You stupid, stupid fool!* "I love you," Ryan spit out and mashed his finger into the one button. He wasn't sure if he'd recorded a very good message, but if he didn't like it, he could always re-record it. The cell phone didn't mind if he made mistakes. He was only human after all. And soon, very soon, the phone would ring. And on the other end would be an incoming call, and

Ryan knew that when that moment came, everything would be okay. He smiled again just thinking about it and held the cell phone in both hands. He stared at it, not moving, for hours, as the sun reached its high point in the sky, and continued to sit and stare long past sunset.

7.

Everyone got Ryan's cell phone number. He made very sure of that. He called them all (on his home phone, of course - he didn't want to ruin the cell phone) and recited the number, and made them recite it back to him.

"Call anytime!" he said.

He'd picked out his ring, the theme from Looney Tunes, and played it for anyone who would listen.

"This is what it'll do when you call!" he said.

He started going out with the guys again, phone always in his pocket, never far from his mind. When he'd see other people talking on cell phones, he'd wave and give them a knowing wink. *We're the same.* He'd think. *Cell phone brothers.* He'd point these people out to his friends.

"That guy got an incoming call!" he'd say. "I heard it!"

Every ten minutes, sometimes every five, he'd pull the cell phone out of his pocket and make sure it was still on. It was always on, but it was important to check. Wouldn't want to miss an incoming call.

"Doesn't matter if I miss the call," he'd tell his friends, even though they never seemed to show any interest. "Cause I've got voicemail. It's the latest thing."

When the guys went to the movies a couple of days later, a cell phone rang a couple of rows behind Ryan.

Ryan's heart swelled. When a thoughtless person to his left hissed at the person on the phone to shut up, Ryan angrily shouted at him. "You leave that man alone! He's on the phone! You keep your nose in YOUR business!" Later on, as they left the theater, Henry walked alongside Ryan.

"I'm not so curious why you yelled at the guy in the theater. No, I'm more curious why when you were yelling, you were pointing your phone at him."

Ryan shrugged. "I didn't realize I WAS pointing the phone at him. I must've just happened to have it in my hand."

"You've got it in your hand right now!" Henry said. "In fact, I haven't seen you release your death grip on it all night."

"Maybe not," Ryan said. "But I'm not going to miss MY incoming calls!" He stomped away and for the rest of the night, Henry noticed that Ryan made a special point to leave the phone in his pocket. He never let go of it, but the phone and his hand were both out of sight. Also for the rest of the night, whenever Henry looked at Ryan, he noticed that Ryan was glaring at him. Ryan wasn't a big guy, and not aggressive in any way, but Henry decided that Ryan's glaring was making him feel extremely uncomfortable. It was at that moment that, for the first time, Henry began to think that giving Ryan the cell phone might have been a very bad idea.

8.

The phone wouldn't ring.

Ryan laid there in bed, staring at the ceiling. Something had been bothering him for days now, and he'd finally put his finger on it.

The phone wouldn't ring.

It's not like he hadn't done his part. He'd programmed it, given out the number, made it PERFECTLY CLEAR that he wished to be called… but it wasn't doing any good, because the phone wouldn't ring. Ryan turned his head and looked at the cell phone, sitting on its charger. The red light shined, unblinking. It made him angry, because he knew the red light was mocking him.

I COULD ring, Ryan, but it's more fun to watch you stew in your own thoughts. Don't you think?

Ryan turned back towards the ceiling and said nothing. He wasn't going to give the phone the satisfaction of seeing him angry. But no matter how hard he stared above him, or how hard he tried to focus on anything but the cell phone, he couldn't help but turn his head back toward that taunting red light.

What's the matter, Ryan? You seem angry. It's not something I did, is it?

Ryan hated the phone's sarcasm. It didn't seem appropriate. Not considering the circumstances. He slit his eyes and clenched his fists. "Why don't you stop being a jerk and ring, you stupid jerk? That's what you're for, you know. Not to sit there, all silent, shining your damn red light in my face."

Oh, Ryan. Don't be that way. I'm not doing anything wrong. I'm just recharging so that when you DO get a phone call, I'll have plenty of power and you can talk for hours and hours.

"Whatever." Ryan rolled his eyes. "You act all innocent. It really gets under my skin."

The red light continued shining, and Ryan closed his eyes. He was tired of looking at it. He knew he could make the light go away. All he had to do was unplug the charger.

But if he ended up missing an incoming call, just because the phone wasn't charged, he knew he wouldn't be able to live with himself. It was a vicious unfair catch 22.

Suddenly, the cell phone rang. The Looney Tunes theme filled the room. Ryan sat bolt upright in bed, then launched himself over to the dresser and grabbed the phone. He pushed the receive button, put the phone to his ear and shouted, "Hello?! Hello?!" The sound he was met with wasn't the sound of an incoming call, but the sound of a dial tone. Not sure exactly what he was hearing, Ryan pulled the phone away from his ear and looked at the screen. According to the screen, he was about to MAKE a phone call, not receive one. *That doesn't make any sense*, he thought. *I HEARD the ringing!*

And it was then that he heard another sound over the dial tone. It was a hearty laughter, a laughter which seemed to be coming from... THE PHONE! *The damned phone TRICKED me! That son of a bitch...*

Ryan fumed. To be toyed with by a cell phone was more than he could bear. He gritted his teeth and pulled the cell phone close to his face. He spoke through a clenched jaw. "Don't you EVER do that again, you understand me?! I'll throw you down the garbage disposal! I'm serious!" The phone seemed to stare at him, uncaring, not at all afraid. "You think I won't do it?! Don't TEST me!"

If you do anything to harm me, you'll miss your incoming call, Ryan. Do you want to miss your incoming call?

Ryan's left eye twitched. The phone had him by the balls. He couldn't deny it. He loosened his grip on it and lowered his arm. He only muttered one word. "Damn..."

Now put me back in my charger and go to bed. And if I ever see an outburst like this again, you can FORGET about ever hearing me ring. Do you understand ME?

Ryan didn't have to say anything. The phone already knew the answer. Ryan did as he was told. He put the phone back in the charger. The red light came back on. It stared accusingly at Ryan as he turned around and crawled back in bed. He laid on his back and resumed staring at the ceiling. As he laid there, tears began to run down his face. It was a long night.

9.

And so it went. Sleepless nights turned into endless days. Ryan began to despise the phone, but he had no choice but to take it with him wherever he went. He'd come too far to give up now. He knew that if he was good, the cell phone would ring, and that was the only thing that kept him going. But he had to be careful, because so many things would draw the cell phone's ire.

He was jumpy. He was losing weight. He was spending more and more time staring at the phone, even though the sight of it made his entire head ache. He wanted it to go away, but when he couldn't see it, he began to panic. Sometimes, in dead of night, the phone would make him promises. *Tomorrow, Ryan. Tomorrow's the big day. I'm gonna ring off the HOOK!* But it would never happen. There were always excuses. Always with the excuses.

Ryan's friends didn't notice the severe change in him, because he seemed to have dropped off the face of the Earth. Calls to his home phone were met with the operator's voice informing them that "This phone has been disconnected". They all figured it was a mistake. They all seemed to think that Ryan was just in "one of those moods." When they would drive by his house, his car would be in the driveway, but he would never answer the door. "Probably out with someone else," they'd say. And it made sense. Ryan had a lot of friends.

Ryan heard the people knocking at his front door. And deep down, a part of him wanted nothing more than to go to them, to open the door and ask for help. But the phone wouldn't allow it. Making that journey to the front room was a sure fire ticket to losing any incoming calls, and he knew it. That red light meant business, and he just couldn't take the risk.

10.

It had been twenty-three days since Henry had given Ryan the cell phone as a gift. Ryan opened his eyes, not sure where he was. It took several minutes, several long, confusing minutes, to realize he was sitting on the toilet. He looked around, his mind moving incredibly slowly, when he remembered the cell phone. It was in his room. How long had he been gone?!

He jumped off the toilet and dashed into his room, stubbing his toe on the bedpost and not even feeling it. He grabbed the phone out of the charger and looked at the screen. "NO NEW CALLS!" it read.

"Thank God," Ryan sighed, and collapsed onto the bed. He laid there for a few minutes, eyes open but seeing nothing, when he saw the phone in his hand light up. Ryan moaned. The phone was all charged up, and when it got fully charged, it got frisky.

Ryan! Ryan, wake up, you lazy fool! I'm bored! I want to go for a walk.

This was new. The phone usually forbade Ryan from

setting foot outside.

"I don't really think I've got the strength to walk."

Don't lie to me, Ryan. I saw you run in here. You think I'm blind? Or maybe you think I'm stupid, is that it? Do you EVER want to get your incoming call?

"I'd really just like to be able to lie in this bed and sleep for a year. I'm really tired. Unbelievably tired…"

Aw… poor Ryan. You've really been through a lot. I feel bad for you.

Ryan's ears perked up. The phone sounded sincere. This was a real change from its pompous teasing. He didn't trust it one bit. There had to be a catch.

Listen, I'll make you a deal. If you take me for a walk in the park, I promise you that I will ring before we get home. I'll ring, it'll be an incoming call, and then you can finally relax. You're too stressed out, man. It's not healthy.

"How many times have I fallen for your promises? Twenty? Thirty? I'm tired of being your plaything."

Oh, everything seems bad if you REMEMBER it. You're just going to have to trust me, though. I hate seeing you like this, and if giving you an incoming call will make you feel better, than that's what I'll do. But I really need my walk. In the park. Now.

Ryan tried to swallow, but his throat was completely dry. With a great effort, he rolled over on his back and sat up. He held the phone in his right hand. Wobbling slightly, he lifted the phone to eye level and said, "No games. If we go to the park and you don't ring, that's it. I can't handle this anymore."

The phone didn't respond right away. There was a brief stare-down, and just as Ryan was about to put the phone back on the charger and lay down, a message appeared on the screen. "INCOMING CALL COMING" Ryan cocked his head. He wasn't sure what to make of this.

The phone NEVER used the screen to communicate. It was totally out of left field. And then it dawned on him... the phone was serious this time. He knew it.

Ryan bounded to his feet, forgetting briefly how weak he really was, and with the phone in hand, he ran out the front door. The park was less than a block away, and if he got there as fast as possible, Ryan estimated he would have an incoming call in as little as ten minutes. He bolted across the street, not seeing the people staring and pointing at the skinny, disheveled man in ratty clothes and no shoes. He only saw the phone and the relief of finally getting that call. For the first time in weeks, he smiled, and for a fleeting moment, he had an inkling that he might be completely insane.

11.

It was a beautiful day at the park, but Ryan barely noticed as he trudged along the walking trail. He was excited about his incoming call, beyond excited, but not even the thought of that could speed him up much. He was just too exhausted. *This damn phone call better be worth it*, he thought, but immediately put that out of his head. Of COURSE the incoming call was going to be worth it. It was going to be the answer he'd been looking for. The relief he so desired. He licked his lips with anticipation and pulled the phone out of his pocket.

The phone looked as it always looked. Nothing different. Even the message he'd seen was gone. But it was warm in his hands. *Warming up to ring.* He let out a girlish giggle as he passed a mother pushing a stroller. The mother looked at him, frowned, and sped up down the path. Ryan didn't have a clue.

He and the phone walked for about an hour, around the trail, passing the same landmarks three and four times. Ryan, who had been staring at the phone the entire time, blinked and looked up. He was thirsty. He was incredibly hungry as well, but what he needed right now was a drink. A water fountain sat off the path slightly ahead, and he steered himself in that direction. There was a park bench near the fountain, and an elderly couple sat there, holding hands and eating ice cream cones. They were watching their grandchildren play on the playground about ten feet away. They gave Ryan a slight glance as he reached the fountain, but nothing more. Ryan simply shifted the phone to his left hand and used his right to push the button. Cool water sprayed into his mouth and he sighed audibly, drawing another look from the old people.

He drank in huge gulps, savoring each swallow. He hadn't realized how thirsty he really was. It felt like it had been several days since he'd had anything to drink. The phone was picky about that sort of thing. But with no objections coming from his left hand, he was free to drink as he pleased.

He drank for three minutes, not realizing it. And he would have continued drinking, probably on and on until water came out his ears, if he hadn't heard the ring. It was a cell phone ring. It was a Looney Tunes cell phone ring. His whole body convulsed for a moment, then he stood up ramrod straight. Water dripped down his chin. He looked at the phone in his hand, jaw wide open, and began to pull it to his face. But before that journey could be completed, his brain made a connection. An unpleasant hateful connection, but one that couldn't be argued with. *That's not my phone*, he realized. And then he realized something else. Something worse. *It's NEVER going to be my phone.* He slowly turned his head and caught a glimpse of a lady answering her cell phone. It was her phone that had rang, not his. SHE had gotten an incoming call. Why hadn't he?

"So... what? I'm not good enough to get a call on my cell phone, is that it?" he said it to himself, loud enough that the elderly couple turned and looked at him again. The lady leaned in to her husband and whispered something. He nodded and they got up and walked over to the playground, away from Ryan. Ryan noticed this, and his head began to get very hot. He was furious.

"I've got lots of friends!" he said, not bothering to keep his voice down. "And they've all got my cell phone number. So why don't they call me?" He pointed at the lady on the phone. "Why do they call YOU? How are YOU better than ME?" She rolled her eyes, uttered something into the phone, laughed, and turned away. Ryan turned toward the playground, where several people were now staring at him. "Do you people want my number? I'll give it to you! It's really easy to remember." Nobody responded and Ryan threw his hands in the air. "Of COURSE not! And you know why? Because nobody calls RYAN! Screw him! What does he need an incoming call for? He's only got a CELL PHONE!!!"

He swiveled around and began stomping down the trail. His mind was racing and he'd never been so angry in his entire life. He felt used. He felt betrayed. He felt violated. Why hadn't any of his friends called him? It had been WEEKS, and yet his phone remained silent. *Some friends I've got,* he fumed. *Heartless, senseless, hateful* "...SONS OF BITCHES!!!" He'd shouted the last part, and a nearby crow flew away.

Ryan wished them all dead. All of them. And

everybody. He didn't deserve this. He was a decent human being, and he only wanted one thing. A single, solitary incoming call. What in the hell was stopping these people from calling him. It didn't make any...

Ryan stopped dead in his tracks. His eyes grew wide with understanding. He'd figured out the answer without even meaning to. He HAD been getting phone calls. Lots of them. But something WAS stopping these people from calling him... it was the phone.

He suddenly had a vision in his head, one that he knew had been played out countless times. His friend Henry, sitting around the house. He grabbed his phone and dialed the number to Ryan's cell. He just wanted to see what was up. In his ear, the phone rang once... twice... three times. Then a voice popped into Henry's ear (or whoever was trying to call him. All his friends had tried). It was the pre-recorded woman. "I'm sorry," she said. *But she wasn't REALLY sorry.* "But the cellular customer you're trying to reach is out of service. Please try again later." And the phone would disconnect, just like that. But he WASN'T out of service. He was completely available. But the call had been blocked... by the phone.

Ryan squeezed the phone in his hand and held it above his head. He pointed at it and hissed under his breath. "You bastard... You've been blocking the calls since day one. All for your SICK amusement..." Some spittle flew out of his mouth and landed on the pound key.

I never blocked any calls Ryan, and I'm hurt. How could you possibly accuse me of something like that? I want you to GET calls. You know that.

"LIAR!!" Ryan shouted. "LIAR!! You get some sort of sick thrill out watching me dance for you, but I'm THROUGH dancing for you. It's OVER!!"

Ryan was standing in a fairly populated part of the park by this time, and everyone was staring at him, this wild looking man shouting at a cell phone.

You're hurting my feelings, Ryan. I thought we were friends.

"I WANTED to be your friend! I gave you every chance in the world! And how do you repay me? By blocking all my incoming calls! My INCOMING CALLS!"

I never blocked anything. You just never GOT any calls.

"Fuck you!" Ryan bellowed, and a man in a tank-top pulled out his cell phone and dialed the police. "FUCK... YOU!!! I did TOO get calls, and you know it! I'm POPULAR!!!"

You never got a single incoming call.

Ryan threw his head back and shrieked. "LYING CELL PHONE SON OF A BITCH!!! EVERYBODY gets incoming calls, you deceitful thing! Look around us! Do you see one person that isn't on the phone? On the CELL PHONE?!" Ryan pointed the cell phone in the direction of the gathering crowd. "You SEE! The ugly woman is on a cell phone! The fat guy is on a cell phone! The old people are on a cell phone!" He looked over at the playground, where a young boy was merrily chatting into a toy phone, oblivious to what was going on. Ryan gasped. "Even the fucking FOUR YEAR OLD is on a cell phone, so don't you tell ME that I didn't get any incoming calls, because I'm not falling for it, you BASTARD!!!"

The phone sat there in his hands, unmoving, and its silence only infuriated Ryan further. He grabbed it with both hands, held it directly up to his mouth, and shouted at the top of his lungs. "ANSWER ME! ANNNNNNSWEEERRR MEEEEE!!!"

You never got a single incoming call, Ryan. I'm sorry.

Ryan emitted a deafening bellow and punched the phone as hard as he could. The faceplate shattered and the phone itself bent in half. He then pulled his arm back and threw the phone as hard as he could towards the street. It sailed end over end for what seemed like forever. Ryan stood there watching it fly, the same as everyone else was doing. And as the phone sailed through the air, right before it hit the street, Ryan heard it ring. It rang as loud and true as anyone else's cell phone ever had, informing the world that Ryan had an incoming call. Even after it hit the street and bounced several times, Ryan could still hear it ring. He stood in place for a moment, then began sprinting towards the street.

"I'm sorry, I'm sorry, I'm sorry..." he chanted with each step, running faster and faster. He had to get to it before the fourth ring or the voicemail would pick up and he'd miss his one incoming call. The incoming call the phone had promised him. Why hadn't he believed the phone? Was he out of his mind?

He was still ten feet away, still gaining speed, when the white Lexus came from the left and drove right over the phone. The driver, talking intently into a cell phone, didn't even see it, and once he ran over it, he didn't even stop. Why would he? He was in a Lexus. Ryan screeched to a halt and collapsed onto his knees. He grabbed his head with both hands and howled. "NOOOOOOOOOOOO!!!!" After he'd screamed himself hoarse, he fell over, pulled his knees to his chest, and wept until the police arrived.

12.

Henry turned on his blinker and got off of the

freeway. He stopped at the red light and continued talking into his cell phone, the one he had bought the same day he bought Ryan's.

"I just got off the freeway. I'll be at Ryan's place in about five minutes."

On the other end of the phone, Henry's friend Adam replied. "You think he's gonna recognize you?"

"Geez, Adam, he had a slight breakdown. He didn't go through some major amnesia-producing trauma."

"That was not a slight breakdown. He murdered his cell phone in the middle of a park. That's not normal."

"He's never BEEN normal. That's the point. Sometimes he attacks cell phones, sometimes he attacks Planters displays. It's all about getting it out."

Adam laughed. "Yeah, well, if I were you, I wouldn't take YOUR phone in the house with you. You don't want to set him off again."

"I'm not even going to utter the WORDS 'cell phone.' I'm just going by to see how he's doing. Simple as that." Henry made a right and headed down a smaller side street.

"Hey, Henry. Did you ever try calling him on his phone after you got it for him?"

"Of course I did. I probably called the damn thing a hundred times. Always got an 'out of service' message. It was really driving me nuts."

"Yeah, I got the same thing. None of the guys ever seemed to be able to get through on the cell. I just figured he always had it shut off."

Henry stopped at a stop sign, looked both ways, and proceeded with caution. "I actually found out why that was, though."

"Really? Why?"

"The dope gave us all the wrong number. The last

four numbers he gave us were 0127, but it turns out his ACTUAL last four numbers were 0126."

"How in the hell did you find that out?"

Henry shook his head and glanced in his rear-view mirror. "It was a total fluke. I just misdialed one day. I hit send, realized my mistake, then just as I started to hang up, it started to ring. Rang four times, his voicemail picked up, and I left a message. His voicemail message was REALLY weird, but it was him. The mystery was solved."

"Well, good work, Shaggy. You tell him I said hi, all right? I gotta run."

"Cool. Will do. Later." Henry pressed the end button just as he reached Ryan's house. He pulled into the driveway and put the phone in his glove compartment.

Henry rang the doorbell and shifted his weight from one foot to the other. He was a little bit nervous. He'd never dealt with a friend post-mental breakdown before. He wasn't sure how he was supposed to act. Still, he planned to be as normal as possible, just like always. He reached in his jacket pocket and grabbed the small package, just to make sure he hadn't forgotten it. Just as he did, Ryan opened the door.

Ryan looked good, but very tired. He had lost a lot of weight and was still quite pale, but behind all the fatigue, Henry could see the old sparkle in his eyes. When he spoke, his voice was scratchy, but he seemed clearer headed than he'd been for a while. They sat and talked for about ten minutes, and conversation left what had happened and moved on to other topics. Ryan was right in the middle of asking a question about one of the guys when Henry snapped his fingers.

"Hey! Sorry to cut you off, but I want to give you this before I forget."

Ryan looked at Henry with mock distrust and his usual grin. "You got me something ELSE? Are you sure that's such a good idea?"

"Well, it's not just for you. We all got one of these, and since you're part of the group, we got you one too. It's what we decided to do instead of getting giant tattoos on our necks."

Ryan frowned. "Yeah, but I really wanted a giant full color eagle on my neck. Patriotism is in this year, you know."

"So is sanity." Henry sucked in a breath and shook his head. "I'm sorry. That didn't come out right."

Ryan waved his hand. "Whatever. Doesn't bother me. I'm not insane. I just had a bad couple of months. Nothing more, nothing less. Now, come on, what's this big group gift you got me?"

Henry pulled it out of his pocket and handed it to Ryan. Ryan looked at it, then his eyes got wide. He looked up at Henry. "It's a..."

"Pager. Yes. It's a pager. Same general communication principle, less pressure. And I personally passed out the number, so we won't have any more mistakes."

Ryan looked back down at the pager. It was green, his favorite color, and the screen said "HELLO RYAN." He forced his eyes back upward and met Henry's gaze. "It's great," he said with a slight grin. "I can't wait to get a page..." His voice trailed off.

Henry laughed and slapped Ryan on the shoulder. "And you're going to get a bunch. In fact, that thing'll probably go off so much you'll get sick of hearing it."

"Maybe..." Ryan whispered.

If you're good, the pager said.

The following True-Life Tale is being brought to you by…

The Dog Says "Bark"

People hate to hang around people who are smarter than they are. When someone is smarter than you, you feel dumb, and there ain't nothing worse than feelin' dumb. If you suddenly discover that the people you associate with are smarter than you, it's pretty easy to stop hanging out with them. But what do you do when you get home and find that your loyal pets are ALSO smarter than you are? That's where PetStupid® comes in.

PetStupid® is a new kind of pet store. We're the kind of pet store that doesn't insult your intelligence by assuming you have any. Our store is laid out so that even the most ignorant doofus can walk in, find what they are looking for and then walk back out. At which point our helpful staff will run out and remind the ignorant doofus that they forgot to pay. And the best part about PetStupid® and our number one source of pride is that we only sell the dumbest possible animals. You know those dogs that can sniff out drugs or apprehend dangerous criminals, making you feel dense and worthless by comparison? You don't have to worry about accidentally purchasing a dog like that from PetStupid®. It's more likely that the dog you buy from us will spend most of its time walking headfirst into walls.

Every PetStupid® animal goes through our rigorous "Brain-Smarts" test and if it passes, we send it right back. Every single time. This means that any and every creature at our store is dumb as a rock, therefore making you, the owner, feel superior in every way. "I may not be able to keep a job at Burger King® for more than a week," you will say, "but at least I don't spend all day staring at my tail!"

We carry a wide selection of great pets at PetStupid® and each one is easily identifiable because we put a big colorful picture of the animal on a sign right next to it. For instance, if you want a kitty, you don't have to get a pounding brain headache trying to find the word "cat" written somewhere. Just look for the picture of the kitty and that's where the kitty will be! That's just a small example of the kind of slow-witted service we provide at PetStupid®, and now here is an example of some of the great moderately retarded animals we are offering for sale this week:

Doggy - Our doggies like to bark at tree stumps and try to eat the rat poison, even though the dog food is six inches away.

Kitty - PetStupid® kitties enjoy rubbing against lit candles. They also believe every inch of your house is a bathroom, except for the litter box.

Fishy - When you buy a fishy at PetStupid®, it will spend most of its time trying to leap out of the fishbowl and onto your carpet. Also, if it sees a kitty, it will desperately try to get the kitty's attention, because fishy loves to say "hello."

Bunny Rabbit - All of our bunny rabbits like to jump on the stove and sit in empty pans. Many of them will marinate themselves in teriyaki sauce. They will also spend long period of time just sitting completely still in the middle of the room, then leaping ten

feet in the air for no apparent reason.
Panther - (Due to customer complaints,
PetStupid® regrets to announce that we
have discontinued selling panthers. No
matter how hard we tried, we couldn't
find a panther that was dumber than a
family that would buy a panther.)

That's only a small sampling of what we have to
offer, but you get the idea. Come on down and finally get
that dumb little pet you've been meaning to get for your
two-year old that will get bored with it in three days and
then accidentally crush it to death. We don't sell dolphins or
gorillas or Lassie-type dogs. We just sell idiots to idiots, and
we do it better than anyone!

PetStupid®
Our Name Says It, Our Stupid Pets Prove It!

Massive Spastic Freak Out

In general, I'm a very mellow person. I try not to let bad things bring me down too far, just as I try not to get too worked up when something good happens. My reaction to discovering a money clip full of hundreds in the gutter ("nice") should not be too different than my reaction to finding out my entire family had just been eaten by wolves ("bummer").

One of the exceptions to this rule, however, is food. For as far back as I can remember, I have been a picky eater on a level that is just stupid. What I have is an exceptionally refined palette. So refined, in fact, that basically nothing tastes good. I would make a wonderful food critic because I could just re-run the same review every week, regardless of where or what I was eating ("Yuck!").

A few years ago, I tried to find out if perhaps something in my youth led to my food quirkiness. I asked my parents, separately, why they thought I was so picky, and the results of my survey were quite enlightening: My mom said it was my dad's fault. My dad said it was my mom's fault. Neither one gave me a whole lot of evidence to back up their claims, but they both seemed so sure of themselves. I wasn't any closer to getting to the bottom of the food question, but I was learning a lot about why my parents got divorced.

I don't hate ALL food, of course, but I do find myself gravitating towards a fixed list of what I think of as "safe" foods. These are certain entrees that I'm reasonably sure I will like, no matter where I'm getting them from. One of these is Chicken Parmesan. Chicken Parmesan is always delicious, and it usually comes with pasta, which is also "safe." I can ask for Chicken Parmesan in several different languages, depending on what sort of restaurant I am in during that meal ("Donde esta Chicken Parmesan?").

One of the things I hate the most is condiments. I hate condiments the way that Hitler hated the Jews. Mustard, mayonnaise, relish, secret sauce, ranch... the list goes on and on. I hate the way condiments completely take over the taste of anything you're eating and then just for good measure, make it soggy. "Soggy" is not one of my favorite adjectives for something I would enjoy eating. As far as condiments go, I like barbeque sauce and that's about it.

This condiment-phobia leads to a major problem that I have to deal with two or three times a week. I like hamburgers, and when ordering a hamburger at one of your leading fast food chains, you have to slowly and loudly explain how you want your burger prepared if you want it in any way different than it appears on the menu. I often find myself talking to the drive thru speaker in a way I would not talk to a retarded monkey. "I would like... my HAMBURGER... PLAIN... with only MEAT and CHEESE. MEAT... AND CHEESE. I do not want ANYTHING ELSE... on my burger... unless it is MEAT and CHEESE!" Occasionally, the drive-thru speaker will ask for some clarification, having never heard such an insane order in all its years of being a speaker. "Okay," it will say, sounding unsure. "Just meat and cheese and that's it?"

"Yes!" I will bellow, encouraged by the progress I am making. "Nothing except for the meat and the cheese!"

"Just meat and cheese?" the drive-thru speaker will repeat, as if it's afraid that this whole order is some sort of trick.

And even though go through this every SINGLE

time, no matter how clearly I state my order, they still manage to get it wrong. How the hell do you screw up what is essentially the easiest version of a hamburger?

So I'm aware that, because this is the life I have chosen, this is the price I must pay. The constant terror every time I unwrap a burger, heart pounding, on the verge of hyperventilating, as I slooooooowly lift up the top bun to see what sort of non-meat-and-cheese ooze these morons have slopped onto my burger, thereby making it completely inedible.

But I sometimes forget how this looks to other people, who were lucky enough to grow up with non-mutant taste buds. I usually do a fairly decent job of hiding this freakish personality trait from others, but sometimes it slips out. Take the other day... (dreamy music plays as we dissolve to a flashback sequence)

On a lunch break from work, I stopped off at the nearest Carl's Jr. and ordered a Famous Star combo, going through the whole "Look, I'm begging you. Just meat and cheese. PLEASE!" routine. The guy seemed very sympathetic to my plight, even telling me that there is a different burger on the menu which is only meat and cheese, and it's cheaper, and asking if I'd rather order that instead. "Of course I do," I told him, and drove up to the window to collect my meal from my new best friend.

A few minutes later, I was back at work, and I walked into the office, where two of my co-workers were sitting at a nearby desk involved in an important work discussion about that night's Dodger game. We all sort of grunted at each other and I sat down to eat my lunch. Now, having really connected with Carl's Jr. guy on my order, I unwrapped my burger without my usual fear. I took a huge bite, ready to savor the glorious meat and cheese flavor I was about to enjoy. Instead, all I tasted was mustard. It tasted like betrayal.

I reached for the bag and made a noise that sounded like "Plarrrggghh" as I spat the foul burger out of my mouth. "Plarrrggghh!!" I repeated, as I licked the inside of the bag, trying to get the mustard off my tongue. I reached for my Coke, took a huge drink, and reached for the burger, which I had dropped on the desk. I lifted up the top bun and sure enough, sitting there, on top of the cheese, was a dollop of ketchup and a dollop of mustard. Soaked into the bun, making it useless. There are three things in life you can be sure of: Death, taxes, and you simply can not get mustard and ketchup out of a bun. I took the bun and threw it in the bag.

Completely agitated but still hungry, I decided to try and save the burger. I grabbed a bunch of napkins and started to blot at the offending sauces, trying to remove them from the innocent meat and cheese, which had done nothing to deserve this. The ketchup came off fairly easily, but I was having a hard time with the mustard, because it was the same color as the cheese. Muttering to myself under my breath, I grabbed another handful of napkins and continued my work. Blot, blot, blot. Eventually, I had a bunch of greasy, cheesy, mustard-soaked napkins, and when I went to throw them into the bag, my hand brushed up against a glob of sauce. "Dammit!" I shouted. "Now I have to wash my friggin' hands!" And I slammed my other fist on the desk, causing my box of fries to fall over.

As luck would have it, there was a bag of hamburger buns in the office, so I grabbed the limp meat patty, which I had blotted until I was blotting individual mustard molecules, and shoved it between a fresh set of buns. I took the original bottom bun and the other napkins and threw them into the bag, which was now almost full of trash, all of it stemming from my reaction to mustard and ketchup on a hamburger. And it was at that moment when I realized I was being watched.

I looked up and there sat my co-workers, no longer discussing baseball, but instead silently watching me lose my mind over a burger. In my rage, I had completely forgotten they were there. After a moment, one of them says, "Um... are you okay?"

To which I meekly replied, "I just... I don't like condiments."

Yes, this is completely ridiculous. I'm not going to argue with that. But I can't HELP it. About the only thing I can do is keep it to myself as much as possible. My success rate on that is pretty decent. But if you happen to be eating a meal with me at some point in the future and I start convulsing in disgust because a tomato passed within ten feet of my plate, just let it go. I know not what I'm doing.

The following True-Life Tale is being brought to you by...

The Best A Mouth Can Get

If you walk down the toothbrush aisle of your local supermarket, or if you visit one of those toothbrush-only superstores like The Toothbrushery, you will see hundreds of different toothbrushes. It can be overwhelming to try and find the exact right brush for your tooth cleaning needs. We here at Gillette® feel your pain, and since we've pretty much cornered the market on razors, we thought we might try and work on developing a superior toothbrush. We sat around a conference table for fifteen minutes or so and talked about how to improve upon the concept of the toothbrush, but we couldn't come up with anything new. Then somebody ordered a keg. Not long after, one of our vice presidents stopped swinging his pants over his head and drunkenly slurred, "You know what we should do? The same thing Gillette® ALWAYS does. Let's add more razors to it!" And then he tried to get one of the secretaries to make out with him.

Introducing the new Gillette® ToothRazor, the world's most advanced toothbrush! It's never been easier to get a clean close shave... inside your mouth! The Gillette® ToothRazor features extra-long nylon bristles, set in a unique crisscross pattern to help lift out and sweep away plaque. In addition, there's an ergonomically designed FlexGrip handle with front and back thumb stops to give you a firm grip and extra control. Finally, we added three razor sharp titanium blades to help get those hard-to-reach areas. It's exactly what the toothbrush has been missing all these years!

The best part about the Gillette® ToothRazor is that

you don't have to brush very hard to get the job done. In fact, you're probably better off being as gentle as possible. The ToothRazor is great for removing pesky plaque and tartar, but it also takes off enamel, taste buds, chunks of your gums... you know, whatever gets in the way. 4 out of 5 dentists prefer the Gillette® ToothRazor to a regular toothbrush, but only after they've been to one of our drunken product development meetings. Another benefit of the ToothRazor is that you don't even have to use toothpaste for it to be effective. The titanium blades do all the work! It's like having a serial killer inside your mouth, but the kind that murders gingivitis instead of hitchhikers.

Yes, we briefly toyed with the idea of developing an ELECTRIC ToothRazor, but the idea of sending 20,000 volts through a toothbrush seemed a little excessive, even to us.

So if you care about oral hygiene, there's only one logical move to make. The move that gets you to the store and makes you purchase a shiny new Gillette® ToothRazor. It's the toothbrush that makes that horrible scraping noise across your teeth every time you brush! And once you experience the satisfaction of a freshly ToothRazored mouth, the tears you are sobbing will be tears of joy.

The Gillette® ToothRazor
Because We Love Adding Razors To Things!

<u>Snow Problem</u>

I survived Death Storm 2010.

I was originally under the impression that what happened last week here in Southern California was several days in a row of some fairly heavy rainfall, but I made the mistake of turning on the news, and it turns out that it was actually much more dire than that. Apparently, we are lucky to still be alive. There should be a steady stream of waterlogged corpses floating down the gutters toward the ocean. What I've learned over the years is that every storm we get is basically going to be The Day After Tomorrow according to the local news. The general consensus in the middle of this one was that, yes, what happened in Haiti was a tragedy, but a tree fell on someone's SUV in Santa Monica! Let's go there live! We've got team coverage!

To be fair, this WAS a pretty gnarly storm by SoCal standards. The rain was pretty unrelenting, plus we had some hail and tornadoes and a lot more snow than any of us are really used to. It was the snow that got my attention. I was made aware on Friday that it was snowing at my mother's house, which is not exactly an unheard-of occurrence, but it's rare enough that it's always interesting when it happens, so I hopped in my car and drove out to Yucaipa. Also, she was out of town all week, so I had to run over there anyway and take care of her cat. It's the whole two-birds-with-one-stone thing.

Now, the thing is, I like the snow. I find it to be sort of pristinely beautiful. I enjoy the sight of everything suddenly just being draped in white. But my love of the snow tends to be purely theoretical, and it falls apart once it actually gets put into practice. In other words, I'm a huge fan of snow until the moment that I am in snow, and then I'm extremely annoyed by it and I wish I was not so cold. This is exactly what happened as soon as I parked the car in my mother's driveway. I took a brief moment to appreciate the quiet majesty of a winter's morn, then stepped out of my car right into a puddle of slush that went up to my ankles, instantly soaking my shoes and socks, at which point the magic was over. It had been nearly three seconds and I had pretty much had it.

But as much as I thought I'd had it with the snow, I was nowhere near as irritated as the cat, who'd been outside during the whole storm, taking refuge under the patio cover. As soon as he saw me, he ran to the back door and gave me a look that said, "I know you did this, and I will never forgive you." I let him in the house and he began loudly telling me off via a series of increasingly pitiful meows. I told him that sometimes snow just happens and he should actually be grateful that I drove forty miles just to let him in, but he was hearing none of it. He quickly ate and then dashed under the bed, where he stayed until I left, lest I try and grab him by the tail and throw him back out and into the frozen powder. I followed him down the hall, giving him my side of the story, and it dawned on me that I'd reached a new low point in my life, wherein I was trying to give a rational explanation to a cat about how the weather is not something that I personally have any control over... and failing. After that, I let him go pout, grabbed my camera and went back outside.

I always take pictures when it snows, but I don't know why. Every picture ends up being exactly the same. It's the house, but whiter. Pictures I've taken of the snow in 2010 don't look any different than pictures I took of the snow in 2005, or 2002, or 1997. But dang it, I've got it documented on film, just in case it never happens again. My grandkids aren't going to care, but I'm going to show them anyway, again and again, long past the point when I've become senile.

I decided to take a walk up to the park, which would give me a better view of the city, thereby possibly adding some variety to my stale old snow pictures. But right as I started my trek, I tromped through another slush pile, and it dawned on me that there had to be a better way to walk through the snow. The problem was that my tennis shoes were not providing adequate protection from the elements. The solution I came up with almost instantly (which goes to prove yet again that when you are a genius, answers come fast), was to take two plastic grocery bags, wrap them around my shoes, and then rubber band them to my shins. No, seriously. This is what I came up with. And it wasn't until I had put on my fashionably functional footwear and walked all the way up to the park, plastic crunching with each step, that I began to realize that this might not be some of my best work. Within the first couple of minutes, I strolled past a family playing in the snow, and they all looked at my feet. And I saw myself through their eyes and realized with a slowly dawning horror, "Is it possible that I look ridiculous? Oh no... I might just be a moron!" From that point on, I tried to intentionally walk in the deepest snow possible so that it would hide my redneck white-trash snowshoes. Also, my shoes were already drenched and frozen before I put the bags on, so the whole thing was pointless anyway. What, I didn't want my feet to get WETTER? Those grandkids of mine better have looks, because Grandpa ain't givin' 'em brains, that's for damn sure!

I stomped around the park for twenty minutes or so,

got some good pictures, then decided to go back home. Halfway there, a lady looked at my plastic bags and said, "Hey, that's a great idea! I wish I'd thought of that!"

For a second, it seemed like my invention had been validated by the public, but when I lifted my foot to give her a better look, it turned out the plastic bag had been torn to shreds. Apparently, grocery bags are not made for the harsh terrain of a snowy countryside. Go figure. I gave her a weak smile and tried to save face. "They're... um... only temporary," I said, but it was too late. She was no longer impressed, and I was making a mental note that next time I would need TWO bags for each foot.

A few minutes later, I made it back to mother's house, apologized to the cat one last time and hightailed it out of there, leaving Snow Country in my rearview mirror, passing a CBS news van on my way down the street, who had come to town to try and put the most apocalyptic spin possible on the fact that there was snow, snow everywhere! Snow, I say! Won't somebody please save the children?! That's just an uneducated guess, of course, but I'll bet I'm not too far off base.

As for me, as soon as I was no longer in the snow, I instantly became nostalgic for it again, regaining my romantic notions of just how wonderful a gentle snowfall can be. But it's a short-lived feeling, because according to the news, there's another storm coming in on Tuesday, so I'm going to take their advice and go hole up in my bomb shelter...

Shadows of the Invisible
(a tale told in "real-time")

Week Eight: Gunfight At The Kaffa Corral

"Two weeks ago, an assassin attempted to assassinate the president of Antarctica. For the second time. It appears that people that I work with may be involved. My name is Librarian of Congress Jacques Vargas, and these... are the longest eight weeks of my life..."

FRIDAY, JANUARY 3, 2003

11:45pm - Kaffa House, Washington D.C. (parking lot)

Jacques Vargas and Irma Damole walk up to the entrance of The Kaffa House restaurant. Jacques is holding a suitcase with "Ransom Munny" written upon it in oil-based paint. Irma wrings her hands nervously together. They haven't said a word to each other since they left the L.O.C. Jacques is too nervous about finally solving this case to speak, and Irma, being the mole within the agency working for the bad guys, is dealing with several conflicting emotions of her own. After all, if everything goes as planned, Jacques and the President of Antarctica will be killed, but if something goes wrong and she gets discovered, she might just lose her job.

They reach the front door and Jacques snaps his fingers, causing Irma to jump slightly. "I remember why this place is so familiar! This is where we had my party when I got promoted to the head of the Library. That was quite a shindig."

Irma glares and says softly, "You were kind of rude to the waitress that night."

"Did you see how much I had to drink, Irma? I was rude to EVERYBODY that night. And I think I might've relived myself in the woman's bathroom, now that I think back on it."

"Actually, Jacques, according to the police report, it was the kitchen. Now can we focus on the issue at hand? We need to go over this one more time to make sure everything goes as planned."

Jacques points at a sign in the front window. "Okay, there's the first hitch in our plan right there. That sign says "closed". How could you possibly make reservations for after the place is closed, Irma? You see, this is why I got promoted over you. I'd never make a silly mistake like getting AM and PM mixed up."

Doing a particularly good job of keeping calm, Irma shakes her head. "I DIDN'T get anything mixed up. We can't possibly be making a ransom exchange like this when there are customers in the restaurant. Think, Vargas, think! I got them to agree to let us in after hours so that we could do this with a minimum of public involvement." She points at the suitcase. "When we go in there, William Williams is going to be waiting for us. We give him that suitcase, he gives us the name of the person that hired him to kill President Kemo, and we leave. There's no reason for us not to be out of there by midnight."

"Then we'd better get in there now." Jacques reaches out and opens the door, which is unlocked. He and Irma enter the Kaffa House for what may be the last time.

11:49pm - Kaffa House, Washington D.C. (main dining room)

Sitting at this usual table, William Williams stands up as he hears the front door open. He sees Jacques and Irma, grins, and holds out his arms. "Mr. Vargas! So glad to finally meet you. I wish we could have met under better circumstances, but you kept refusing to die." He chuckles and motions towards some chairs. "Please, have a seat."

Irma sits down, but Jacques does not. He just stands there, sizing up Williams. "If you don't mind. I feel like standing. I have a hard time accepting an invitation from someone who tried to blow me up with a bomb."

Williams smiles and takes a seat. "That's up to you, Mr. Vargas, but for the record, we never intended for you to be killed. We were only going to frame you for the murder. It was your utter incompetence that changed our carefully constructed plans. But now, right here, we're going to finish what we started. May I have the suitcase full of..." He looks at the word written on the side. "... munny?"

"I'll give you this suitcase after you tell me one thing. Who are you working for? Who hired you to kill the President of Antarctica."

"Fair enough. My employer happens to be here right now, as a matter of fact. She's here five days a week, serving good and bad customers alike. And you, Mr. Vargas, were a very bad customer. Francine! We're ready for you!"

The door to the kitchen opens, and President Dennis S. Kemo walks out. He's holding his hands in the air, because right behind him, holding a gun, is Francine, still dressed in her waitress uniform. Kemo sees Jacques and gives his typical and slightly disturbing "Huge Grin Under Terrible Circumstances". "Jacques, my friend! It is so good to see you again! They kidnapped me right from my home, if you can believe it!" He laughs. "I never should've answered the front door, but they said I had a candy gram. A common mistake, I'm sure."

Jacques frowns and looks at Williams. "You went all the way up to Antarctica to kidnap him? If you're going to go to all that trouble, why not just kill him there?"

"We kidnapped him at his house, Jacques. Not his work. He WORKS in Antarctica, but he LIVES in Cleveland."

President Kemo reaches the table, still trailed by Francine, and shakes Jacques hand. "I would have been more on alert, I suppose, but the Browns had just clinched a playoff spot, so I was too excited to think straight."

Suddenly, Francine shrieks and fires the gun twice, striking Kemo at point-blank range. The smile on his face turning to confusion, Kemo grabs his side and collapses to the ground. Before Jacques can react, the gun is pointing at him. "You PEOPLE!" she spits. "You think you're so great, just because you came to a restaurant? You think you can treat the waitress however you want, just because our job is to get you stuff? Well it doesn't work that way! We're people too!"

"Wait a minute... this whole thing is because I was rude to you during that promotion party? Are you kidding me?"

"See! There you go again! You think it's all about you!" Francine waves her hands in circles and makes some noises that aren't exactly words. Jacques thinks to himself that she looks like somebody being rewound. After a moment, she comes back to reality and points the gun at Kemo. "It was a really bad night for me. Between your drunken party, dealing with my usual tables, and having to jump through hoops for this guy, just because he's the president of the South Pole, I'd had enough! I'd had it, do you hear me?! And then, when it couldn't have gotten any worse, neither one of you left me a tip! What the hell is WRONG with you people?! Not even a tip!"

Williams leans forward in his chair and puts his elbows on the table. "You see, Jacques, you stiffed the wrong waitress, and now, your karma is coming back to haunt you." Williams pulls out a gun of his own and points it at Jacques. "Funny... I'll bet you never thought you'd be shot with the same gun... that killed your mother!"

"My mother? What are you talking about? My mom lives in Boise. I talked to her an hour ago. She told me to wear clean underwear and asked when she was ever going to get a grandkid."

Taken slightly aback by this new information, William shakes his head as if it doesn't matter, cocks his gun, places his finger on the trigger... and with an impossibly loud crash, a pickup truck drives through the side of the restaurant. Shattering the front window, it takes out several tables and chairs before screeching to a halt ten feet in front of Jacques. Chuck Williams jumps out of the driver's side, gun drawn, and Todd Herring weakly gets out of the passenger side, after first disentangling himself from the air bag.

"Jacques! Irma's the mole!"

"What?"

Irma jumps up. "Lies! He's lying, Jacques! He's the mole! Him and William are brothers! That means he's got a family connection! He's the snitch, Jacques, not me!"

Chuck shakes his head. "I did some research on her past, just on a whim, and I discovered that her real name isn't Irma. She changed it when she applied for the L.O.C." On the other side of the truck, ignoring the head wound on his forehead from the crash, Todd pulls out a gun of his own, looks around, and finally decides to aim it at William. "Jacques, listen to me. Her real name is Ima. Ima Damole. It makes better sense if you say it out loud."

Irma slams her fist on the table. "Why did you have to go there, Chuck? WHY? Now you have to die!" Irma pulls out a gun and points it at Chuck, who is pointing his gun at Francine, who is pointing her gun at Jacques, who's still holding the briefcase. He turns back to Irma with a quizzical look on his face. "But why, Irma. You've always been the best Librarian we've had. How could you do this?"

"Because, Jacques, I AM the best Librarian we've got. There was no reason for you to get promoted over me! I should be in charge of the L.O.C. Not you. It's completely unfair! The only reason they gave you the promotion is because you're a man!"

"Geez, Irma. Of COURSE that's the only reason I got the promotion. I do good work, but I'm certainly not qualified to run the division. We all know that. But we can't have a woman in charge of the L.O.C. What kind of example would that set? Next thing you know, women will want to the senators and firemen and, perish the thought, doctors. No, that's not the kind of world for me. That's not MY America."

Chuck briefly points his gun at Jacques, then thinks better of it, and returns it to the waitress. Francine shrieks again. "I'm done screwing around! It's time for me to get my tip!" And she squeezes the trigger. And then lots of other triggers get squeezed.

11:57pm - Kaffa House, Washington D.C. (parking lot)

There is lot of gunfire coming from inside the restaurant. Just for a second, it's probably safer for us to stay out here.

11:58pm - Kaffa House, Washington D.C. (main dining room)

The silence is twice as loud in the aftermath of all the shooting. As the smoke begins to clear, Jacques Vargas becomes aware of two things. One, he seems to have escaped without being shot, and two, President Kemo is standing in front of him holding, you guessed it, a gun. Jacques throws his hands in the air. "Am I the only one who doesn't have a friggin' gun?!"

Kemo looks down and smiles. "Yes, Jacques, but you're the only one with a briefcase."

"I can't believe you're still alive, Mr. President."

"I was wearing a bullet-proof vest."

"She shot you twice. From point-blank range. With hollow-tipped bullets."

Kemo sighs and rolls his eyes. "Then I was wearing TWO bulletproof vests. Let it go. We need to wrap things up."

Stumbling over, no longer holding his gun, Chuck grabs Jacques by the shoulder. "Are you okay? I took about four rounds, but I think they're all non-lethal. How many did you take?"

"I didn't get shot at all, Chuck." He shrugs. "Just lucky, I guess."

Chuck stares at Jacques for a second, then spits out some blood and curses under his breath. He walks away, towards the men's room. Jacques puts the briefcase down for the first time and looks around. He can hear the sound of sirens approaching, which is good, because it appears everybody BUT him took at least one bullet. He smiles at his good fortune. Jacques reaches into his pocket and pulls out a cell phone, dialing quickly. He holds the phone to his ear. "Yeah, this is Head Librarian of Congress Jacques Vargas. I'm going to need some police backup. We've had a... um... minor shooting incident at the Kaffa House. Lots of people down, but it doesn't appear there are any fatalities. And could you get an urgent message to the president. The American one. Tell him the threat against the Antarctican President has been eliminated... courtesy of Jacques Vargas." Satisfied that he has made himself sound like an action hero, Jacques walks towards the front door of the Kaffa House, passing the gigantic hole made by the pickup truck. He thinks to himself that he could use a vacation. Nowhere fancy. Just maybe a few days at home, with a good book. He happens to know a place where the selection is quite good.

Behind him, amongst the shooting victims, both good guys and bad guys, all of whom will survive, a grandfather clock begins to chime. It is now 12 midnight, and a Saturday begins, one in which the shadows have faded, and the invisible has become visible.

The End

Director's Commentary

There's more to writing a book than just putting together some random words. No, you have to put together a LOT of random words, not to mention all kinds of different punctuation marks. And the rules for all the punctuation marks are extremely specific. It's kind of exhausting. I'm working on developing an app that does all the writing for you, but it keeps turning into a cheap Angry Birds knock-off (I am calling it "Not-Happy Burds").

For a collection such as this, you have to come up with quite a few ideas, and this section is meant to shine some light on the origins of a handful of the stories. It's like that movie "X-Men Origins: Wolverine," except without any X-Men or Wolverines. On second thought, that was a terrible analogy, and I probably should've just quit after the first sentence of this paragraph. Oh well. Live and learn...

Shadows of the Invisible

During its entire run, I was a massive fan of the show 24, reacting in the same way to it that tween girls act when they are at a Justin Bieber concert. If the Supreme Court let me, I probably would have tried to marry 24. I'm still hoping that I can get that case pushed through the system. So Shadows of the Invisible was both my love letter to/spoof of 24 and also an attempt to try an experiment, which was to write a story that took place and would be read in "real-time." The idea was that each part of Shadows would take 15 minutes to read, so the action within it would happen during those 15 minutes. At the time, my friend Pat and I were putting out a weekly comedy newsletter every Friday, so when you see that Part One takes place on December 15th,

2002, it's because that's the date we released that issue. "Right now! This is all happening RIGHT NOW!" was what the reader was supposed to be thinking. Basically, it was my version of what later would become liveblogging.

I spent about a month beforehand sketching out the plot and characters, and outlining how each of the eight parts would unfold over the eight weeks, because even though it's a silly little story, I still wanted it to work on a bunch of different levels. All these years later, sitting down and reading it as a whole, I feel like I was about 75% successful pulling it off, which isn't bad. It's not my absolute favorite thing I've ever written, but it's probably the most ambitious, so I'm glad it was able to find a home throughout this book.

I am still, however, endlessly tickled by the idea that the Library of Congress is just a front for a covert government anti-terrorist agency. I wish that were true in the worst way...

You Can't Spell Can't Without Ant

I've often considered purchasing another ant farm to try and make a second attempt at managing a loving and nurturing home for ants, but I just know it would go badly, and I'll forever be branded as some sort of ant serial killer. On another note, I can give the following update, which is that the Home of A Million Animals now only contains two dogs, which is far more normal, so there is no need to contact PETA.

A Lover, Not a Fighter

After the events of this story, I'd done an admirable job of not getting struck in the face anymore. That was, until about three months ago when I accidentally smacked myself directly in the mouth with a metal pole. I hit myself so hard that I was fairly certain I had knocked out some teeth, but was relieved to discover I had only split my lip open and was bleeding like a stuck pig (I do not know how much a stuck pig actually bleeds, because I have never researched the expression, but I can only assume it is "a lot"). There is not much to say about this incident except that unlike my boxing match with Jason, in the battle of Me Vs. The Metal Pole, is it hard to argue that I won the fight.

The Dinner Party

In a way, The Dinner Party is both the oldest AND newest story in the entire book.

There was a great Saturday Night Live sketch from the mid-90's where Will Farrell plays Unabomber Ted Kaczynski visiting his class reunion, and none of his classmates seem to have heard about his little run in with the law. That sketch was the little seedling that implanted itself into my brain, although it took about ten years before it sprouted into what would eventually become The Dinner Party.

I wrote the first few pages of The Dinner Party by hand one night and then about halfway through, my hand got sore and I stopped and shoved the pages in a drawer. As time went by, I kept taking it out and thinking "I should finish this," and then I would shove it back in the drawer. This went on for years.

Flash forward to a couple of months ago when I decided to put this book together. It occurred to me that if I was ever going to finish the tale of Adam the Axe Murderer, there was no better time. Out came the hastily handwritten pages and two days later, it was finally complete. If you really want to get technical, I started this story in 1996 and it took me 17 years to finish it. But let's not get so technical, because that sounds AWFUL.

The Shadow Knows

For the sake of accuracy, I have to point out that there is a factual error in this particular True-Life Tale. After he read this account, Alan sent me a message and pointed out that his 1984 Honda Accord was actually an automatic and not a stick shift. Time can sometimes fog a memory, but I personally blame this mistake on the whiplash I received every time his car violently switched gears and my head lurched forwards and backwards. Automatic, manual, it doesn't matter... his car gave me brain damage. I could've been a professor of nuclear physics, but noooooo...

The Big Dumb Goat

I have to be honest with you. I have no clue where this story came from. I mean, it's in the "Stories" folder on my computer and I have a vague recollection of the act of physically sitting there and writing it, but as for what was going on in my head creatively at the time, I couldn't say. I do like saying "Meh-eh-eh-eh!" to goats when I see them, so maybe that has something to do with it, but I also like saying "Mooooo!" to cows and I've never written anything bovine-related. I shrug and accept that this may just have to remain one of those eternal mysteries.

A Story About Badgers

I have a friend named Rachel who tends to inadvertently inspire me from time to time. A Story About Badgers is a perfect example of this. We were having a conversation once that logically wound its way around to talking about badgers, and more specifically, one named

Billy. In the midst of that exchange, I absentmindedly jotted down the "traditional children's rhyme" that leads off the story. Later on that night, the opening couplet got stuck in my head (*"Billy Badger, Billy Badger had a badger life. Billy Badger, Billy Badger had a badger wife"*) like some awful Top 40 pop song and A Story About Badgers followed soon after.

Rachel had some sort of magic power where she could make me want to write verse about animals for no apparent reason. There was another chat in which we pondered whether or not one could milk a moose, and if one could and was to market this beverage, would one call it "Moose Juice?" Moments later, without even really thinking about it, the ad jingle for Moose Juice fell out of my brain, which was: *"There's no excuse! Get off your caboose! And go get the juice, that comes from a moose!"* Sometimes, even to this day, that gets stuck in my head even worse than the Billy Badger thing.

The Time Time Flew

Several years ago, I read a novel by Dave Eggers called "What Is The What," which is the loosely fictionalized story of a young Sudanese refugee whose village is attacked by a militia and who must endure various hardships as he tries to get to a refugee camp and later on, the United States. Heavy stuff.

Rachel was reading it at the same time, so we had a number of discussions about the book. At some point during all that, I thought it might be interesting to take the exact same story and add a single love-struck girl, completely oblivious to everything going on around her. It would be a true account of the Second Sudanese Civil War, just with one character written by Nicholas Sparks. Once I'd conceived of the concept, The Time Time Flew came to me almost fully formed from start to finish and my only real issue was typing fast enough so that I didn't forget anything. It's one of my personal favorites.

It also contains the song "Love Inside A Jar" which I hope one day plays over the trailer of countless insipid romantic comedies.

Lounging

The significance of Lounging is that it was the only thing I ever wrote for a college class. I had enrolled in a creative writing course and the first assignment was to write a descriptive story about a special moment in 1,000 words or less. It was implied that the story was supposed to be something that had really happened, but the professor never explicitly stated that to be the case, so I turned in Lounging instead. To his credit, he gave me an A. To my (whatever the opposite of credit is), I decided college was not exactly my cup of tea and that one-and-a-half semesters was plenty. But at least I have the memories... (Note: I do not actually have that many memories, because I was only there for one-and-a-half semesters)

Cell Phone

I like to think of Cell Phone as my Twilight Zone story.

Right off the bat, it's more than a little apparent that it was written pre-iPhone and right before cell phones joined "keys" and "wallets" as things that always go with you whenever you leave the house no matter what. Back when people with cell phones were the exception more than the rule. Heck, back when people actually felt like they had to specify "cell phone" instead of just saying "phone." It's a tale of a bygone age. But reading over it now, in addition to being my take on the encroachment of a new technology, I think it may have been a little bit of a cry for help (Don't worry, we're not going to get TOO deep here, I promise).

When I wrote Cell Phone, I was living by myself for the first time, and anyone that was around me during that period would agree that I starting acting funny. But not funny ha-ha. I became somewhat reclusive and antisocial, often preferring just to stay at home by myself, taping newspaper to the walls and collecting Pepsi boxes in a cabinet until I had enough to build what I called The Pepsi Shrine (No, really. There are pictures). I was going through some sort of weird adjustment that I was not aware of at the time, and the main character in Cell Phone does seem to be a thinly veiled version of myself, especially because at the time I wrote the story, I had just gotten my first cell phone.

Is it possible Cell Phone was what could have happened to me if I'd continued heading down the slightly unhinged path I was on at the time? No, probably not. My friends and family are too good to have let all that nonsense go on much longer, I think. They gave me the space I needed to work it out for myself, but would certainly have been my safety net if I'd plummeted off some sort of edge of madness. But it's kind of interesting to look back now and consider the possibility that even my subconscious knew something was up and was quietly trying to make a point.

Although mostly what jumps out at me is that there is a pager in the story. Pagers! Remember pagers? We seriously used to live in caveman times, am I right?!

Index of Advertisers

Like the low-quality daytime programming that you get stuck watching when you're home sick from work, Accidentally Clever was made possible by the generous support of our illustrious advertisers. They gave us wads of sweaty cash and in turn, we gave them a forum to advertise their companies with the promise that we would neither fact-check their ads, nor even read them before we put them in the book. We hope you will find it in your hearts and wallets to frequent the following businesses, even though we have virtually no contact information for any of them. But that's what Google is for, right? We just wrote an entire book here. We're exhausted…

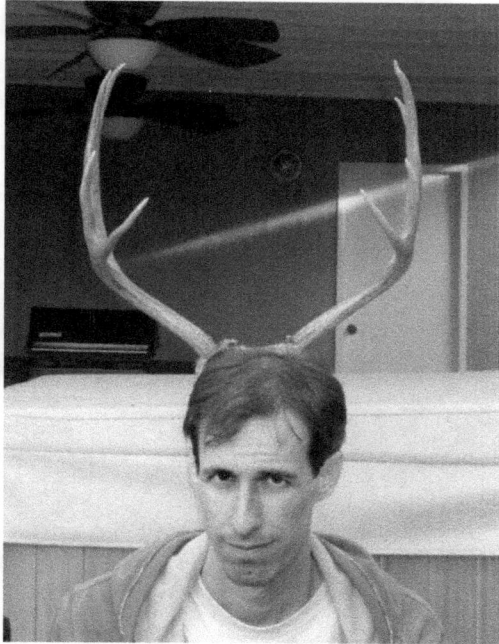

Matt Bates is best known for the story collection Accidentally Clever. Prior to the book, he was best known for being tall and skinny. Matt has written stories and sketches and songs, but is often distracted by bright lights or butterflies. Sometimes people tell him he should do stand-up comedy. These people are sadly mistaken. He is the founder of the Commercial Parodies comedy website which might still online somewhere, but it just as likely might not. Matt currently lives in Yucaipa, California, a city you have never heard of and have no idea how to properly pronounce. Matt also wrote the Harry Potter book series under the pseudonym "J.K. Rowling."*

*(*This statement has not been independently verified by our lawyers and is almost certainly a blatant lie)*